Mask Making Techniques

Mask Making Techniques: Creating 3-D Characters from 2-D Designs for Theatre, Cosplay, Film, and TV, introduces and demonstrates a variety of mask making materials, techniques, and styles to bring extraordinary characters to life.

A foundation reference for mask making and design, the book features over 700 color photos and illustrations of different masks, as well as diagrams of construction and finishing techniques. It provides a wealth of practical information about material options, safety, how to build large- and small-scale masks, how to build armatures for appendages, options for coverings, and finishing techniques. Readers will learn how to use a wide range of materials, including latex, paper and fabric mâché, cold foam, thermoplastics, urethane, ethylene vinyl acetate (EVA) foam, resin, found objects, and organic materials. The book also provides tips on topics such as how to create rigid polyfoam head forms and three different ways to create eyes, as well as step-by-step instructions to construct 13 different masks.

Mask Making Techniques is written for intermediate mask makers, students of theatrical mask making, costume crafts, and prop making courses, as well as prop builders, costume designers, and artists who create Halloween and cosplay costumes.

Mary C. McClung is a professor of costume design at West Virginia University and the author of *Foam Patterning and Construction Techniques* (Routledge, 2016). She has designed costumes, puppets, masks, and sets for theatre, video, and television for over 20 years. As artistic director and crafts artisan for Animax Designs, she had the opportunity to design and build for companies such as Disney, Children's Television Workshop, and Universal Studios. Freelance work includes productions with the Dallas Children's Theatre, Trollwood Performing Arts School, and the Colorado Shakespeare Festival.

Mask Making Techniques

Creating 3-D Characters from 2-D Designs for Theatre, Cosplay, Film, and TV

Mary C. McClung

NEW YORK AND LONDON

Designed cover image: © Dodo mask. Design, construction, and image by Mary C. McClung.

First published 2024
by Routledge
605 Third Avenue, New York, NY 10158

and by Routledge
4 Park Square, Milton Park, Abingdon, Oxon, OX14 4RN

Routledge is an imprint of the Taylor & Francis Group, an informa business

Library of Congress Cataloging-in-Publication Data
Names: McClung, Mary, author.
Title: Mask making techniques : creating 3-D characters from 2-D designs
for theatre, cosplay, film, and TV / Mary C. McClung.
Description: New York, NY : Routledge, 2023. | Includes bibliographical
references and index.
Identifiers: LCCN 2022059355 (print) | LCCN 2022059356 (ebook) |
ISBN 9780367149048 (hbk) | ISBN 9781032379913 (pbk) | ISBN 9781003343264 (ebk)
Subjects: LCSH: Mask making. | Plastics craft. | Costume design. | Theatrical makeup.
Classification: LCC TT898 .M357 2023 (print) | LCC TT898 (ebook) |
DDC 731/.75--dc23/eng/20221212
LC record available at https://lccn.loc.gov/2022059355
LC ebook record available at https://lccn.loc.gov/2022059356

ISBN: 978-0-367-14904-8 (hbk)
ISBN: 978-1-032-37991-3 (pbk)
ISBN: 978-1-003-34326-4 (ebk)

DOI: 10.4324/9781003343264

Typeset in GillSansStd-Light
by KnowledgeWorks Global Ltd.

Dedicated to my husband Alan, my one and only partner in crime.

In memory of Scoutdog.

CONTENTS

PREFACE

The use of the mask and its many iterations has been around for thousands, perhaps hundreds of thousands of years, whether it be for entertainment or religious ceremonies – some might even say that to our ancestors and to some of us, these meant the same thing!

Many archeologists have speculated that early humans may have worn them as a disguise for hunting by wearing the real heads and skins of animals.

Masks could also have been a part of spirit dances or ceremonies anthropomorphizing animals into a human-like characters. Early cave paintings and artifacts suggest these practices, and it is not that far of a leap of the imagination, because many cultures that exist today use masks with costumes in similar ways. Some of these cultures and ceremonies include the Mesoamerican *Dia De Meurtos*, the transformational masks of the Native American Kwakwaka'wakw tribe of the Northwest American Coast, and the funerary rites masks of the Dogon Tribe of Mali in Africa.

The Mesopotamians and the Myceneans sometimes buried their royal dead wearing full bronze or gold helmet-like masks or partial masks, and we know that Greeks used them commonly for staged theatrical performances.

Early Asian, Indian, Native American, South American, and African tribal cultures have used masks similarly. There are some of these masks and mask making traditions still in existence, but unfortunately examples from many cultures have not survived because they were made of degradable, fragile materials or they were destroyed during wars or invasions/colonization. Luckily, some hints from lost cultures exist in the forms of frescoes, relief sculpture, artifacts, and, frankly, common sense.

Looking forward, these masked ceremonies and practices in all their forms, developed over time into traditions, which led to the birth of mask theatre (such as utilized by the Greeks and many other cultures), and even puppetry. These art forms are about telling stories by using an item that transforms a person or object into something else that is seemingly real. Having said this, it is easy to imagine an early human relating the story of a big hunt or a vivid dream by wearing a mask made from the head of an auroch festooned with special beads, feathers, or stones. The use of a mask can make a huge impact on a performance!

When wearing a mask, it can be something of a spiritual experience. When a person puts on a mask, they begin the layering process toward building a character; they are encased in a protective shell, which is dark on the inside, with sometimes limited sightlines. This can make the wearer feel safe and free, and, even if they cannot see themselves, they begin the transformation. The second layer develops when the actor sees their reflection and/or observes the reaction of those seeing the mask. That reaction ultimately feeds the transformation and performance, especially when it is augmented by the third layer: sound/music, costumes, and the audience.

Personally, my first memories of mask-wearing characters were while watching television. I can still remember the dragon from *H.R. Pufnstuff*, the Sid and Marty Kroft series from 1960s and 1970s. I didn't know *Pufnstuff* was a person in a mask and suit; I thought the character was a real being. Halloween was the next step, and then theatre and film. I have never lost my interest in seeing a character come to life wearing a mask: how the actor transforms, and how the audience reacts to the person wearing the mask. There are so many styles, materials, and sizes of masks that can be built and used to transform and/or enhance storytelling. I am constantly searching and learning new techniques for designing and creating them. I hope with this book to share my love of the art form and to shed some light on some of the design and building techniques I have learned over the years. I am still eager to learn more!

Mary McClung
Artist/Storyteller/Explorer

CHAPTER 1

WHAT IS A MASK?

Ultimately a mask is a covering that goes over the face and head and can even extend partially over the body. It can be in the form of (A) a half mask; (B) a three-quarter mask; (C) a full-face mask; (D) a full head mask; or (E) a partial head and body mask.

Masks can be any size from very small to extremely wide, tall, or long (see Figures 1-1A–E). Anything is possible if the mask can be worn or held. If it cannot be worn and/or is not functional as a mask, i.e., a wearable, transformational

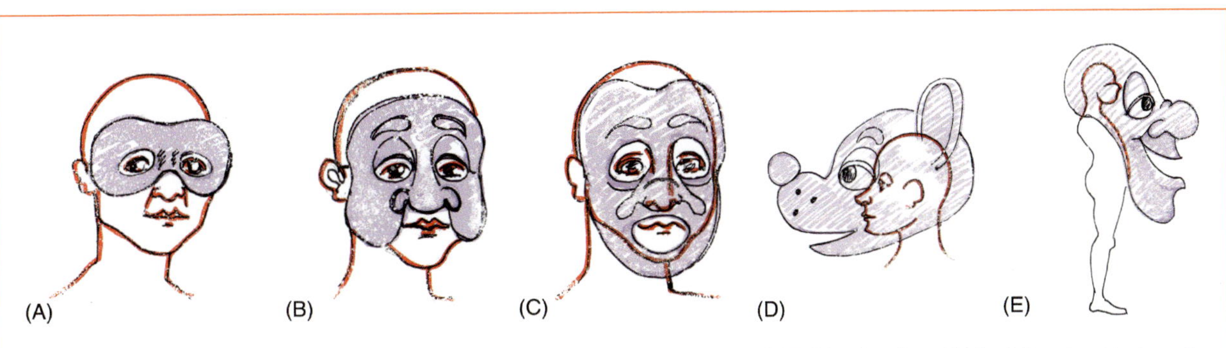

FIGURE 1-1 *Types of masks. A) Half mask; B) Three-quarter mask; C) Full face mask; D) Full head mask; and E) Partial head and body mask*

DOI: 10.4324/9781003343264-1

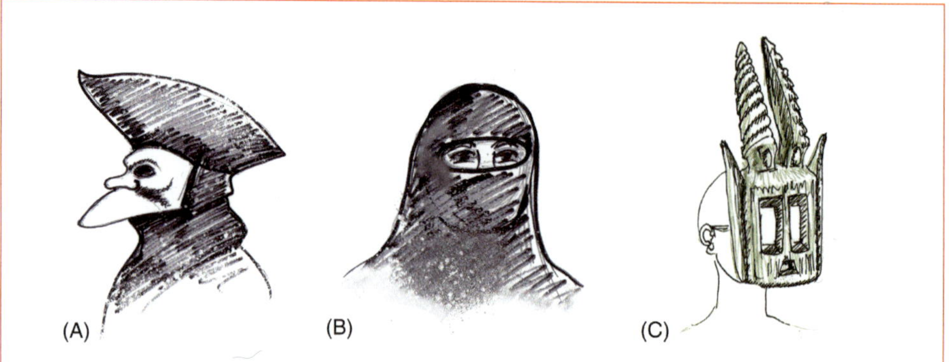

FIGURE 1-2 *Masks used for cultural and religious purposes. A) Sixteenth century Italian bauta costume; B) Muslim niqab; C) Walu antelope mask, one of many worn during Dogon tribe funerary ceremonies*

tool, then it could perhaps be considered a puppet or a piece of art.

It is important to note the difference between a facial prosthetic and a mask. What is the difference? The determination is the permanence of the facial prosthetic versus the immediacy of being able to remove the mask. Is the item adhered to the face? If it is glued to the face, then it is a prosthetic; if not, then it is a mask. However, there are certain types of masks that might employ temporary adhesives in selected places on the face. This book does not go into the art of makeup appliances; however, it will discuss some techniques that occasionally cross over into other crafts and art forms.

MASKS IN EVERYDAY FASHION AND CULTURE

Sometimes masks can be considered a fashion or cultural and/or religious clothing accessory and an item worn for safety (see Figure 1-2A–C). For example, in sixteenth century Italy, the *bauta costume* (half masks with cowls; the masks could be black or white) were worn to disguise the identity of those who might be participating in sordid situations. Another example is the Muslim tradition of wearing a *niqab*. The purpose being to modestly shield the face to demonstrate religious faith. Yet another example is one form of Dogon mask worn during Dama, a funerary rite supporting the passage of the deceased.

CHAPTER 2

MASK DESIGN

READY, SET, GO

One of the most challenging aspects of mask making can be producing a strong design in a timely manner. A mask can be well crafted and comfortable, but if the design falls short, then the story might not be supported to its fullest. To complicate matters, the design may need to be done swiftly. For example, if the mask is a part of a collaborative team for storytelling, the developmental process may be more involved and have a tight deadline, whereas a personal project might have an unlimited time span to flesh out ideas. If the design process is daunting, detailed steps and methods are provided in this chapter that may help jostle and open the mind for creative action.

THE DESIGNER'S TOOLBOX: THE MIND'S EYE, IMAGINATION, VOCABULARY, RESEARCH, AND THE ELEMENTS OF DESIGN

Our brains are the best and most unique design tool we possess. The way in which our individual brains interpret all the gathered information is what sets us apart from everyone else. To that end, it is important to keep our brains continually loaded by reading, looking at images, talking, smelling, touching textures, and learning new strategies for utilizing raw information to express an idea more fully. In addition to expression, these *strategies* or approaches may be employed to jostle the brain out of a habitual pattern, to come at an idea in a different way, such as collage, shadow box, vocabulary, and interpretive dance.

DOI: 10.4324/9781003343264-2

TIP BOX

The Steps When Designing a Mask in a Collaboration

1. Read the play or see the dance rehearsal or art piece.
2. Read any historical information or analysis that pertains to the piece.
3. Meet with the director, artistic director, choreographer, and/or the collaborative team.
4. Begin filling your mind with research and ideas.
5. Take a break!
6. Put together "emotional response" charette/collage.
7. Get feedback by meeting with the team and see what they are thinking.
8. Acquire more specific research and/or initial sketches
9. Get feedback from the artistic team.
10. Produce sketches.
11. Get feedback from the team.
12. Produce more sketches as needed with color and some sense of texture.
13. Meet with the team for a final "touch base."
14. Produce designs in color.
15. Present the final design to the team for the director's approval.
16. Produce working drawings.
17. Estimate the budget.
18. Start building!

I often refer to these tools or strategies as the basic contents for the *mental toolbox* or the *designer's toolbox*. To articulate, stay relevant (and avoid burnout), storytelling designers must stay fresh and open to concepts and new ways to communicate. Storytelling is as ever changing and dynamic as language and culture, and designers must be ready to meet the challenge.

STRATEGIES FOR DESIGNING

When putting together a design for a mask based on the visual, psychological, or emotional needs of a performance, all design practices including the *elements of design* come into play and meld (hopefully) seamlessly. For the practiced designer, these fundamentals are unconsciously combined and utilized. But for the beginning designer, it is important to start adding to the *mental toolbox* by learning various design approaches as well as the elements of design. These are strategies that may be utilized in any order to help solve the challenges of design.

It's Alive! Imagine the Characters in Their Own Environment

After mentally digesting the story, one good approach toward designing a mask is to imagine the character as a living being: how it moves in space and how it might interact with others. When designing anything, be it a mask, costume, puppet, etc., always give it a reality. In the mind's eye, it has its own rhythm and movement patterns – it breathes a certain way. Sometimes it might be helpful to stand and move your own body to get the feel of the character. I have often found myself frowning when I am sketching an angry character or hunching my shoulders when a character seems shy. This may seem like an actor's movement exercise, but it also wholly informs the design.

It is also important not to forget to lean on story and not try to impose too much of our personal taste onto a design: what is the character's purpose or intent? What kind of physical energy does it communicate? Such factors can help shape the character's being and thus the design.

Conceptual Approach: Where and When Do They Live?

As we think about the attitude and reactions of a character, we will inevitably start thinking about what the character is reacting to and how it lives. What does the character eat? Where does it sleep? What is the period? All these and similar factors are the building blocks for the character's design.

Discussions about environment (time and place) correspond to the overall *conceptual approach* of the story.

The *conceptual approach* or *concept* will help determine the *style* or how *stylized* a design should be, i.e., how removed from reality (see the section "Research" later in this chapter). The mask and character should meld with whatever environment or conceptual approach is determined by the needs of the story, and the mission of the collaborative team is to find ways to best create a design that will communicate the story.

For example, if a character is an upbeat, chatty rabbit that lives in a geometric world with sharp angled lighting, this could be echoed in the mask design. It might be as simple as reflections in the eyes of the mask or as complicated as changing the line and shape to become a stylized, geometric interpretation of a rabbit. Conversely, to tell the story of an outsider, it could also mean that the rabbit is soft and fluffy. Considerations as to color and texture would also help this approach. Inspiration for this style could come from charette images of abstract paintings, crazy quilts, kites, geodes, or stained glass.

Again, with practice all these suggestions will flow together as an organic process. However, it is important to delineate and specify terminology.

Use Your Words: How Vocabulary Can Help Shape a Design

Another approach to designing is to ask yourself and/or the director pointed questions about the character within the story. The answers to these questions can then be broken down into single-word adjectives that pertain to the character. This may seem mechanical; however, it is a nuts-and-bolts approach, as it assigns literary attributes that can then be broken down into wonderfully detailed descriptors that help with shape, texture, line, color, and so forth. *Hint:* a thesaurus is a huge help!

TIP BOX

The Power of Vocabulary: Ways to Begin to Assign Adjectives by Asking Questions

1. *How does the character interact with others?*

   Does the masked character argue, or physically attack another character?
   Do they look others in the eye when speaking or do they look off into the distance?

2. *How does the character move?*

   Is the masked character slow or bouncy?
   Does the character dart about and seem elusive?

3. *How is the character described by others?*

   Do they make positive or negative comments?
   What are the comments?

   Is there talk of fearfulness, or "eagerness to be with" or "loath to be around"?

4. *How does the character speak (the rhythm)?*

   Does the character speak fast or slow?
   Do they slur their words or have a staccato, clipped way of talking?

5. *What does the character say?*

   Do they speak of hate, fear, hope, or passion?

6. *What emotional colors or shapes come to the director's mind when they think of this character?*

   Are the colors bright or muted?
   Are the shapes smooth or jagged?

7. What is the character's posture?

How to Use Adjectives

Character example:

Mary Shelly's monster from *Frankenstein* (see Figure 2-1).

Adjective(s) as a result of pointed questions:

Innocent, crafted, sewn together, stumbling, fumbling, clomping, rotting, dangerous, fearful, lonely, loud, wide-eyed, mournful, vengeful, growing, resigned, smart, independent, etc.

Dr. Frankenstein's skills as a surgeon (translated into elements of design adjectives):

Asymmetrical, bumpy, large, stinky, droopy, stiff, angular, coarse, bulbous, tattered, patchwork, stringy, solid, earthy, human-like, bent, etc.

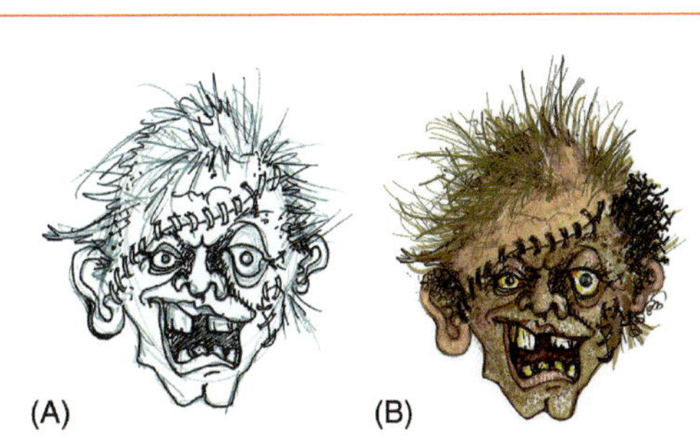

FIGURE 2-1 *Design for Frankenstein's monster using vocabulary: A) sketch; B) with color*

Research!

It is often surprising how little time some designers and artisans spend on research. The research process should never be bypassed, as it is one important way to prepare the mind for creation. Research can include reading (without pictures); looking at magazines and books (without reading); watching and looking at real people, animals, plants, clouds, water, molecular structures, etc.; surfing the internet; talking to experts, such as those from indigenous cultures; and touching, listening, smelling, and sometimes tasting. After all, our brains are fleshy hard drives that never stop learning, and we need to upload as much sensory information as possible to help formulate ideas. Even though we all have different brains, artistic ruts do occur. If we are unable to overcome or diverge from repetitive styles and motifs on project after project, then we may be in a rut.

Taken from the *Oxford Languages English Dictionary*, the word *style* is defined as "a distinctive appearance, typically determined by the principles according to which something is designed." *Merriam-Webster* offers this definition: "a particular manner or technique by which something is done."

There are different disciplines of artists who count on a definitive style – it's one of the things that sells their art and what some people want to buy into. But if you are an artist and/or a designer who is engaged in telling different genres of stories, then having a *style* might become a detriment to the truth of each story. The advice here is to keep the mind fresh, open, and replenished with information.

Many designers mention existing in a "designer frame of mind," which is similar to being "in the zone." In this state, the brain is primed with research and ideas and is very susceptible and open to formulating connections. The designer might look at a table leg and somehow connect it with another idea or shape; or the way another person says something might link another thought, and then that thought creates a new idea. This frame of mind can be amazing and incredibly beneficial, but the mental earth needs to be fertile – tilled and mulched with information – in readiness to catch the seeds of imagination.

Time to Rest and Germinate: Giving the Mind Time to Work

One of the best ways to come up with ideas is taking a break. Step back from the flood of information and let your brain digest and do its work. This can happen during any relaxing pursuit, i.e., during a dog walk, taking a drive, dinner with the family, etc. Perhaps it is no surprise, but sleep and dreams are also very helpful. There is a presleep stage called the *hypnogogic state* that is the space just between wakefulness and dreaming (I know, Peter Pan!) when our minds tend to wander and conjure hallucinations. The brain floats out flotsam-like research and ideas, assembling them in different ways. I can't count the number of times that ideas have come to me in this presleep state.

The Charette or Mood Board: The Tangible Interpretation

Architects, artists, and designers in the areas of fashion, theater, interior decoration, and other disciplines will at some point utilize the *charette* or *mood board*. These are types of collages or visual lists that assemble optical, emotional responses and ideas for projects. The process can help communication with fellow artists, but it also can lead the mask designer down some inspirational rabbit holes, especially if a director or another collaborator submits an image that is unexpected and insightful. A charette/collage/mood board should not go into specific research; however, it should deal with your emotional interpretation of the story. It is the very beginning of visual interpretation of the project for an artist – a literal gut reaction.

What to Wear?

Because a mask is only one visual part of a character, the *costume design* must be considered to help complete the transformation process. Even though masks correspond in design with the costume, sometimes the design of the mask is a separate category of worn items. If you are only asked to design the mask, then for it to be cohesive and successful, you should be working closely with the costume designer to collaborate on texture, fabrics, movement, size, ornamentation, color, etc. Depending on the venue, at least half if not more of the effectiveness of the character could be impacted by the costume design. This might be less impactful in film, because close-ups are frequently used and little of the costume might be seen.

However, if you are designing the entire character (always my preference), then you still need to consider the integration of both mask and costume. If a character is moving about in your mind's eye, then you are probably already thinking about hands, feet, toenails, movement of fabric, hair, eyes, food stains, style of clothing, trim and ornamentation, and so on.

It is important to note again that the more you design, the more all these techniques will become second nature and an automatic part of the design process. Practice does make perfect, or at least it can sometimes create good habits.

PUTTING IDEAS ON PAPER

After gathering as much mental and physical information as possible, it is time to push forward with creating the two-dimensional (2-D) mask design. Before jumping in, it is important to review the elements of design. This is the foundation terminology that will help the designer compartmentalize and consider all aspects of the design as well as assist when discussing and explaining ideas to the conceptual team.

EOD: The Elements of Design

Though masks are specifically discussed in this book, the *elements of design* (EOD) are the building blocks of all art and design. This collection of artistic components includes *line, shape, space, color, scale, mass, value, texture*, and more. *Movement* is also added to this list because masks, like costumes, are made to be worn and sometimes move in conjunction with the actor's response.

1. **Line:** *Line* is one of the most basic of the design elements (see Figure 2-2). It is the quality of the line that helps define the initial impression. How linear, broken, curvilinear, and so on a mask is determined its emotional attitude. Line can also be described as the type of *line quality*: how the line is drawn, whether thick, thin, blunt, wavy, and so on.

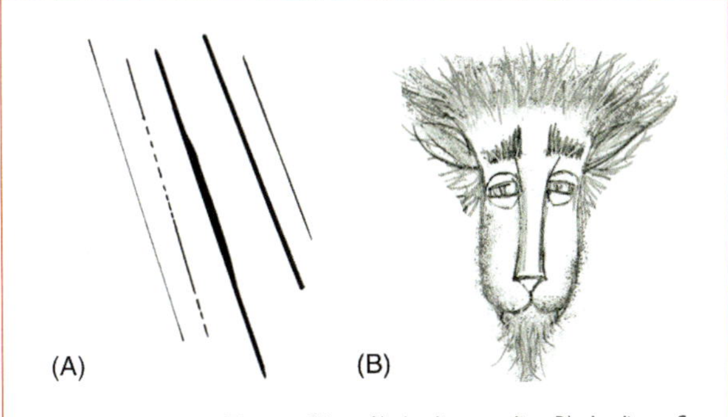

FIGURE 2-2 *Types of line: A) the line quality; B) the line of an object*

2. **Shape:** This refers to the overall shape of a mask (see Figure 2-3). Is it triangular, square, circular, oval, etc.?

   Considering a broad view of a *shape* can help when determining how a single mask might work or how a group of masks might work together on stage.

3. **Space:** This deals with the area within and around a shape. *Positive space* is that area contained within a shape. *Negative space* is the space around the shape. Question to ask is whether the exterior space or negative space is affected by the object (see Figure 2-4). This is especially important when designing for shadow theater or other applications when a silhouette needs to be emphasized.

4. **Scale:** The *scale* of a mask is its height and width. How big or small is the mask? This might seem a like an obvious consideration, but bear in mind the power of the unexpected when dealing with size. Figure 2-5 depicts the difference between tiny versus large. Pushing the boundaries of a conventional mask, which is often about the size of a human face, can jangle perceptions. Consider the impact of a giant mouse head or a very small rhinoceros mask.

5. **Mass:** The *mass* is the bulkiness, density, and solidity versus the airiness of a mask. Even though a mask is small, it might look heavy depending on the corresponding details of the material it is made from, the texture, or the line and shape. On the other hand, a large mask that might be porous or floating may look very lightweight (see Figure 2-6).

6. **Texture:** One of my favorite elements of design, the *texture* of an object deals with the surface

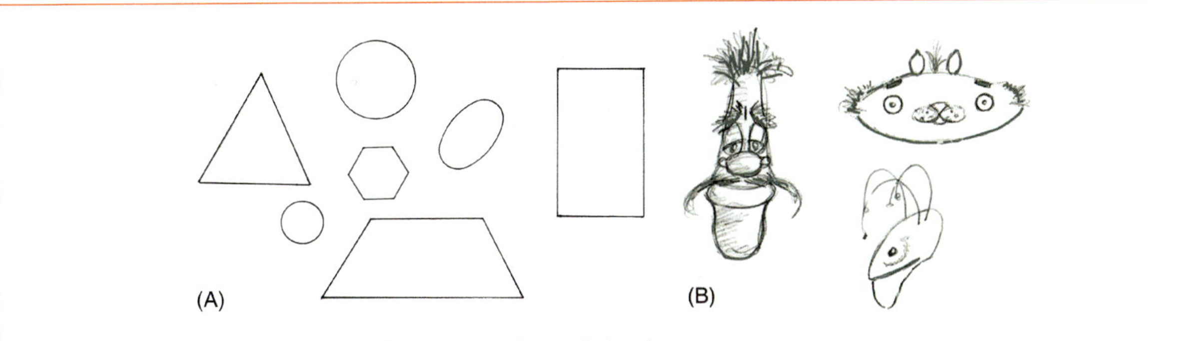

FIGURE 2-3 *A) Different shapes; B) different shapes when applied to characters*

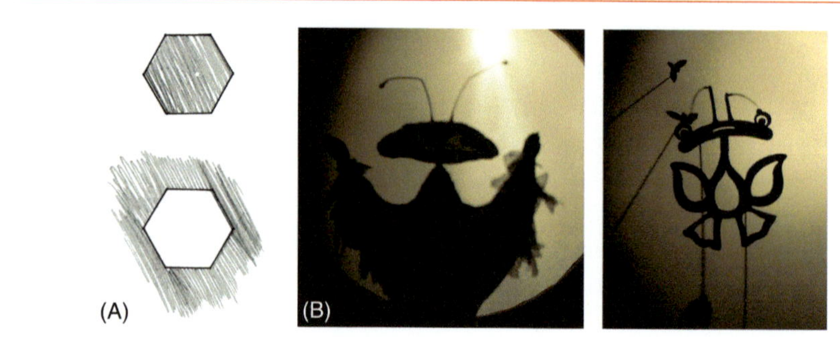

FIGURE 2-4 *A) Positive and negative space; B) shadow puppetry using positive and negative space*

FIGURE 2-5 *The impact of small versus large*

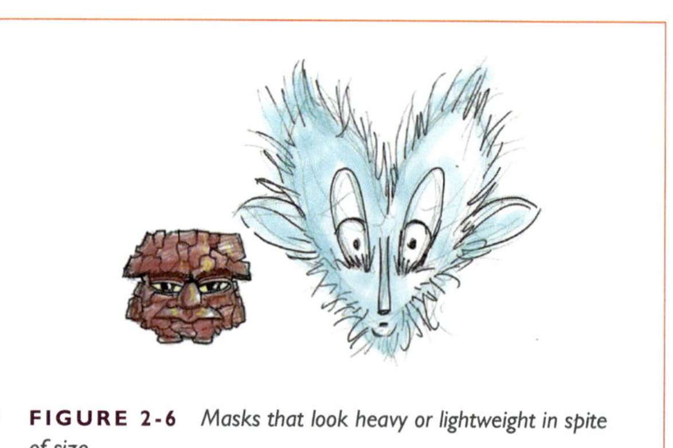

FIGURE 2-6 *Masks that look heavy or lightweight in spite of size*

treatment (see Figure 2-7). Is a mask slick and glossy, cracked, or spikey? This is all determined by the textural finish.

7. **Color:** There are many *color* scheme choices, including *complementary, analogous, monochromatic, neutral, triadic,* and more (see Figure 2-8). The color of a mask and/or its color arrangement can have quite an emotional impact on an audience.

8. **Value:** This term is associated with the light and dark qualities of a color or hue (see Figure 2-9). Use it when discussing contrast. Remember: *value* deals with light and dark, whereas *intensity* deals with the vibrancy of a color.

9. **Movement:** This is not normally considered an element of design; however, masks are three-dimensional (3-D) worn objects that may depend on ancillary movements to help enhance the character. Adding decorative items such as feathers, shredded silk, grasses, horsehair tubing, the actor's fingers, and such can add a floating or "living" movement. This has sometimes been called "sympathetic movement," that is, when a decoration or attached feature echoes the movement of the original object.

FIGURE 2-7 *Different textures on the same design*

FIGURE 2-8 *Different color schemes on the same mask: A) complementary, B) analogous, C) monochromatic, and D) neutral*

FIGURE 2-9 *Value differences on the same mask*

TIP BOX

Style: Interpreting the Human Face in Different Ways

The power of the *elements of design* (Figure 2-10).

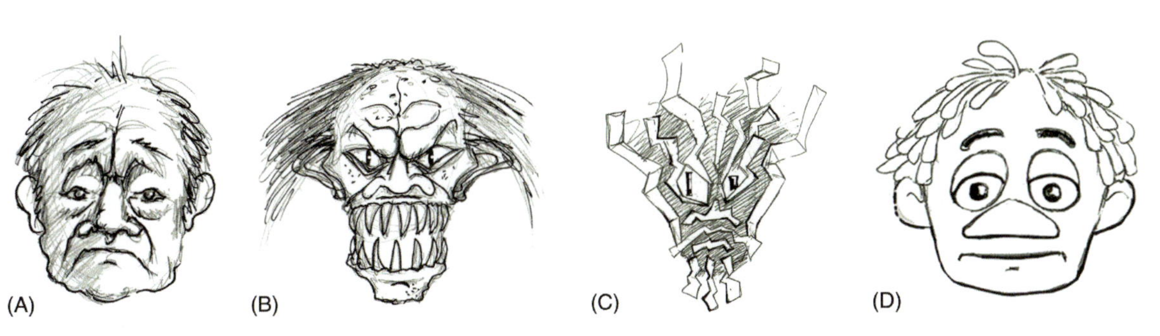

FIGURE 2-10 *A) Realistic, B) horror, C) deconstructed, and D) cartoon*

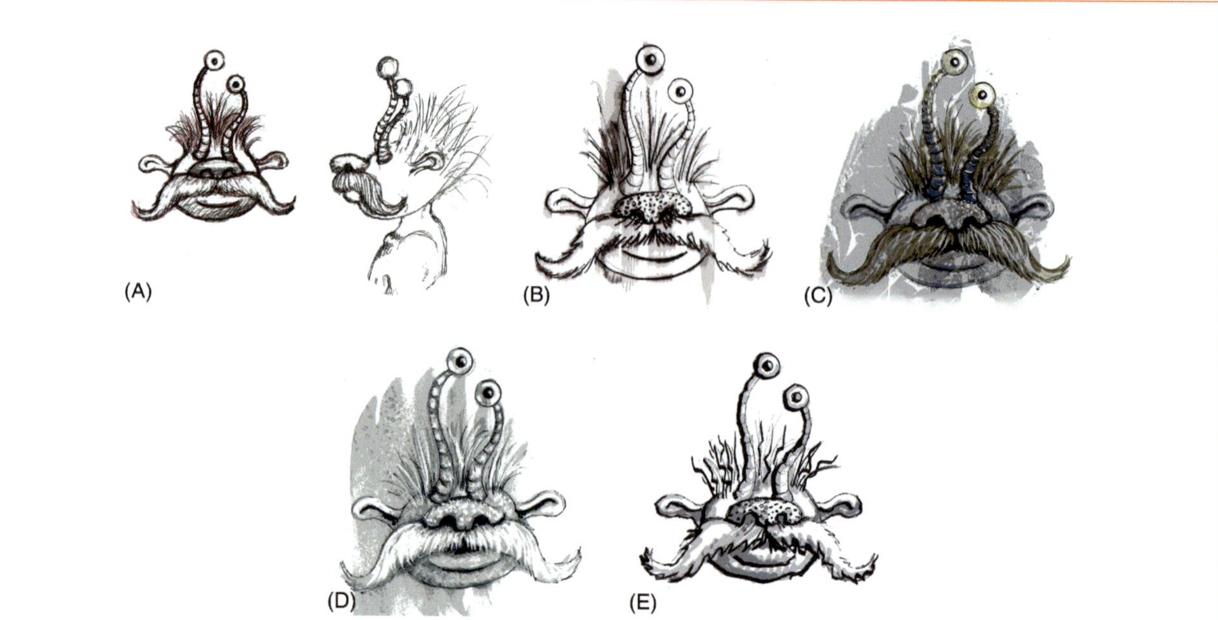

FIGURE 2-11 *Drawing techniques for emotional impact: A) front and profile line drawing; B) bleeding pen technique; C) capillary technique; D) salt; E) beveled marker*

PRESENTING THE DESIGN

After conceptualizing and while physically sketching, some deliberation over the presentation of the design might be considered. A finished rendering may be used to help emote and translate the concept to the actors and the audience. To help communicate the mood of the design, often a specific technique might be employed to help tell the story. This may be achieved using hand drawing, digital techniques, or a combination of them both. Don't forget to do working drawings to help communicate your ideas to the shop. A swatch board with fabrics and painted samples is also helpful (Figure 2-11).

PRACTICAL FACTORS WHEN DESIGNING A MASK

Practical factors should always be taken into consideration when designing a mask. These factors include 1) character movement; 2) the venue; 3) and the size of entrances and exits (Figure 2-12). Other factors, such as sightlines and making the mask wearable, will be explained in Chapter 4.

1. **Character Movement:** One of the most important considerations is how the character needs to move. If the character needs to do cartwheels or flips, then the mask will need to be very secure and squashy, and some thought about size should be considered or tested. If there is time in the production process, a sample mask of different sizes can help determine how big the design could and should be and the type of materials to use.
2. **The Venue and Space:** When designing, consider the type and size of the performance space and if it is inside or outside. With regard to film, designing can be different from designing for theater because the distance the audience (the camera) is away from the actor. Additionally, when using masks for film, there might need to be several dozen copies used for different scenes. Those used for close-ups can have microfinishes done with an airbrush and layers of translucent glazes. They may require many thousands of seamless hand- or laser-cut and glued pieces that are for only one shot. There could also be dozens of these to account for accidental damage. Conversely, in a theater setting, generally the actor cannot stop in the middle of a scene onstage to find a detailed mask or put on the one that spouts blood. So, the mask for that venue/genre should be designed, painted, and finished for what the entrances and exits allow (or clever use of slight-of-hand and blind spots). Though there are exceptions, in general theater does not often allow the luxury of changing duplicate masks and costumes for a certain effect, therefore the effect is often built in and waiting to go.

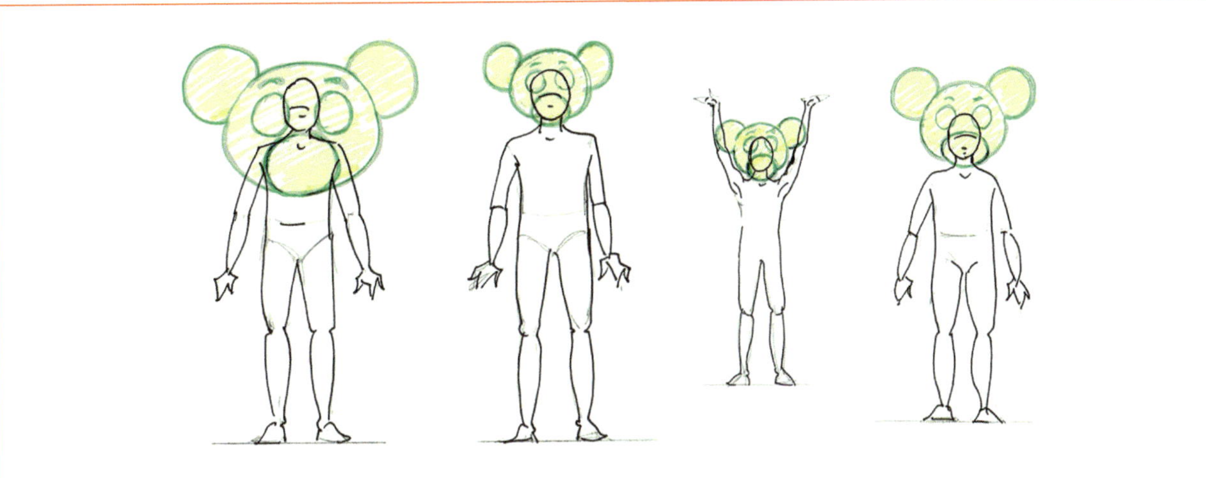

FIGURE 2-12 *Logistics of mask size, human anatomy, and movement*

In terms of detail for theater, the middle of the house or the middle row of seating is commonly the distance for which theatrical designers gauge their level of detail. The audience will not necessarily see microdetail such as an abundance of very fine wrinkles or tiny scales, but they will see the bolder strokes of paint and any 3-D shapes needed to communicate age or expression. This is especially important for large venues. Unless there is a video screen projecting the show above the proscenium, bolder shapes and high-contrast painted finishes are often used to communicate the design, or the work will be lost. For any theatrical space, time should be dedicated to viewing the finishes and textures from a distance (see Figure 2-13). This is commonly the case with most feature films because of big investments: many screen tests are done before filming to prescreen the *look* of what the characters are wearing.

Another important aspect of venue and space is the difference between 2-D painted details and three-dimensional (3-D) layered or carved details. I always lean toward 3-D texture as a rule. This is because the mask is a real shape moving in space under angled lighting. If 3-D details such as wrinkles, pustules, and bulging eyes are present, the lights will cast shadows and enhance the shapes. Painted dimension is still vital to enhancing the object and should be integrated with texture and sculptural details.

3. **Indoors or Out:** In addition to spatial considerations, thought should go toward whether the mask will be used in an outdoor or indoor performance space. The environment, i.e., weather and light, can impact the use of a mask. Lighting can play a huge part of how a mask might be seen, but if you are outside in the daylight, the variations a lighting designer can contribute to support

FIGURE 2.13 *Painting on a mask used in a large venue needs to be pronounced: A) mask for Dracula; B) close-up of a three-quarter mask, the West Virginia University Production of* Dracula*; C) full head mask for Marley from the West Virginia Public Theatre's Production of* A Christmas Carol *(2018)*

the performance will be missing. Also, if a mask is used outside in an area where there is a lot of wind, rain, or extreme heat, thoughts toward using materials that are water resistant or that will let the wind pass through, or adding a fan for your actor, will be important. This is not to say that the masks should not be worn outside. Native cultures have been using them for thousands of years with total awareness and acceptance of the environment. Though Western fire codes might have a lot to say about it (safety should always be a major consideration), masks worn lit by firelight can be both truly haunting and inspiring.

4. **Entrances and Exits:** Communication is always key. If there are tall or wide masks used in a show, then this needs to be communicated to not only the director and actor but also the scenic designer and the scene shop. There are many comic scenes with characters straining to get through doorways because their hair is too tall or their costume is too wide. Not all theatrical shows need or want a comic scene with Jacob Marley straining to get through a tiny door or to see Aida get down on hands and knees because her collar and headpiece is too tall. *Rule of thumb*: plan and communicate with all the parties. The good news is if you ever make this painful mistake once, you will never make it again … hopefully.

CHAPTER 3

SAFETY

Anyone who makes a mask will at some point encounter a tool or material that might not be 100% safe. The goal of practicing safe building techniques is to protect you and everyone else in the room so we all can keep doing the things we love to do. If you are missing an eye because you did not wear goggles or are unable to breathe properly because of not wearing a dust mask, then this will become obvious and cumbersome when you are later trying to build another detailed mask. I look at our bodies as wonderful tools that we need to keep clean, honed to perfection (… as much as possible), rested, and energized in equal amounts.

STAY AWARE

Almost all human-made chemicals, including some of those in cosmetics, detergents, foods, and especially those made from petroleum, have Safety Data Sheets (SDS) or Materials Safety Data Sheets (MSDS). These are required by law to be available to the consumer in the United States. Many other countries have similar required documents.

A casual read of food additives and other everyday chemicals we commonly encounter may be eye opening (and perhaps horrifying, to say the least), but it is better to know what we are exposing ourselves to than to skip through life and then wonder why our left arm suddenly dropped off. Admittedly, this is an extreme illustration. However, I have had acquaintances (all "makers" stay in touch) who have mentioned that they were experiencing allergic reactions to materials that previously did not affect them. I also have many colleagues who are now suffering horribly debilitating diseases wherein they have lost control of their bodies. I do not pretend to be a diagnostician, but even now there are

DOI: 10.4324/9781003343264-3

pesticides and herbicides that are being recalled because they are suspected of causing similar symptoms. Who's to say that, while working in a theater shop, these acquaintances did not encounter some sort of chemical that was at the time believed to be safe? The message here is to be aware and do as much as you can to protect yourself and others.

SOLID AND GASEOUS INHALANTS

Though inhalants are mostly defined as fumes that can make a person high, *gaseous inhalants* generally include those chemical fumes that stay in the air unless diffused or sucked away. They are not always invisible and do not always have a bad smell. Some gases such as volatile organic compounds (VOCs) in foam do not have a smell but still may cause respiratory and neurological damage. Therefore, it is important to read the MSDS or SDS of all the materials used and wear the recommended safety equipment. On the other hand, solid inhalants can include fumed silica, glitter, plastic dust, Styrofoam dust, glass fiber dust, baby powder, alginate, plaster, etc.

EXTERIOR AND INTERIOR ABSORPTION

Often unknown to the enthusiastic mask artist, the skin, throat, lungs, and other organs are capable of absorbing and sometimes storing chemicals in fumes, liquids, and dusts. Large particulates can be inhaled, stored in the lungs, and/or absorbed into the bloodstream. It is also possible to swallow particulates, which are digested and absorbed into the bloodstream, then stored in the liver and kidneys. Even though fat layers and mucus membranes are there to help, this is still fair to those organs!, absorption through the skin and eyes is also possible. Wear protective safety gear!

An Additional Note: The most unfortunate aspect of many forms of mask making is the use of toxic and unsustainable petroleum-based products: dreaded plastics, foams, resins, etc. There are still many individuals and native cultures who use wood, natural floral fibers, natural pigments, and animal by-products. Even though I write this book about using many harmful and dangerous materials, I recommend and support that we all try to invent solutions (for example, supporting sustainable construction and population control and resisting overconsumption) to change our outlook for a healthier world. There are still ways we can curb waste and practice more care when using potentially dangerous chemicals. I added these suggestions throughout in the Tip Boxes.

THE MOST COMMON REASONS FOR *NOT* WEARING PROTECTIVE GEAR

1. ***We forget to do it.***
   When we creators are "in the zone," it is extremely difficult to remember to think ahead or stop and put on a mask. I genuinely did not think about it until I smelled the fumes or felt the dust flicking against my face. Since then, I have heard so many horror stories about damaged eyes, breathing problems, and cumulative allergies that I have made putting on my protective gear a regular part of my process. I am planning on having a functional body for a long time.
2. ***The safety items were not available.***
   This is a matter of developing the habit of including the items in the budget and on the shopping list and then restocking them regularly, just like you keep toilet paper and soap in stock at home. It needs to become a part of the routine, and the only way to establish this routine is by starting it.
3. ***It wasn't convenient to the process.***
   Safety wear for the eyes used to be one of my least favorite things to wear because they fogged up and/or the lenses became scratched and useless after I put them away carelessly. Since then, I have discovered many varieties of safety glasses, with and without side panels, and elastic goggles (like diving masks) that have small air holes on the sides for ventilation. I prefer the second style, as they block all the dust, and the holes vent moisture. I now also take steps to either slip them in a case or keep them in my work apron to protect the lenses.

   If it seems inconvenient to the process to wear a particular style of safety accessory, keep looking until you find what works. Luckily, there are now different sizes of latex, vinyl, and nitril gloves (hooray), there are wonderful paper-based protective sleeves with elastic on the top and bottom (hooray again), and there are different sizes of fabric and paper coveralls as well as fabric bib overalls (my personal favorite). Respirators not only come in different sizes with soft rubber face masks but have different kinds of cartridges for a variety of materials (hip, hip, hooray!).

VENTILATION

I believe that ventilation is one of the most important forms of safety. If there is good ventilation, then fumes and particulates can be abated. It lessens the chance of inhalation in case a respirator or dust mask is forgotten, and if there are other people in the room they are protected too.

Options include portable dust and fume collection units (resembling a Dr. Seuss gadget), big ventilation hoods and paint booths, a room such as a garage with the door open and one or more fans behind the workspace blowing outside, or … working outside. Living in the Northeast can present problems with ventilation as a lot of the chemicals used do not cure below 60 degrees. If this is a problem, try and do the fume-intensive work during warmer months, or make certain no one else is in the building (while you wear a respirator and get your work done – ha, ha!). But seriously, you might be able to lay on a layer of fiberglass outside when it's below 60 degrees, then bring the item back inside to a warmer temperature so it can cure while it gases off in front of a portable ventless fume hood designed to filter noxious fumes. This is wildly inconvenient, but it will save your brain and lungs down the road.

RESPIRATORS AND DUST MASKS

Respirators are an essential piece of personal equipment (Figure 3-1). These come in a variety of sizes. The better kind have wonderfully flexible, and comfortable, rubber masks for the face. MSDS or SDS sheets say exactly what chemicals are in the material being used and commonly recommend what type of filter cartridges are needed for the respirator. If these documents do not list the cartridges, then call the manufacturer's *technical support* who specialize in safety equipment (such as Lab Safety) and ask them for help. There are places that will test the fit and filtration quality of your respirator. Check the web for *respirator test fittings* or contact the Occupational Safety and Health Administration (OSHA) for locations.

FIGURE 3-1 *Respirators and dust masks*

Note: Depending on the chemical that is being filtered, the *longevity* of cartridges may be shortened to only a few hours of use. Keep a taped schedule on or in the respirator storage bag to keep track of the time used. Also always store the respirator in an airtight bag, as the cartridges are always filtering air and particulate even when not being worn, and the lifespan of cartridges might therefore be shortened.

Dust masks are also essential. Because of COVID, even the greenest layperson knows something about disposable filtration masks. Dust masks come in a variety of filtration capabilities, shapes, and sizes. Keeping one in a bag (to keep off the dog hair and work dust) in your work apron pocket is helpful and makes it more convenient. Remember: Dust masks only filter large particulate (what you can see); they do not filter gases or fumes and could even make inhalation worse by trapping fumes inside the mask with you.

TIE UP HAIR

Hair, scarves, dangly jewelry, and loose clothing can easily get wrapped around and sucked into machinery and even hand tools. You can still be pretty and stay safe; just use common sense.

EYE PROTECTION

Goggles and safety glasses should be kept close to where you are working so you can conveniently grab a pair when needed (Figure 3-2). There are also face shields with eyeglass arms that are helpful, but take the time to store them upright, hanging, or in a cloth bag so the lenses do not get scratched.

PROTECTING HEARING

Hearing loss is a common problem and many people do not know they have it (Figure 3-3). It's hard to imagine that the tiny and delicate membranes in our ears are constantly

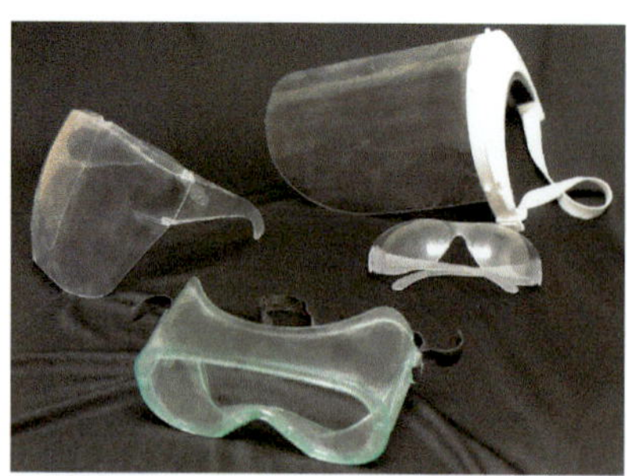

FIGURE 3-2 *Different styles of eye protection*

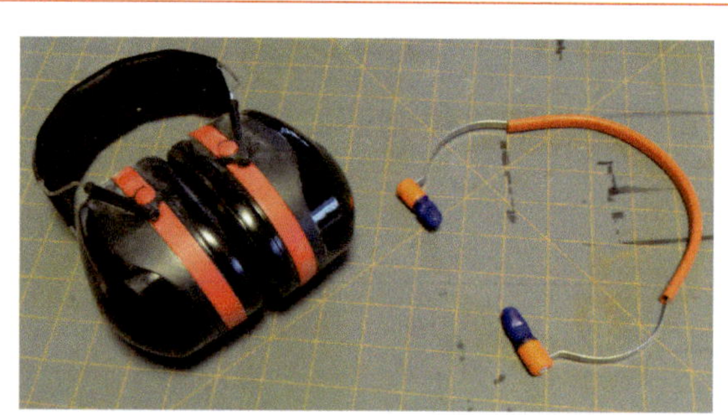

FIGURE 3-3 *Types of hearing protection*

vibrating and conducting sounds for us and that we can lose our ability to hear over time by being exposed to loud music, noise from equipment, and sometimes from genetic predisposition. The noise from power tools can be easily diminished by wearing ear protection, and it is available in a variety of forms.

HANDS, ARMS, AND BODY

Hands

I have a slight phobia about losing parts or the use of my hands. These are a big part of my income, so I pay special attention to interior aches, pains, and skin. There are several different kinds of flexible safety gloves available. Latex is still around, but now there are gloves made of thin vinyl and nitrile. There are four sizes available (small, medium, large, and extra-large) and different thicknesses for dealing with toxic substances and those that might be more abrasive. I find the heavier 9-to-11-millimeter nitrile gloves sold at Harbor Freight are perfect for all sorts of procedures. They last much longer than others. I don't normally throw away gloves unless there is a hole or they are covered with goo. They can be washed with soap and water while you are wearing them, just like you wash your hands, and can be dried with a towel.

> TIP BOX
>
> **Clean Off Sticky Chemicals**
>
> 1. Warm soapy water.
> 2. Pumice-based automotive cleaners such as Permatex. Always make certain that the "pumice" is not microbeads (plastic particles) but rather ground nut shells or fine milled sand.
> 3. Acidic acid (vinegar).
> 4. Citrus-based removers. These use citric acid as their base.
> 5. If none of those help, try a quick wipe of 91% or 99% alcohol, then wash with warm soap and water.
> 6. For dry skin issues, use Vaseline, Utter Cream, Cornhuskers, or Cetaphil lotion.

Arms

Disposable safety gloves never go high enough on the arms, and I am always getting paint and other materials on the bottoms of my lower arms. Options include 1) using disposable Tyvek sleeves available by the bag; 2) wrapping and taping plastic bags on the arms; and 3) cutting the sleeves off an old shirt or unitard or using a long sock with the toes removed (Figure 3-4). These are at least washable and will to some extent protect from abrasions and paint.

Body Protection

It is possible to purchase disposable Tyvek body suits, aprons, and gowns, but these are hot and have no pockets (Figure 3-5). Rubber aprons are also helpful when casting

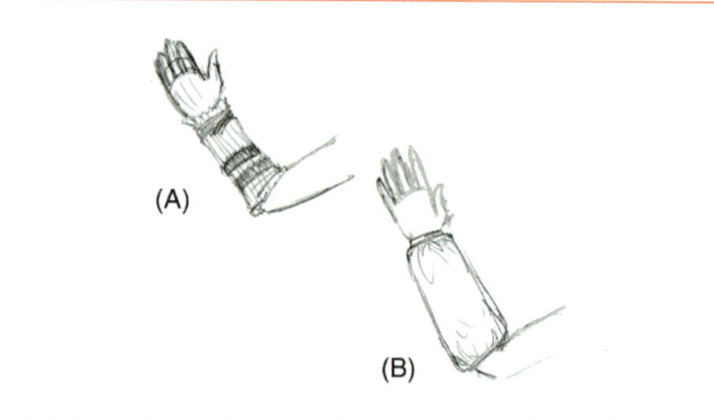

FIGURE 3-4 *Two styles of arm protection: A) a modified tube sock secured with tape; B) a Tyvek sleeve*

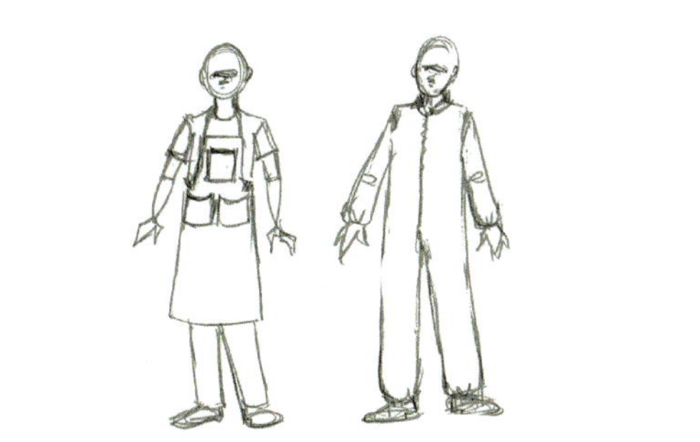

FIGURE 3-5 *Two styles of body protection: an apron and a Tyvek coverall*

silicone and other liquids that might splash. My favorites are full cloth aprons with no sleeves and two pockets. I will also wear additional items over these when using messy resins and glass fiber.

BACK AND FOOT CARE

What do you do when you work? It's mostly standing, sitting, bending, breathing, and seeing. If you stand for long periods of time on a cement floor, this can hurt the arches of the foot and the heel pad. Plantar fasciitis is a common result of standing on cement. Certainly, close-toed shoes (a must!) with a good arch support and thick soles are helpful, but antifatigue mats are invaluable.

- Good shoes along with regular exercise is the best defense against back injuries occurring when moving the bandsaw or unloading 10-to-50-pound bags of hydrocal.
- Lower-back support belts are helpful.
- A seemingly little thing such as proper table height will also help counteract back and neck aches.

Depending on personal height and the application, table heights can vary. I like a taller table (above my natural waist) because I am generally doing things such as patterning, gluing, dremeling, painting, etc. For sanding and styling wigs, the table height is generally lower.

A RECAP OF SAFETY TIPS

1. Wear eye protection.
2. Wear breathing protection.
3. Tie back long hair (head and facial) and do not wear scarves, loose clothing, or dangly jewelry (lanyards with keys included).
4. Wear hearing protection.
5. Wear gloves and arm sleeves when working with chemicals.
6. Wear proper shoes when working with tools and for standing for long periods of time.
7. Invest in padded floor mats (antifatigue mats).
8. Protect the back by exercising and placing the worktable at a proper height.

CHAPTER 4

THINGS TO CONSIDER WHEN CONSTRUCTING A MASK

Consider the job of an actor. Their purpose is to stand in front of a live group of strangers while attempting to convince them that they are a different character in a different time and sometimes a different world. They must memorize a script, remember their blocking and timing as they interact with a bunch of other actors doing the same thing. To that end, in addition to creating an appropriate visual object (the mask), mask makers must do everything they can to make the mask a workable/wearable tool to for the performance. This can include the following:

1. Comfort.
2. Clear sightlines.
3. Being secure on the wearer.
4. Ensuring that vocalization will not be hampered.

If these conditions are not met to the satisfaction of the wearer, director, and the audience, then the transformational performance may not be as complete and successful as needed. For example, if the mask is not secure and the actor is constantly afraid that it will fall off, then they may not feel comfortable moving as freely as the character should. Often, there are compromises to meet both visual and movement needs, but it is the job of the mask maker to produce a mask that is as wearable, safe, and stable as possible.

COMFORT

This includes types of padding, ventilation (and cooling), weight, and cleanliness.

Padding is generally done with raw or covered foam, but in the end whatever works is what you use: this can include

DOI: 10.4324/9781003343264-4

FIGURE 4-1 *A) Open-cell foam and B) rigid closed-cell foam*

FIGURE 4-3 *A) Vinyl nitrile foam and B) polypropylene foam*

layers of fabric, quilted polypuff, rag, straw pillows, and so on. Foams and fabrics can be layered from soft to dense, but the firmer the foam, the more stability on the head.

Note: When surveying interviews and articles related to the best military helmet padding, a combination of the interior hammock style liner with foam padding seems the most popular – for air circulation and for impact resistance.

Foam can come in two forms: closed cell or open cell (see Figure 4-1).

1. *Closed-cell foam* is a dense, meaty foam that has no pores. It can be found in multiple colors and varieties depending on the chemicals from which it is made. It may also be soft or rigid.
2. *Open-cell foam* has air pockets. When sliced or cut, it has visible pores. This style/form can be found with many varieties of foam (rigid or soft).

Ethylene vinyl acetate (EVA) foam (Figure 4-2) is a very common closed-cell foam used to pad out helmets. This foam can range in flexibility: L-200 is very flexible, whereas L-600 is less so. It can be used on everything from fatigue mats to sneakers and flip flops. It comes in multiple colors. Premade EVA foam helmet-lining sets can be found online in different shapes for variations in padding. Because EVA foam can become slimy and slightly abrasive when moisture accumulates between it and skin, most of these pieces, if not all, should be covered with fabric. EVA can be molded/shaped with an even, careful heat distribution or patterned to fit curves, such as those of the human head; therefore, adding this to a helmet or a custom mask interior could be done with multiple fittings and the right adhesive.

Vinyl nitrile and *polypropylene* (Figure 4-3) closed-cell foams are both used commonly in military helmets because they have great impact resistance, can withstand heat, and are durable. Hopefully the masks discussed in this book will not be used for combat or wildly violent activities. If you are needing something to withstand impact, the outside decoration would need to be built with that in mind.

Expandable polystyrene (EPS) (Figure 4-4) is a stiff bead foam commonly used to make coolers and styrene cups. It is lightweight and, in a factory environment, is easily formed for human head shapes. EPS is also sometimes used as a helmet liner for sports and works equally well for masks. Even though it is rated for one high impact situation because it crushes, most entertainment masks are not used for those activities – still, it is good to know a material's limitations.

FIGURE 4-2 *Ethylene vinyl acetate (EVA) foam*

FIGURE 4-4 *EPS or XPS foam*

FIGURE 4-5 *Rigid (white) noncross-linked polyethylene foam and the crosslinked (dark gray) polyethylene foam*

Even with this being the case, thick sections of polystyrene can be cut and spaced around a helmet's interior or solid pieces can be carved into a head shape and adhered inside the mask by itself. It may also act as a foundation for other materials. Everything depends on the space in the mask interior and its use.

Polyethylene foam (Figure 4-5) is another good foam to use as a spacer in its noncross-linked form. This foam is not as messy as EPS but does not have the same positive impact characteristics. It is also great for carving and covering.

Polyurethane foam can also be used for padding. This class includes the small-cell foam *polyether,* generically called "upholstery foam," and a drain-dry, reticulated large-cell foam (Figure 4-6). Polyurethane ranges in softness and can be so soft that it compromises fit and comfort. If the mask's weight causes the helmet to sink down on the head, compressing the foam, then whether the foam is soft or not is irrelevant (memory foam may fall into this category). This foam should also be covered with fabric. Multiple thick layers can be used successfully if there is enough room in the mask to allow for it. Small cell upholstery foam will absorb moisture and bacteria, so it should be covered or replaced often for cleanliness. Note that many foams are antimicrobial, which really helps with smell. The drain-dry, reticulated large-cell version of polyurethane dries much quicker than the small-cell version.

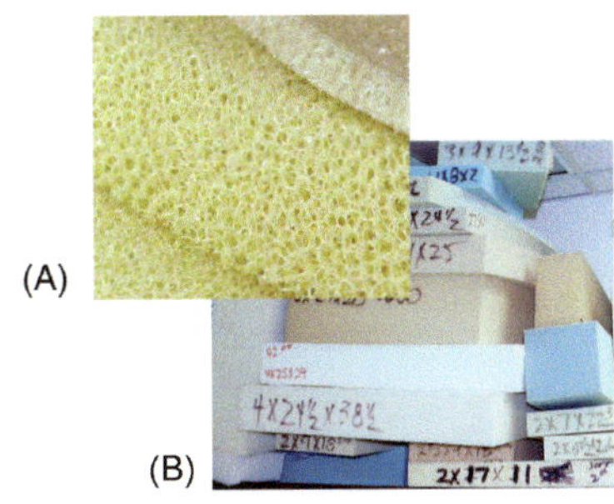

FIGURE 4-6 *Polyurethane foam: A) large cell, drain-dry, reticulated, or "scot" foam; B) small cell "upholstery" or polyether foam*

New Materials

Elastic microlattice material, newly developed by HRL Laboratories, could replace foam for used in sports, outdoor activity, and military helmets. HRL describes it as a "polymer material [that] has an open internal structure not unlike the interlinked struts of the Eiffel Tower. It is claimed that this feature not only allows the material to [absorb impacts, but it also allows] heat and moisture to pass through. By contrast, traditional foam padding simply holds sweat against the wearer's head."

SIGHT

The ability to see out of a mask can be achieved in many ways. The *material* and *location* of the "vision port" should be ascertained during fittings and/or rehearsals with the actor. Materials can include flexible fabric netting, plastic or metal screens, perforated metals, or thermoplastics (Figure 4-7). Whatever material is chosen should meld with the design and be able to be stitched, riveted, glued, or wired into the mask.

In terms of vision port location, it is possible to use the shadows in folds and features on a mask's face, neck, or upper-head area to cut strategic slots or ports. These can sometimes accentuate shadows that will never be noticed during a performance. Suggested areas include

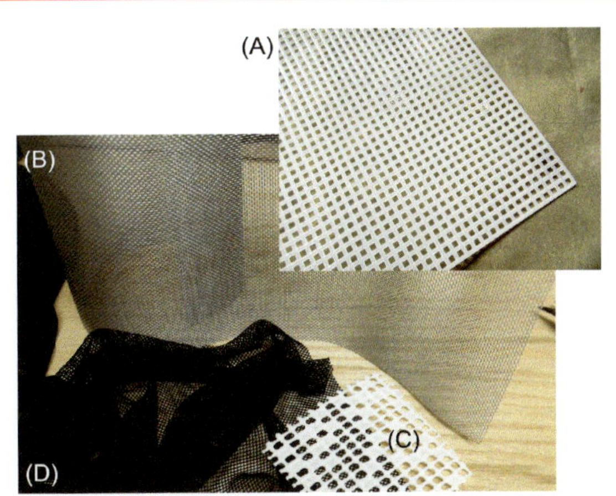

FIGURE 4-7 *Types of materials for a vision port: A) low-density polyethylene plastic latch-hook craft foundation; B) one type of wire mesh; C) varaform (don't use if the mask will be exposed to high heat); D) flexible fabric netting*

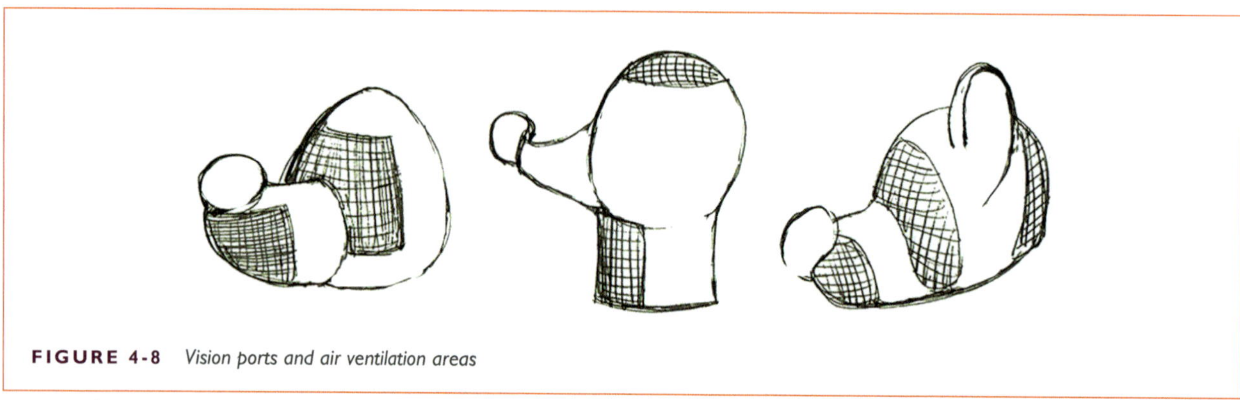

FIGURE 4-8 *Vision ports and air ventilation areas*

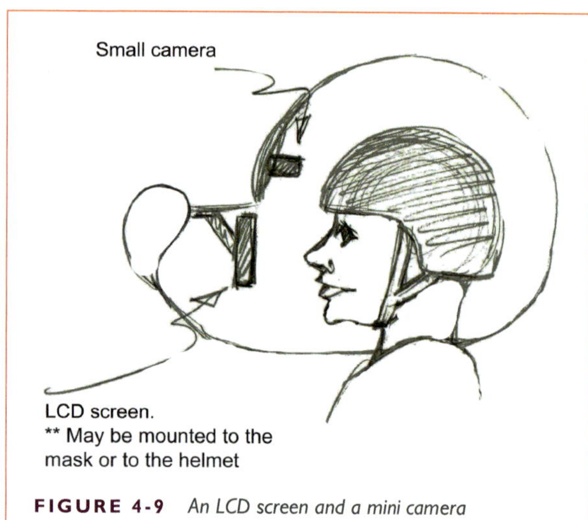

FIGURE 4-9 *An LCD screen and a mini camera*

nostril holes, behind the alae or nostril crease, in or under the eyes, in or behind ears, in areas with hair or fur, open mouths, under chins, etc. (Figure 4-8). If many of these are opened, it can also increase not only sightlines but airflow and ventilation.

Cameras and screens can be an important part of sight (see Figure 4-9). Liquid crystal display (LCD) screens may be used inside the mask to see what the audience sees, or a small camera might be included so that the actor can see what the mask sees. These small monitors and mini cameras are relatively inexpensive. Though many locations will work, cameras should be mounted in the eye area, so you see what the character sees. This will help with focus, giving the actor the ability to address the audience at the correct angle or look another character in the eye.

THE CORRECT FIT

There are really no rules for keeping a mask on an actor's head, but there are many ways to approach solving the challenge. Masks that function well for the performances are those that fit and are balanced well. If a helmet is being used, then padding appropriately can help it fit (more snuggly) and can keep it from slipping forward over the actor's face or backward off the actor's head. Sometimes this can be achieved by only adding padding, but also a combination of chin and rear cranial straps may be used to secure the mask (Figure 4-10). Another suggestion involves correcting any imbalances with a counterweight to the lighter side (Figure 4-11). This can be remarkably effective if the mask tends to tip one way or the other.

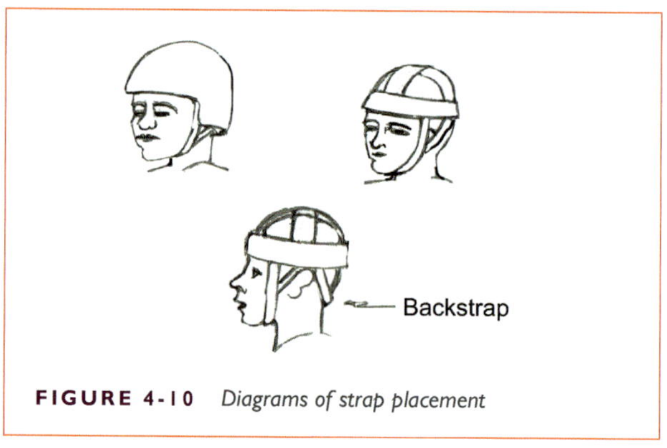

FIGURE 4-10 *Diagrams of strap placement*

VENTILATION AND COOLING

There is nothing like being in a foam head/mask on stage under the lights or outside in the heat. No matter how many ports for ventilation are added, it just never seems like enough. To that end, items for cooling the actor should be added to help support the performance. Small battery-powered fans are low cost and can be attached to the sides of the mask wall to aim at the actor's face or can hang around the neck to blow upward toward the face (Figure 4-12).

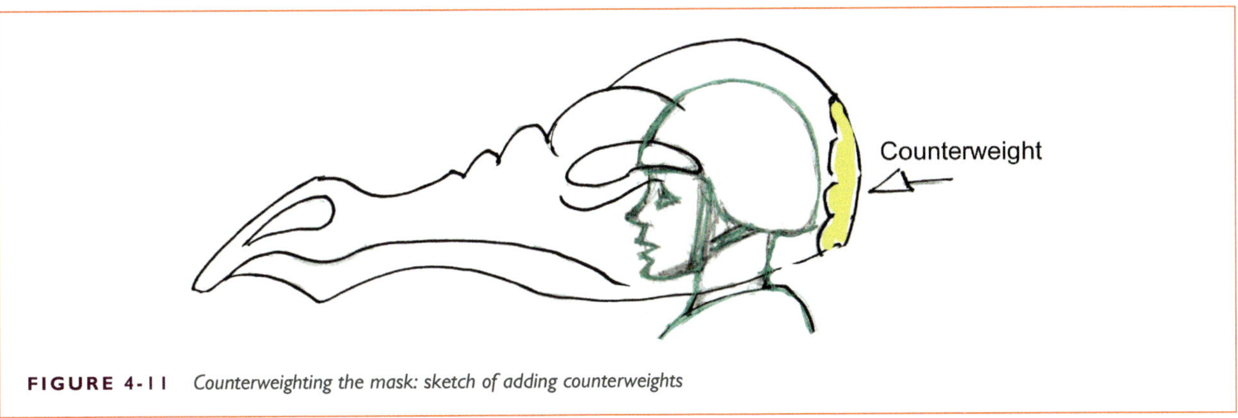

FIGURE 4-11 *Counterweighting the mask: sketch of adding counterweights*

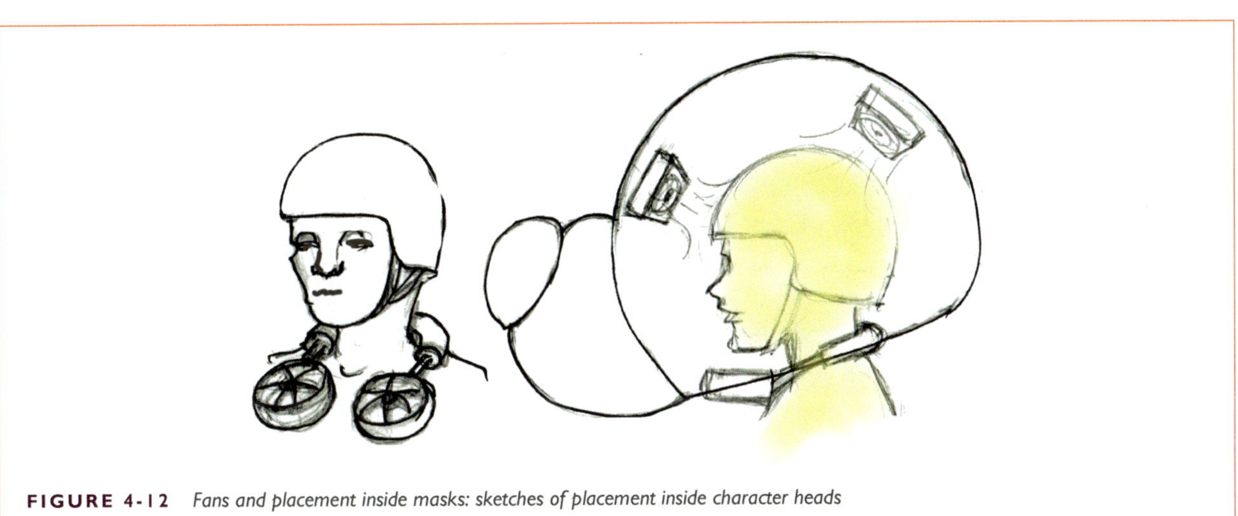

FIGURE 4-12 *Fans and placement inside masks: sketches of placement inside character heads*

Note: Take time to test small fans with the sound technician, as they can sometimes be picked up on wireless mics.

Additional items such as gel-filled bandanas and fabric-covered ice packs are also helpful. These can be placed in a freezer and be ready to use when needed. Place the ice packs in a vest made of "moisture-wicking" fabric. Towels and bandanas made of moisture-wicking cloth may also help keep sweat from running into the eyes and down into the body of the costume (Figure 4-13).

Note: The choice of materials for making the mask should also be considered. Is it possible to build the mask so that it is porous using thermoplastics, fabric netting, or rattan? This might affect the artistic style of the mask, but the comfort of the actor is just as important (Figure 4-14).

FIGURE 4-13 *A sketch of a bandana and vest for carrying cold packs*

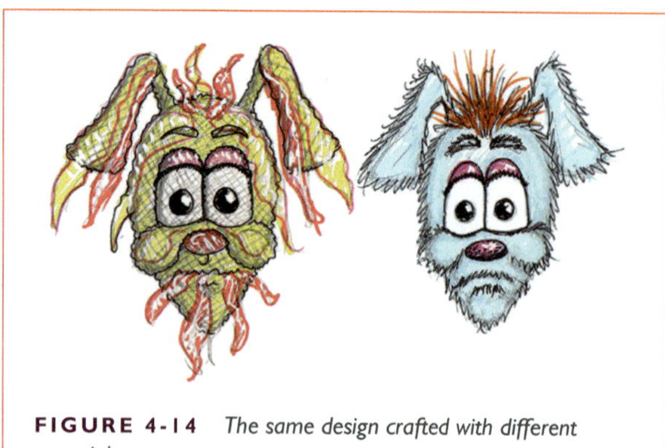

FIGURE 4-14 *The same design crafted with different materials*

TIP BOX

Sprays and Wipes for Deodorizing Masks

1. Vodka spray diluted with one-third water or less.
2. 91–99% alcohol diluted or straight.
3. Febreze – unscented.
4. Soap and water if the inside can be wiped down.
5. Diluted bleach.

WEIGHT

After a while, almost all masks will seem heavy and cumbersome, so when constructing a mask, it is important to consider the type of materials to be used and how long with the actor might be wearing it. The mask might be supported by the head and neck or by the shoulders with a backpack or carried by a stick with their hand (Figure 4-15). These considerations should be taken into account. The good news is that most materials can be made to look like metal, stone, or thick clay without being constructed of the actual substance.

CLEANLINESS

No one wants to put their head and face in an enclosed space that is hot, smells bad, and is potentially loaded with germs. There are different ways to build different types of masks so that they can be disinfected and cleaned. The best way to do this is to make anything that touches the skin removable for washing. Fabric pads and helmet liners can be backed with strategically placed velcro, snaps, or magnets and removed. Then a soft cloth covered with alcohol, or a light solution of bleach and water can be used to wipe down the inside. As soon as this is done, the mask should be put in front of a fan to dry and air out. A pouch of baking soda (which absorbs odors) as well as silica-gel packets can also be placed inside for storage. There are also many kinds of "deodorizing sprays" available, but resist the urge to use highly perfumed deodorizers, as these in an enclosed space (the mask itself) might be annoying or potentially harmful to the actor.

FIGURE 4-15 *Diagram of different masks: A) head and neck; B) Shoulders; and C) held with a hand*

VOCALIZATION

If a masked character is supposed to speak with the actor's live, unsupported voice, then make it easy for the actor to clearly articulate words and be able to project. Articulation and projection are two very different skills: *articulation* is how an actor says a word. It's the ability to enunciate each syllable and consonant; to speak crisply and clearly. *Projection* is the ability to speak with volume – to push from the diaphragm and get sound out to the audience.

Most live performance today is dependent on wireless microphones to increase projection. However, even if the actor can project without a mic (this is becoming a lost craft), if they are unable to enunciate properly, the audience may not be able to understand what they are saying. To support their performance, the mask should not hamper the lip movement or excessively block the mouth. Having said this, I have had success with masks that have covered mouths and touched lips – it just depends on the actor and how well they can adapt to the mask. The trick is to get the mask into rehearsal as soon as possible. It is always important that we help the actor; if we help them, then we help ourselves by successfully communicating the story.

Certain masks might not contribute to clear enunciation or projection. Examples include the very popular masks with moving mouths (based on Javanese wooden masks, which sit under the chin) (Figure 4-16). They move, but unless humans yell, squawk, or burp for effect, we do not normally use our jaws when speaking; we mostly use our lips and facial muscles. Therefore, the actor might need to open their mouth wider (and therefore their jaws) to allow the "mask mouth" to move, and this will invariably distort speech. Try moving your jaw when speaking and see if it distorts speech. These masks are successful in more intimate settings. They are often used in cosplay or close-proximity character interaction at amusement parks. However, unless the mask is used for big guffaws or energetic squawks on stage, the subtly of movement might be lost and the projection may also be blocked. A wireless microphone would be important to aid live performance with this sort of mask. Immortal Masks creates really remarkable versions of this style of mask.

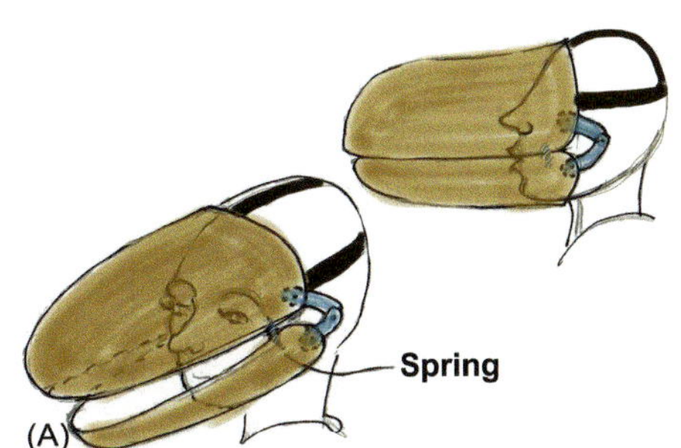

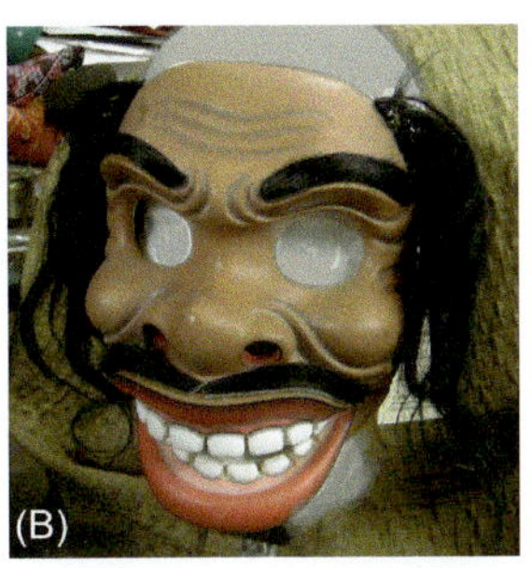

FIGURE 4-16 *A) Diagram of a large moving-mouth mask; B) wooden moving-mouth mask in the traditional style of Bali (created by Newman's Commedia Mask Co.); C) moving-mouth mask with a fiberglass understructure covered with polyfoam (designed and constructed by WVU undergraduate student Toby Francis, 2022)*

If the mouth and facial movement is important, perhaps a form-fitting silicone or latex mask might be a better choice. These are highly flexible and can sometimes be adhered to the face. Another option would be a half or three-quarter mask with an open mouth or one that has an open mouth that is shaped roughly like a megaphone.

Though mask makers do not want to hinder it, an actor's enunciation is not a skill that can be helped with a mask. Masks can, however, have negative and positive effects on sound projection. Mask makers should be aware that if

TIP BOX

When dealing with vocalization and masks, there are occasionally psychological factors at play. Sometimes, even though you can hear and understand the actor, but the lips of the mask do not move, the director will ask you to enlarge the mask mouth. While making the adjustments, remember there are other collaborative areas that find these mysterious factors at play. Recall the lighting designer's maxim: "if you can't see the actor, you can't hear them." This is one reason why you hear directors and lighting designers calling out, "Find your light!"

the mask partially covers the mouth or rests *too far away from the face* at the upper lip, then without a microphone, most of the sound may be trapped inside the mask. Also, if the mask pushes too hard against the adenoid area of the face (the cheeks and bridge of the nose), this could compress the facial cavities and limit sound. Often this can be dealt with by letting the actor practice with the mask and adding a small amount of padding to elevate it. The actor can then learn how to tilt their heads and bodies to project better. In addition to a mask's position, on rare occasions a wireless microphone on the inside of a mask can amplify in such a way that it sounds like the actor is inside a cave. The best way to avoid these problems from the outset is with multiple fittings, tests, and use in rehearsals.

FINAL NOTE CONCERNING CONSTRUCTION

Overall, the most important factor when including a mask in any production is a rehearsal period for the actor to adjust and workout what is best for the performance. A mask maker should *never* introduce a mask for the first time at the first dress rehearsal. If they do, don't be surprised if the mask is cut from the production or that critical and time-consuming alterations will be needed at the last minute.

CHAPTER 5

TYPES OF HELMETS, ARMATURES, AND INTERIOR SUPPORTS

In terms of the art of mask making, the interior structures are sometimes a little boring and tedious to stop and install. However, to make a mask wearable and become animated (one of my favorite parts of character creation) requires a little time dedicated to making it comfortable and stable for the wearer.

HELMETS

Because the mask shell may be more securely mounted to them, full helmets are best used in big costume heads, as they do lend more support and control (Figure 5-1). These are often made of thick plastic (either with high-temperature plastics or cast with resins) with the intention of protecting the head. The durability of the plastic allows for drilling to attach frames, metal, and other plastic struts to center and anchor the helmet inside the mask head.

HELMET LINERS

Strap helmet liners are used in safety hardhats by suspending the head on an interior hammock (Figure 5-2). Welding masks employ the same general idea but are on a more rigid frame, which has the added plus of a built-in "flip up and down" hinge.

Originally this method was used in helmets during World War I and II, before foam was available, and the technique is still used today (Figure 5-3).

Liners can be altered easily with *adjustable webbing tri-glide buckles*, or *lock buckles* (and sometimes a rear knob). Use these in smaller full and half masks, but again whatever works best for the project. Welding masks also have adjustable straps and are good for masks might need to raise and lower onstage (Figure 5-4).

CUSTOM HELMETS AND LINERS

Occasionally there may be a need to custom make a helmet to support the mask, especially if the mask is porous, so that the wearer is partially exposed. The helmet should be as aesthetically pleasing on the inside as the outside, and the helmet material might need to look the same. Thermoplastics (including those used in the vacuum forming process) are

DOI: 10.4324/9781003343264-5

FIGURE 5-1 *Examples of different helmets*

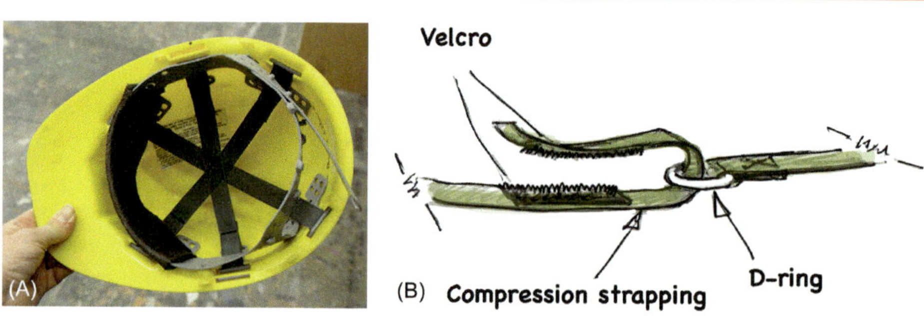

FIGURE 5-2 *A) Example of a strap helmet liner; B) diagram of compression strap and D-ring connection for use on the back of the head or as a chin strap*

TIP BOX

Using the strap helmet liner is basically like treating the mask outer shell as a hard-hat. Buy the helmet with the liner and dremel out the pre-fused or cast slots that are inside the helmet. The liner generally slides or snaps into the slots inside the helmet. Use these cut-out "helmet slots" or "tracks" as attachments for the liner. These may be attached to the interior sides of the mask with epoxies and/or nylon ties, screws, lock washers, and/or lock nuts (Figure 5-3).

designed to melt at a certain temperature and to be hand manipulated or drawn over a form (*buck*). If you double or triple the layers on some thermoplastics (*varaform*), these can be quite strong. The drawback is that some are susceptible to heat as low as 70°C or 160°F, which could melt in the hot sun in a car (hot glue is also a thermoplastic and will also melt in a car!). Depending on the plastic, if this is kept in mind, thermoplastics can be very effective.

Other materials such as fiber-supported resins (fiberglass), aluminum, and rattan are tough materials that can

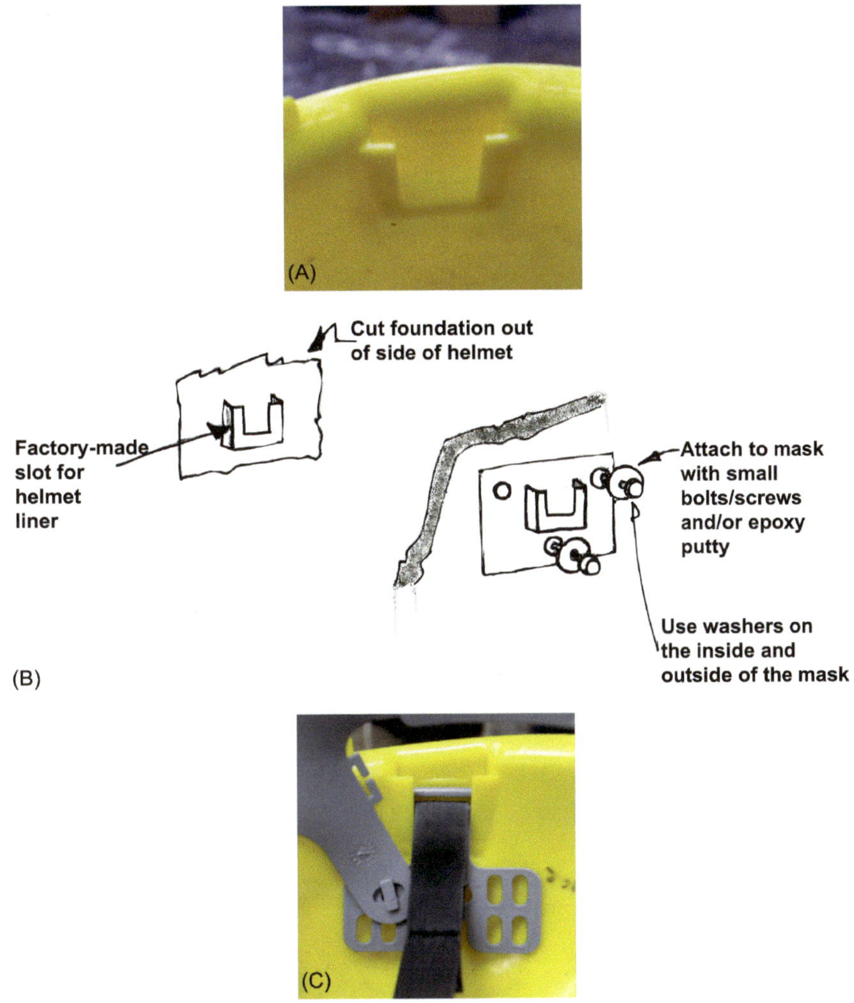

(A)

Cut foundation out of side of helmet

Factory-made slot for helmet liner

Attach to mask with small bolts/screws and/or epoxy putty

Use washers on the inside and outside of the mask

(B)

(C)

FIGURE 5-3 *Attaching a strap helmet liner inside a mask: A) image of a factory-made slot inside hardhat; B) diagram of cutting out a slot and attachment; and C) image of a strap helmet liner attachment*

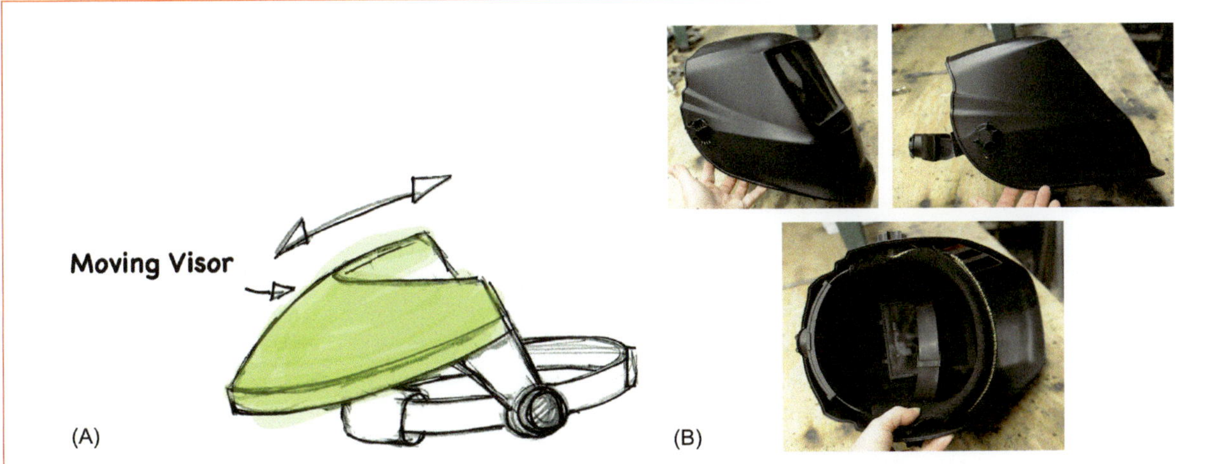

FIGURE 5-4 *A) Diagram of one example of a welding mask helmet liner with a moving panel for raising and lowering the mask; B) image of a welding mask*

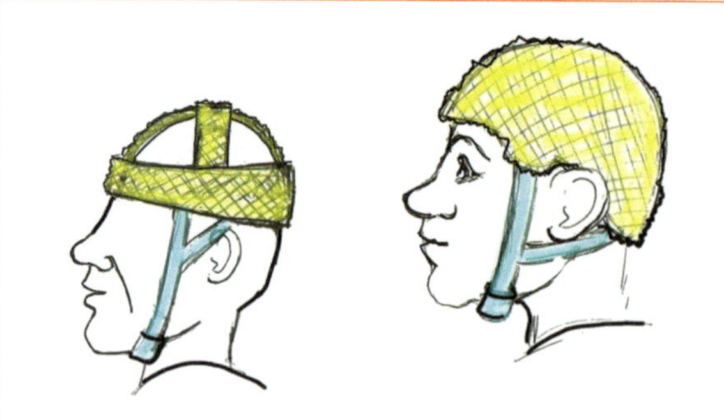

FIGURE 5-5 *Diagrams of custom helmets made with varaform*

be used to make custom helmet-like shapes to support the head in a mask. It just depends on the kind or style of mask, the use, and the time and money available (Figure 5-5).

FRICTION FITTING

Friction roughly means the force created by the action of two surfaces rubbing against each other. In the case of a mask, this simply means that the material hugs the head in such a way that it stays in place, that is, the head will squeeze (comfortably) into a foam-, silicone-, or latex-lined mask. I have found some of these masks, especially silicone masks, to be especially hot – severely increasing sweating. They are very confining and seem to suffocate the skin. As I am not a heavy sweater, the experience of wearing this mask made a lasting impression. Silicone masks, however, look *amazing* because they are slightly transparent – clinging and moving with the face. Often fabric coifs are used to cover the head and hair; these are absorbent and are also washable (Figure 5-6). Note: Hair growing out of the scalp may literally rip out because silicone likes to "grab on" to it.

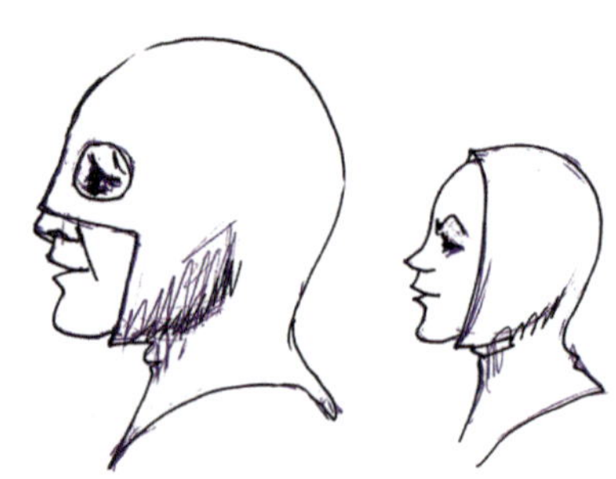

FIGURE 5-6 *Sketch of a fabric coif that goes on before the mask to absorb sweat and as a buffer against possible abrasion*

"STRAPS, BUCKLES, AND CLIPS OLE!"

To keep maintenance time to a minimum, when creating the exterior or interior of a mask, it is best to use materials and construction techniques that will last. Take the time to do it correctly and it will pay off. Materials made of nylon, aluminum, and heavy plastic will not biodegrade or melt and, hopefully, should withstand normal wear and tear.

Machine stitching is very effective. It provides regular, even stitches and can be knotted easily by backstitching. Hand stitching or using a hand "speedy stitcher" and an awl is also effective. Thread should be strong and nonbiodegradable because it might encounter sweat and could rot (Figure 5-7).

ARMATURES AND INTERIOR SUPPORTS

Rigid helmets and strap liners occasionally need extensions to make them "float" or be suspended inside big masks. A *strut* (a rigid beam or shaft extending from the helmet to the side of the mask) might be able to support the helmet by anchoring

FIGURE 5-7 *Examples of strapping, buckles, elastic, clips, and thread*

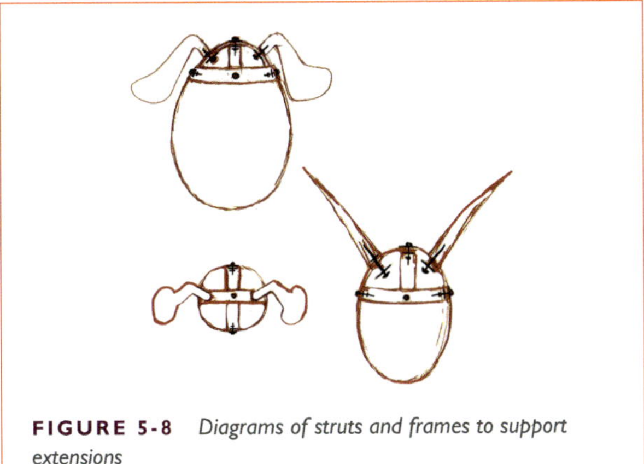

FIGURE 5-8 *Diagrams of struts and frames to support extensions*

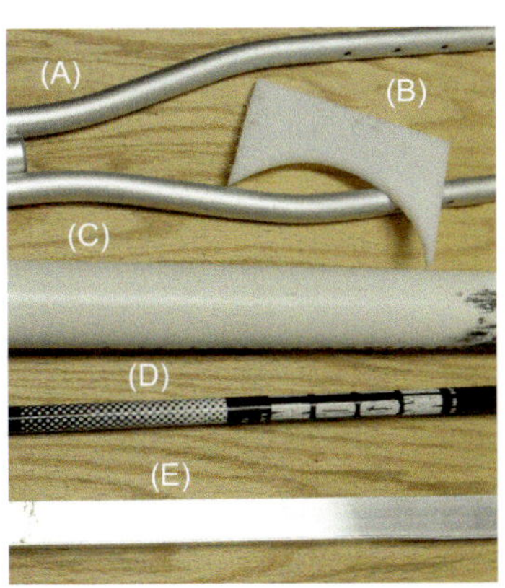

FIGURE 5-9 *Types of materials for creating struts and frames: A) Aluminum tubing recycled from crutches; B) polyethylene plastic sheeting; C) PVC tubing; D) carbon fiber rod recycled from old ski poles; and E) 1/8-inch aluminum strapping*

it directly to the mask material if, for example, the mask is rigid. However, if the outside material is relatively soft (such as foam and fur), then a frame or *armature* needs to be built to support the extensions (Figure 5-8). *Frames* or *armatures* are the skeletons of a mask. They might be used to support mechanisms, the mask material, or the helmet. The best materials are those that are light and tough. This includes aluminum strapping and tubing, plastics such as high-density polyethylene and PVC pipe, and carbon graphite poles (Figure 5-9). Many of these items may be acquired by recycling unwanted objects.

Depending on the mask size and shape, one way to support a helmet with struts is a four-point attachment. This prevents the helmet from moving side to side and up and down (Figure 5-10). Everything depends on the configuration inside the mask, so be prepared to install as many (or as few) supports as needed to make the helmet stable.

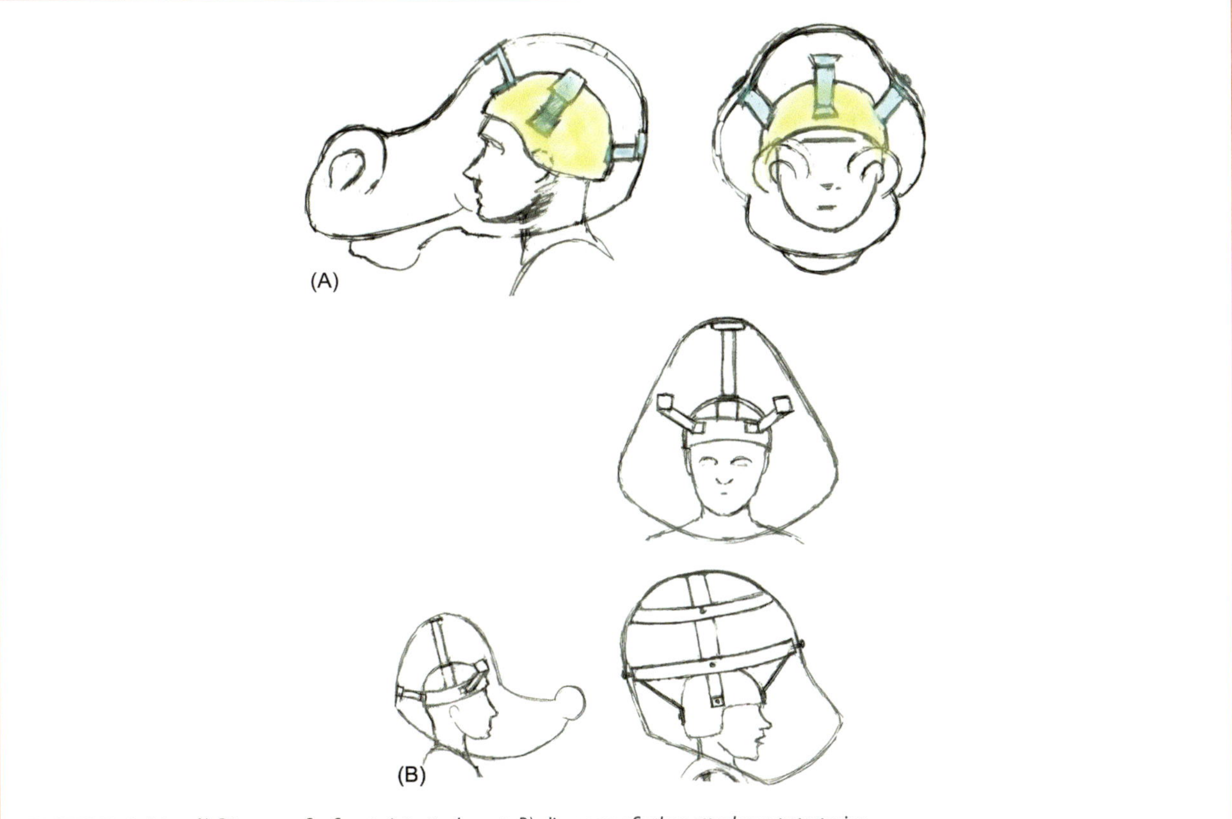

FIGURE 5-10 *A) Diagram of a four-point attachment; B) diagrams of other attachment strategies*

CHAPTER 6

TOOLS AND SUPPLIES

TOOLS

Every craftsperson has their own special group of tools that are a part of their work routine. In terms of hand tools, a collection including a variety of sizes and shapes is helpful. Such a collection includes pliers, clamps, screw and nut drivers, basic cutting tools, hole punch, scissors, and more.

Hand Tools

Hand tools are those that are not directly connected to a power source (Figure 6-1).

Scissors (Figure 6-2). A variety of scissors is good to have on hand: small, medium, and large. Save a couple of pairs reserved only for fabric.

Metal snips and wire cutters (Figure 6-3). Make sure you only use them for wire. Have a separate pair of metal snips for varaform or other materials.

Clamps (Figure 6-4). Develop a collection of different clamp sizes and styles. *Quick-Grip Clamps* are perfect for molds as well as other projects. Big and small C-clamps are sturdy and dependable no matter the size.

Razor blades (Figure 6-5). Two-inch single-edged blades are very sharp and last a lot longer than the 1-inch ones. Do try and sharpen them before disposal. They may also be bent for carving. Such razor blades may be recycled at certain locations.

Screw and nut drivers (Figure 6-6). These tools come in different lengths and sizes and are invaluable for mask making, as no two masks are the same unless they are designed to be. Screw and nut drivers make it easy to get into tight spaces and long noses.

Pliers (Figure 6-7). A good collection of pliers is really helpful for construction. Such a collection may include needle nose, blunt nose, slip-joint, and tongue and groove joint, or channel lock pliers. A collection of jewelry pliers is also handy for small work.

Hammers and mallets (Figure 6-8). These tools are helpful for heat bending plastics and any other pounding.

Center punch and an awl (Figure 6-9). The center punch provides an indentation in plastics and wood for accuracy when drilling. An awl is handy for boring holes through fabrics and other materials.

Hand saws (Figure 6-10). These might include a small hack saw and a keyhole saw.

DOI: 10.4324/9781003343264-6

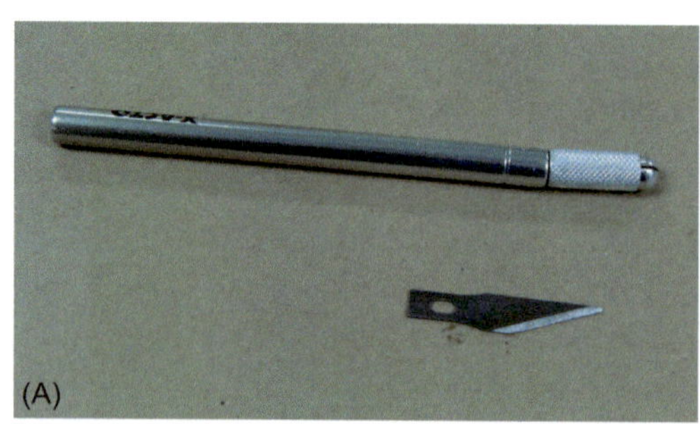

FIGURE 6-1 *A) X-Acto and B) carpet knives*

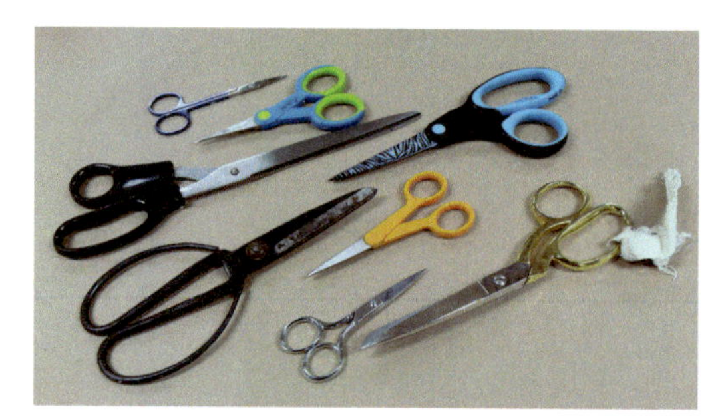

FIGURE 6-2 *A variety of scissors*

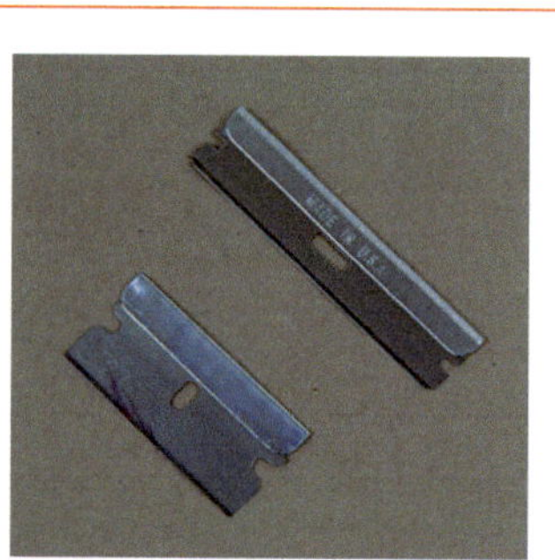

FIGURE 6-5 *Razor blades*

FIGURE 6-3 *Metal snips and wire cutters*

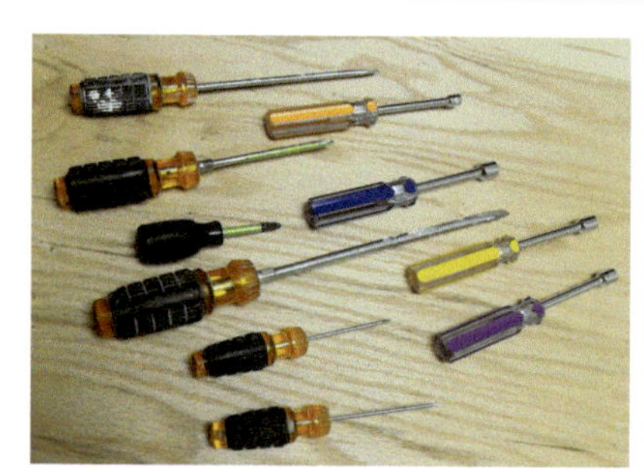

FIGURE 6-6 *Screw and nut drivers*

FIGURE 6-4 *Clamps*

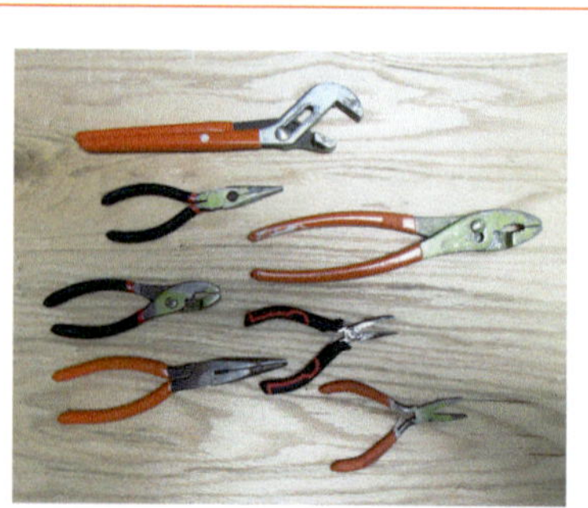

FIGURE 6-7 *Pliers*

FIGURE 6-8 *Hammers and mallets*

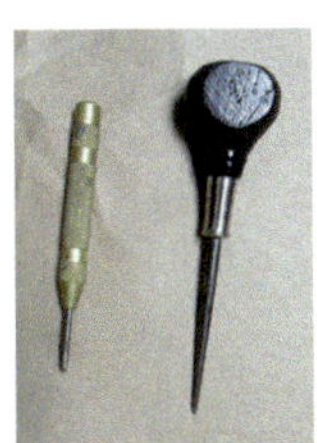

FIGURE 6-9 *Center punch and awl*

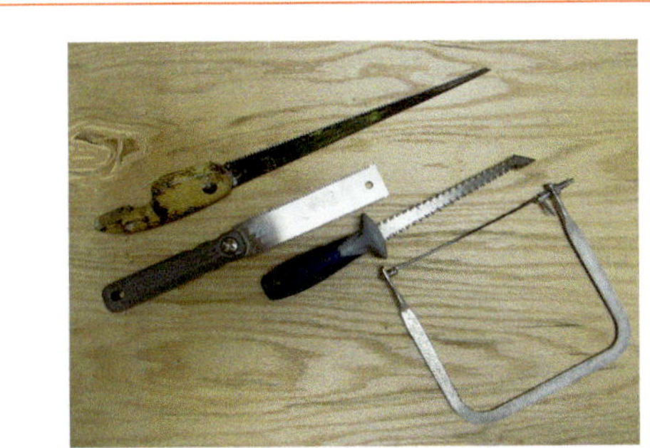

FIGURE 6-10 *Hand saws*

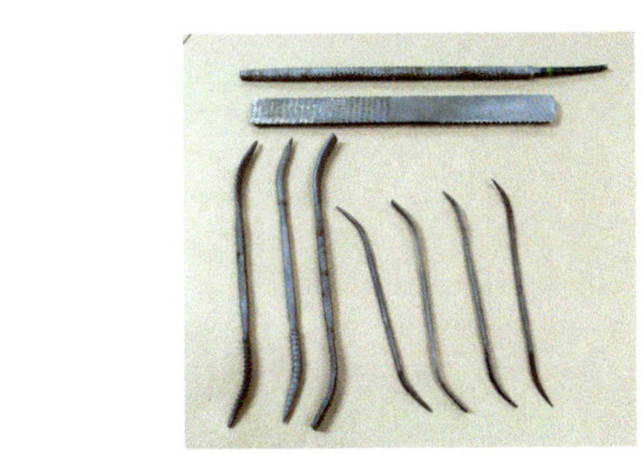

FIGURE 6-11 *Files and rasps*

Files and rasps (Figure 6-11). A big and small collection is great for metal filing needs.

Surform tools (Figure 6-12). Yes, it is "surform," not "shurform." These tools are perfect for taking down sharp sides on plaster molds and for carving foam.

FIGURE 6-12 *Surform tools*

FIGURE 6-13 *Sandpaper*

Sandpaper (Figure 6-13). Use coarse grit (60–80) and fine (150–220).

Power Tools

A power tool is any tool connected to a power source. Common power tools that are helpful to have in stock include Dremel tools (two are helpful), palm sander, band saw, heat gun, battery-operated hand drills (two are handy), hot plate, and several clip-on fans.

Dremel tool (Figure 6-14). Bits that you should buy include aluminum oxide EZ-lock cutting wheels (and

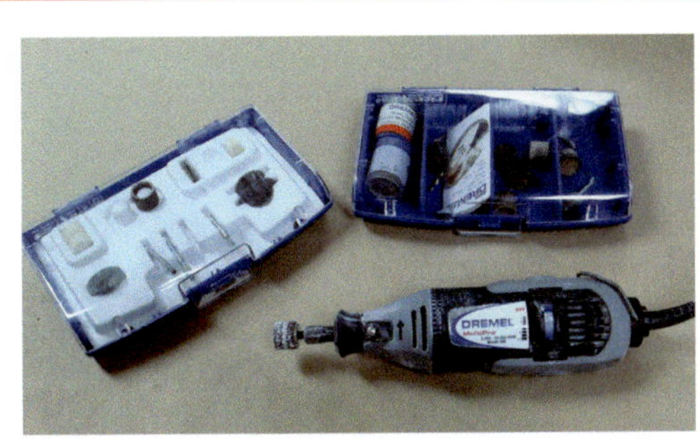

FIGURE 6-14 *Dremel tool*

FIGURE 6-15 *Palm sander*

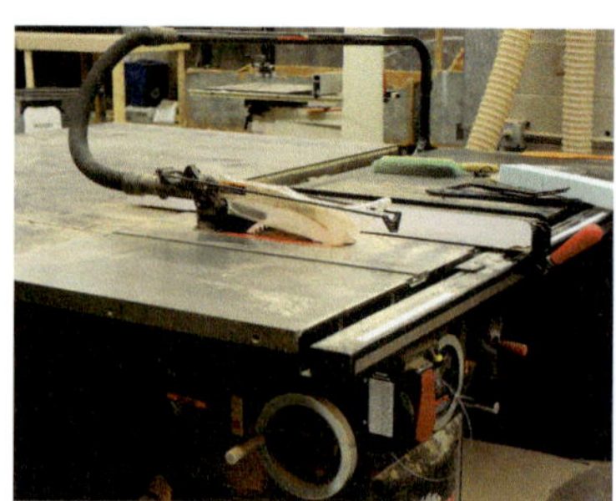
FIGURE 6-18 *Table saw*

connection adapter), cutting bits, sanding drums, and grinding and buffing drums.

Palm sander (Figure 6-15). Rarely do I use fine sandpaper with this tool. I use it to sand big surfaces, such as sheets of plastic.

Belt sander (Figure 6-16). This tool is great if you have the room. Use it for foam, plastic, some metals, fiberglass, and epoxies.

Band saw (Figure 6-17). This is a wonderful tool that I end up using for about every project. Small blades are for cutting tight corners and curves, and large blades are better for thick, straighter cuts. A quarter inch blade is a good all-purpose width.

FIGURE 6-16 *Belt sander*

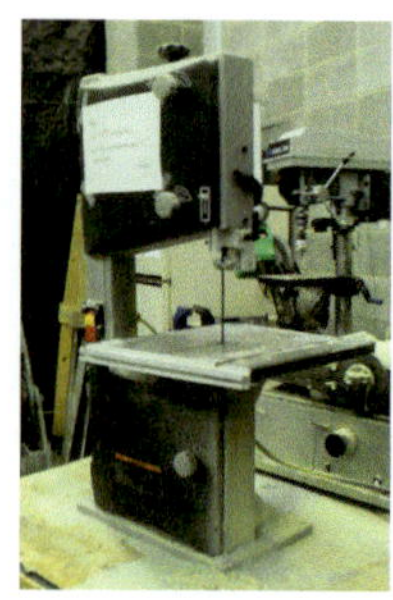
FIGURE 6-17 *Band saw*

Table saw (Figure 6-18). This saw is good for reducing big sheets of wood down to small pieces.

Hot plate (Figure 6-19). This tool is for dying and if you need two pots for a double boiler.

Jigsaw (Figure 6-20). This tool is good if you don't have a table saw. It can reduce large pieces of material down to small enough pieces for the band saw.

Hand drill (Figure 6-21). This is an invaluable tool. I always have two ready at once: one with a drill bit and one with a screwdriver bit. A hand drill can also be used for many other purposes. See "Drill Hacks" on YouTube.

Heat gun (Figure 6-22). This tool is needed for heat bending plastics, working with Worbla and other low-temperature thermoplastics, and modifying plastic fabrics.

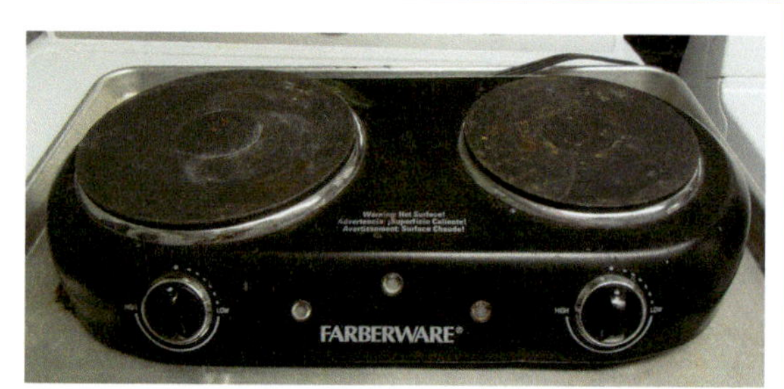

FIGURE 6-19 *Hot plate*

FIGURE 6-20 *Jigsaw*

FIGURE 6-21 *Hand drill*

FIGURE 6-22 *Heat gun*

Adhesives and Glues

Hot glue is a melted plastic – a thermoplastic – and is therefore somewhat outside the topic of this section (Figure 6-23). However, it is used to hold things together. The fine tip guns are good, and the cordless guns are really wonderful, though the chargers are (mysteriously) often sold separately.

Epoxy. This is a two-part adhesive that can have different curing times. I prefer the five-minute variety. It may be made to cure (kick off) faster with Zip Kicker or a sprinkle of baking soda. Epoxy is used primarily for plastics, wood, some fabrics, and metal. It dries hard. Use it in a well-ventilated area.

Super Glue and Super Glue Gel. This is a cyanoacrylate-based adhesive, which means it hardens without mixing a second component. It is not as tough as epoxy but still pretty strong. The gel form is easier to control than the liquid.

Polyvinyl Acetate (PVA). This is Elmer's glue, white wood glue, tacky glue, etc. PVA is a water-based glue that may be used as a coating on fabrics (test it first), a hair stiffener, and a glue. It may be used for wood, some fabric applications, and plastic. Some

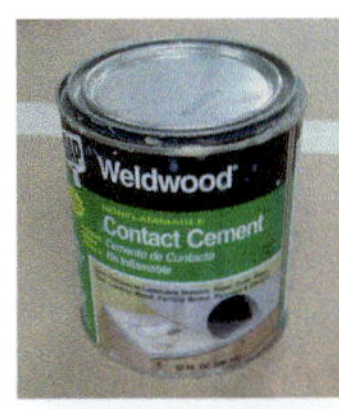

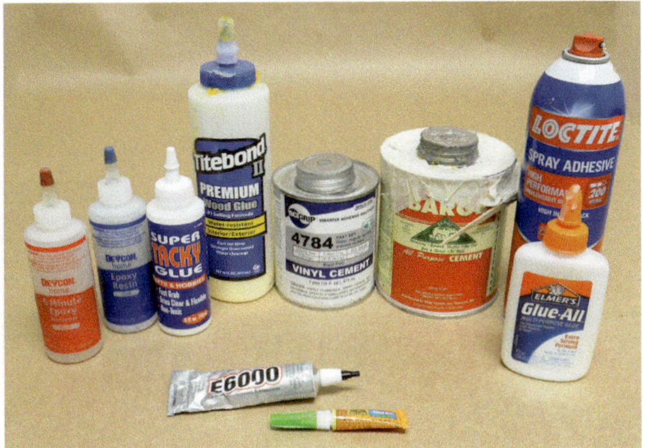

FIGURE 6-23 *A) Hot glue gun and glue sticks; B) low VOC contact cement, flex glue, five-minute epoxy, yellow wood glue, vinyl cement, contact cement, spray adhesive, PVA glue, E6000, super glue gel*

forms are rigid when dry, and others are somewhat flexible. Yellow wood glue has some resin additives.

E6000. This is a type of perchloroethylene adhesive that is used for multiple craft purposes – for ornamental applications, not for structure. E6000 may be used for some fabric applications, plastics, wood, and metal. The adhesive is somewhat soft when dry. (Many people praise E6000, but I have had little luck with it.)

Contact Cement. This adhesive is applied to both sides of the material to be glued, allowed to dry, then pressed together. It can be toluene petrochemical based, that is, it needs ventilation (Barge Glue, Weldwood linoleum cement, etc.); or polychloroprene, that is, water based (Weldwood Nonflammable contact cement, Simalfa 309, etc.), in which case it may be used indoors without a respirator. Both will adhere fabrics, flexible plastics, leather, large cell foam, and latex rubber. Barge Glue is the best of the two types of adhesives (hands down), and it is the one to use with closed-cell foams. Unfortunately, it is really toxic. Wear gloves and a respirator and use it outside or with a ventilation system if possible.

Flex Glue. This adhesive is in the PVA family and may be used as a glue for fabrics and as a coating.

Putty and Spackle

Putties and spackles are used to fill in and repair surfaces (see Figure 6-24). Some may also be used for sculpting.

Epoxy Putties. These include Green Stuff, Plummer's Putty, Apoxie Sculpt, All Game Epoxy Sculpting Putty, and more. They are a two-part mix (resin and hardener) and are generally opaque – though they may come in different colors. They all have different working times, from one to two minutes to 24 hours (depending on the hardener), may be sanded, and are tough. These may also be used as structural adhesives (to some extent). The longer setting putties allow for sculpting of detailed pieces, especially if built on an armature.

Spackles. These are mostly developed to use on drywall. However, the *extra-fast-setting* varieties, such as Dap's Fast and Final, are great for patching papier-mâché. These sand easily but are not structural. Spackles should be coated with a sealant.

WORKSPACE SETUP

The space where you work can be anywhere, but it should be a space that can be adapted for many different mask making projects. The space should be an area where you can leave things to dry or cure. It should also have tables and/or a workbench; places for hanging tools; drawers and bins for holding supplies; a bare wall for hanging drawings and research; a floor that is not precious (because there will be a mess); or a plastic or paper covering the floor. There should also be a place set up that has good ventilation for those projects involving use of chemicals and solvents. This can sometimes be a loading dock or a partially enclosed patio area. It could also be a garage with a fan blowing toward the open door.

Stands and Worktables

Because you are building masks, it is good to have premade stands for holding eyes and other separate features while they dry (Figure 6-25). Also, a worktable or bench with a narrow edge can accommodate a vise for clamping items that need drilling, gluing, or bending (Figure 6-26).

FIGURE 6-24 *Putties*

FIGURE 6-25 *An example of a drying stand for holding eyes*

FIGURE 6-26 *A vice is the third (or fourth) hand that humans don't have; vices may also be used to bend and twist heavy wire, and most have a built-in anvil*

Head Forms

Head forms are essential when building certain kinds of masks. These can give you a sense of the human face as well as a solid base on which to construct.

EPS head forms are sometimes helpful and at present come in two varieties (Figure 6-27). These do damage easily and are somewhat small, so when using them as a base for human heads, make certain to take accurate measurements of the person you are building the mask for; otherwise, the finished mask may be too small. It is possible to cover these with layers of foam putty and tape, tape and compressed quilt batting, or rigid polyfoam to enlarge them and make them more durable. Because the foam forms are so lightweight, stands such as wig stands or custom-made wooden stands that can be clamped to the edge of a table are crucial to keeping them stable.

Plaster head forms are great when working with masks needing some weight to keep them steady. Also, a plaster head form is crucial to those masks that are cast for a custom fit as they become the *core mold* or *interior positive*. The term *core mold* refers to a form (made of plaster, stones or other materials) that is used inside certain types of multi-layer molds being used to create a hollow skin or foam mask/appliance (Figure 6-28).

FIGURE 6-27 *EPS head forms on wooden stands*

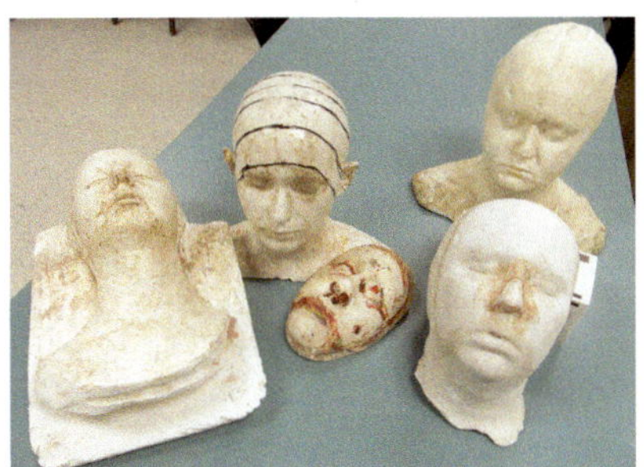

FIGURE 6-28 *Examples of plaster heads and faces*

Custom soft or rigid cold foam head forms are somewhat time consuming and costly to make, but if cared for the molds and the forms will last for years. If stored properly, the molds may be used to make dozens of copies of the same foam form.

TIP BOX

How to Cast a Human Head (see Figure 6-29 A–R)

Head Casting

Allow at least two hours for this process.

1. Prepare your supplies:
    - Alginate.
    - Vaseline.
    - Bald cap or crude plastic head wrap:
        - Adhesive for cap (Pros Aide or spirit gum).
        - Adhesive remover.
    - Mixing bowls.
    - Comfortable chair.
    - Towels.
    - Trash can.
    - Large plastic bags.
    - Masking tape.
    - Extra-fast-setting plaster gauze.
    - One dark crayon.
    - Hydrocal plaster.
    - Scissors.
    - Small lump of clay.
    - Two five-gallon buckets.
        - Two to three lengths of 2 × 4s (no longer than 20 inches).

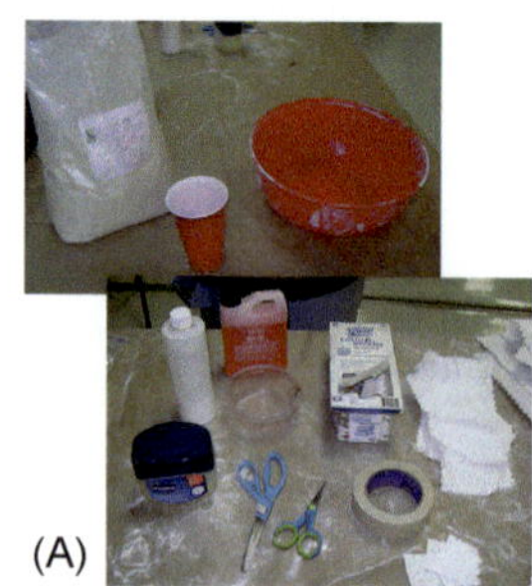

FIGURE 6-29A *Supplies laid out on a table, ready to go*

2. Prepare your space (Figure 6-29A)

   - Set up in a space that is removed from the hubbub. Put up signs that say, "Do not disturb, casting in session."
   - Precut or tear strips of "fast-setting" or "extra-fast-setting" plaster gauze. You may need about six rolls, but it does depend on how much area you will be casting layout craft or newspaper on the floor and table.
   Arrange supplies, such as bowls, a bucket for washing hands, trash can, and prepared strips in a pile.
   Vaseline.
   Alginate.
   Towels.

3. Prepare your subject:

   Discuss the process with the model – make them comfortable, walk them through step by step.
   Prep the model. Cover with a garbage bag (cut out a head hole), tape it to chest and back, and sit the model in a comfortable chair (see Figure 6-29B). They will be there for a while. If your model is sick or sneezy and coughing, then reschedule.
   Ask the model to apply a very thin layer of Vaseline on eyebrows and lashes.

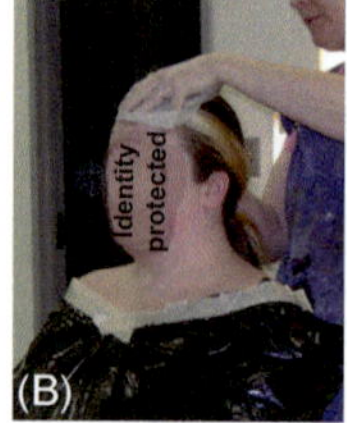

FIGURE 6-29B *Putting on the bald cap*

4. Put on a bald cap (or cover hair with a wig-pattern-style head wrap).

   To smooth down hair, use brush-on conditioner, hair gel, or water to flatten hair to the head. You might be able to separate and wrap the hair around the head. If hair is too thick and long, make a braid and run it down the back of the neck. Cover the braid with plastic wrap.
   Use Elmer's Glue Stick or Gafquat to glue back any stray hairs along hairline.
   Place the bald cap on the model's head.

If you want the actor's ears to be exposed and therefore to be in the cast, carefully draw around ears (using a grease or lipstick pencil) onto the cap and cut away the latex over the ear (see Figure 6-29C).

If you don't want the ears exposed, simply stretch the bald cap over the actor's ears.

5. Adhere the cap using Pros Aide adhesive (or spirit gum if it's all you have).
   - Forehead first.
   - Back of neck and behind ears.
   - Temples in front of ears.
6. Mark the dividing line along the top of the head and shoulders. This line will be called the *dividing edge*.
7. Begin putting wet plaster bandage strips along the dividing line.
8. After the line is complete, fill in the back of the head with at least three layers of wet plaster gauze (see Figure 6-29D and 6-29E).

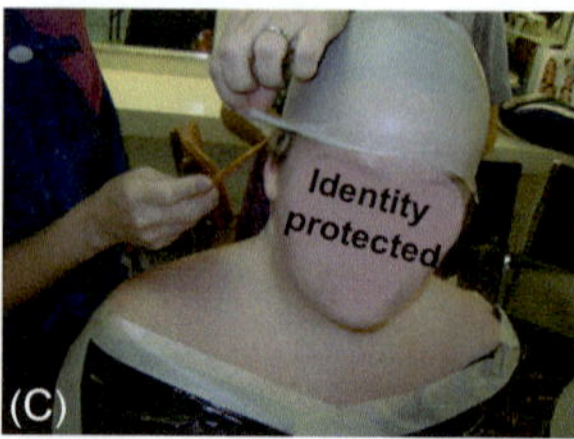

FIGURE 6-29C *Tucking hair under bald cap with a rat tail comb before adhering with Pros Aide*

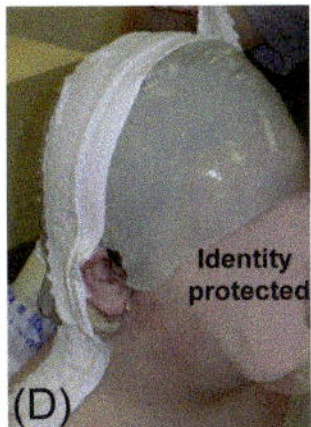

FIGURE 6-29D *The plaster gauze dividing line*

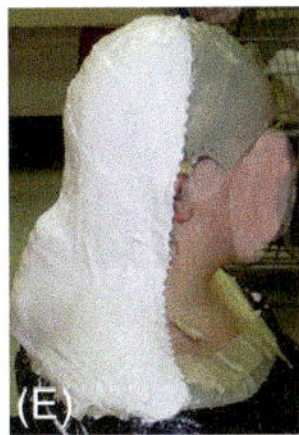

FIGURE 6-29E *Back of head filled in the gauze*

9. After the gauze has hardened, use a grease pencil or crayon to draw a line that is one inch back from the dividing edge of the plaster layer.
10. Coat this one-inch space with Vaseline.
11. Lay down the front frame.
    - Add another layer of plaster gauze over the newly "Vaselined" area.
12. Continue the line of gauze around the front and over the chest of the actor (see Figure 6-29F).
13. Mix the alginate in cold water (see Figure 6-29G). If it's too warm, the alginate will set before you get finished.

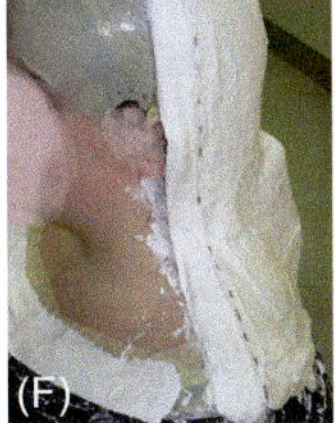

FIGURE 6-29F *The gauze frame nearly complete*

FIGURE 6-29G *Mixing alginate*

14. Cast the face with alginate.
    - Cover the actor's face with alginate, leaving the nostril area until last. Warn the model before you begin and talk to them throughout the whole process.
15. Overlap the alginate (about a quarter inch) onto the "dividing edge" area, making certain to leave at least a quarter inch of the new plaster gauze exposed. This will allow the plaster to create an envelope around the alginate, holding it in place.
16. Before the alginate cures, press small pieces of dry plaster gauze into it. This will cause the final plaster gauze mother mold to bond with the alginate, allowing the front mold to pull off in one piece without separating, tearing, or sagging (see Figure 6.29H and 6.29I).

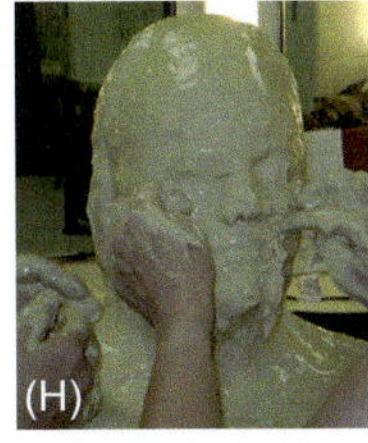

FIGURE 6-29H *Alginate is being applied to model*

FIGURE 6-29I *Small squares of plaster gauze pressed into nearly cured alginate*

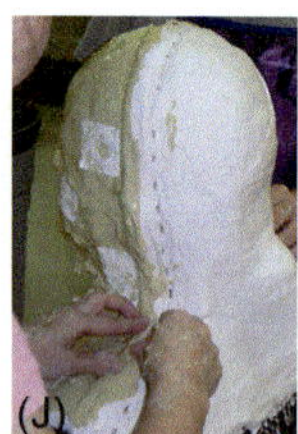

FIGURE 6-29J *Clearing excess alginate to allow some of the plaster gauze to be exposed*

17. In the *dividing line* area, cover the alginate with gauze and press the new gauze into the exposed cured (and ungreased) gauze, thus creating the envelope (Figure 6-29J and 6-29K).
18. Lay at least three layers of plaster gauze over the alginate ending with the nostril area (see Figure 6-29L). This is the *blanket* or *mother mold.*
19. Mark the overlap of each side of the mold with "notches" using a crayon or grease pencil.
20. After the plaster gauze has set, take a blunt metal tool or butter knife and pry open the mold along the dividing line.
21. Ask the model to bend at the waist and nestle the front of the cast in their hands to support its release.

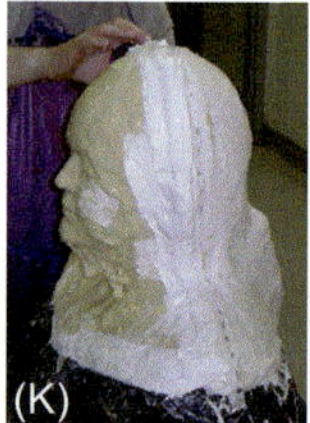

FIGURE 6-29K *Applying final layer of plaster gauze to create the envelope*

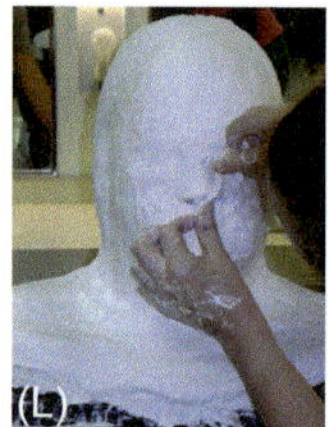

FIGURE 6-29L *Blanket or mother mold*

FIGURE 6-29M *Releasing the alginate from the skin*

22. Ask the model to exhale through the mouth and move the cheeks and mouth to help release the alginate from the skin (see Figure 6-29M).
23. Carefully loosen the front half and pull away the alginate from the actor's face. Place this half plaster-side-down on a *padded* level surface. *Do not flap the mold around; the alginate could tear.*
24. On the *outside of the mold*, block the nostril holes with a small piece of clay, then cover the clay with a few pieces of wet plaster gauze.
25. Pull the back part of the mold off the actor's head.
26. ***Note:*** Brush Vaseline over the entire *inside* of the back half of the mold, that is, all the exposed plaster (see Figures 6-29N and 6-29O).

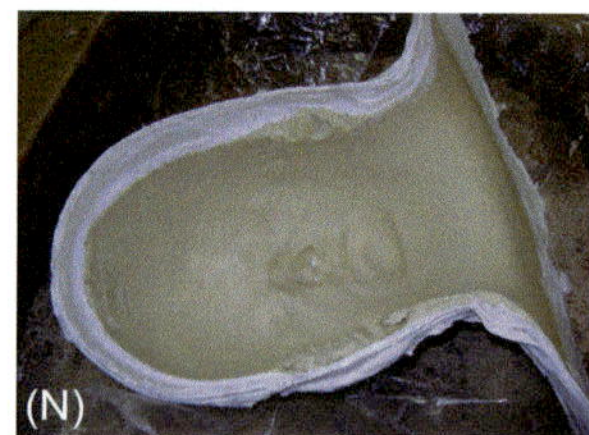

FIGURE 6-29N *The front half of the plaster mold with the alginate cast held in place*

FIGURE 6-29O *The back half of the mold*

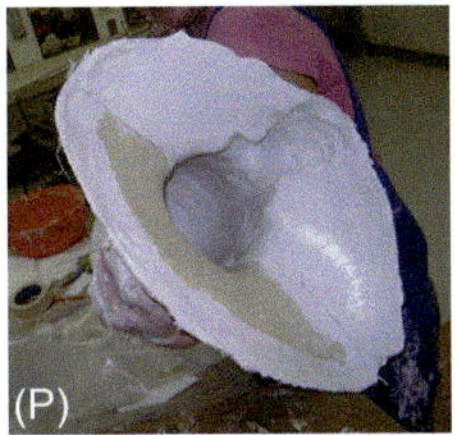

FIGURE 6-29P *The mold reassembled and secured with plaster gauze strips*

27. Using the "notches" you drew on the outside of the mold as markers, reassemble mold halves and seal with strips of plaster gauze (see Figure 6-29P).
28. After gauze strips have hardened, place the mold upside down in five-gallon bucket and stabilize it with wooden blocks as needed. The mold *should not* be resting on the bottom of the bucket but on the shoulder area.
29. Mix (hydrocal) plaster using the "dry creek bed method" and slowly fill the mold up to shoulder area (see Figure 6.29Q). This may take a few batches.
30. A threaded rod may be inserted into the hardening plaster to create a rotating bust.
31. Let the plaster sit until it is hard and cool. This will indicate that the chemical reaction has taken place and the plaster has reached its proper strength.
32. Remove plaster gauze strips that hold the two halves of the mold together. Carefully pry open the mold at the dividing line and slowly release the interior cast. The negative can be thrown away at this point.

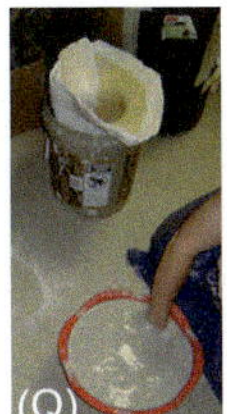

FIGURE 6-29Q *Mixing hydrocal*

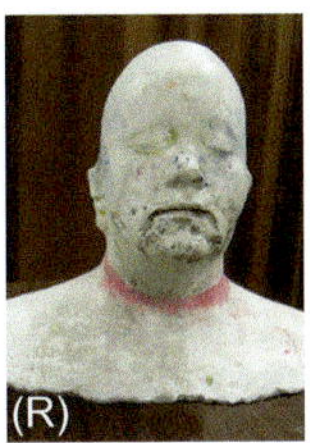

FIGURE 6-29R *The finished bust that has since been used many times for mask making projects*

33. Patch and sand the positive as needed (see Figure 6-29R).

TIP BOX

Steps for Making a Cold-Foam Form

Hydrocal plaster mold (Figure 6-30A–P):

1. Sculpting a positive shape with clay.
2. Divide the sculpt in half visually. Add a dividing shim metal wall and clay keys.

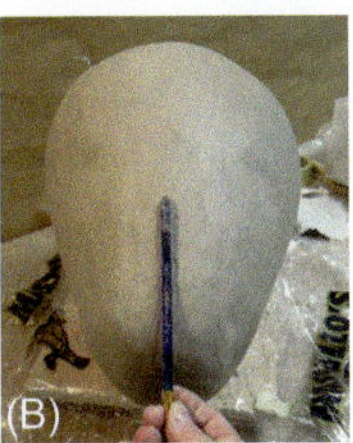

FIGURE 6-30A–C *Creating a two-part mold from a clay positive*

(D)

(E)

(F)

FIGURE 6-30D–F *The first half of the mold is cast with three separately applied layers of hydrocal; notice the shim steel/tin mold wall*

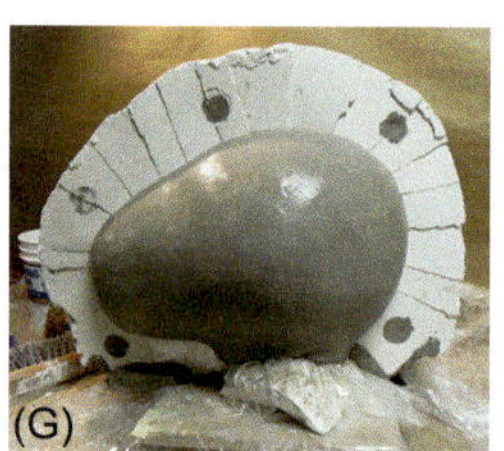
(G)

(H)

(I)

FIGURE 6-30G–I *Completed mold popped open*

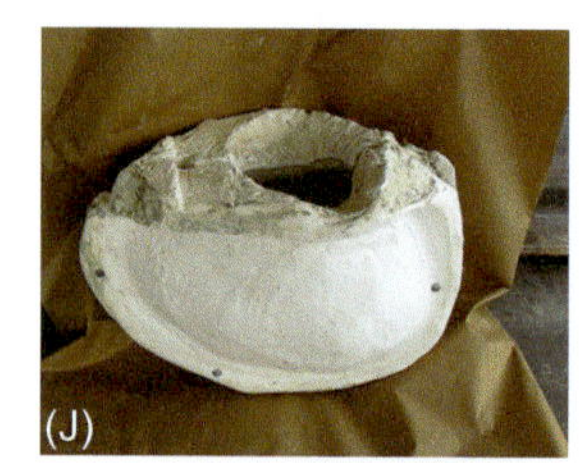
(J)

(K)

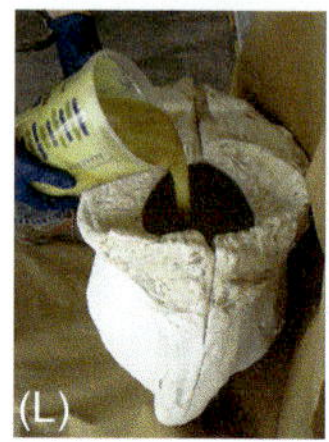
(L)

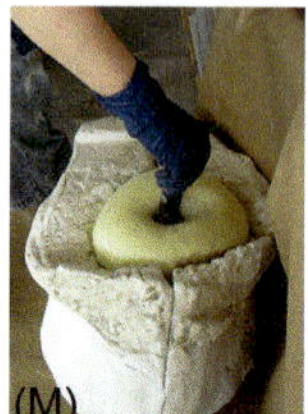
(M)

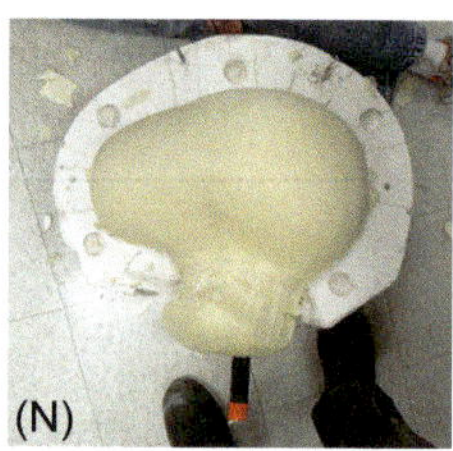
(N)

FIGURE 6-30J–N *The mold is bolted together then the foam is mixed and poured*

(O)

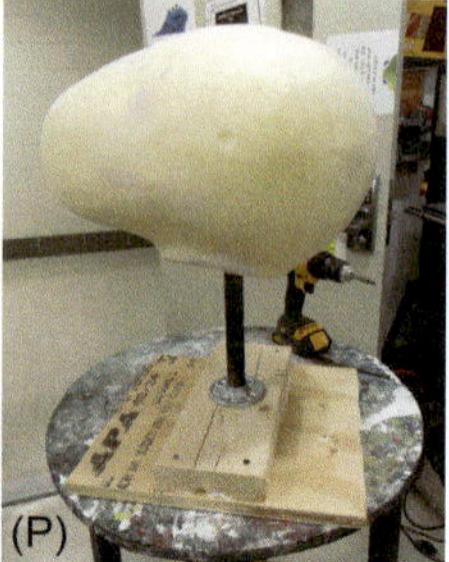
(P)

FIGURE 6-30O–P *The wooden stand with metal socket*

3. If using hydrocal:

   Add release agent over the keys and on a metal shim.

   Layer one is *splash coat*, layer 2 is burlap and plaster, and layer three is final plaster.
4. To cast side two, add release agent to "flange" – the exposed edge of the mold. The metal shim needs to be removed, and the exposed plaster "flange," if not greased with release agent (Vaseline), will bond with the new layers and lock the mold.
5. Repeat the previous steps and cast the second half of the shape.
6. After being cured, surform the shape to refine sharp and uneven edges as needed.
7. Predrill holes for bolting together (no holes are needed if you are clamping the halves together).
8. Patiently pry apart mold halves.
9. Again, Dremel, sand, and refine sharp and uneven edges as needed.
10. Clean out the clay.
11. While the mold is still open, add the release agent to the inside and flange edges of the mold.
12. Assemble the mold (by bolting or clamping), then mix and pour the foam.
13. While foaming, add threaded pipe. This will allow the positive to be mounted to a stand.
14. When foam has expanded and cooled, pop out of the mold.

    If there is damage to the surface, use extra foam, Bondo, or epoxy putty to patch. Cut off any extra expansion (flashing) with a hand saw. Then sand as needed.
15. Attach the inserted rod to the prepared metal socket and wooden stand.

Or, for a ***fiberglass mold*** (as shown in Figure 6-31A–D):

- Add the dividing shim metal wall.
- Add the release agent and keys.
- Add three to four layers of fiberglass and resin.

16. If you are using fiberglass, allow to cure and gas off.

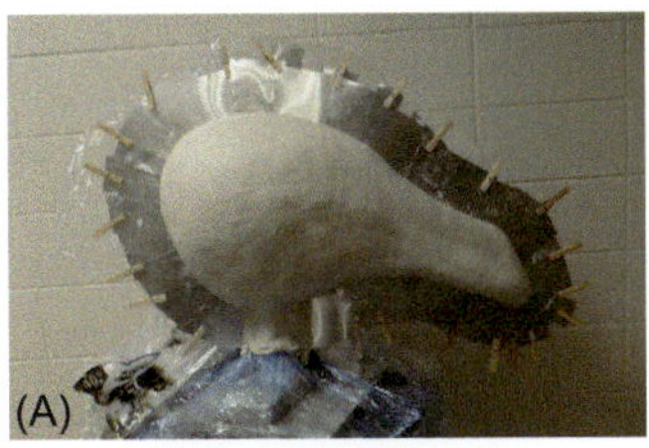

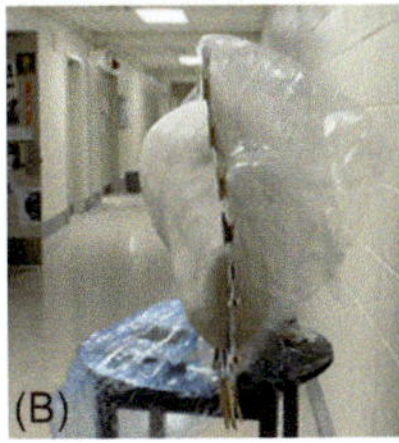

FIGURE 6-31A–B *Water-based clay positive sculpt with metal shim*

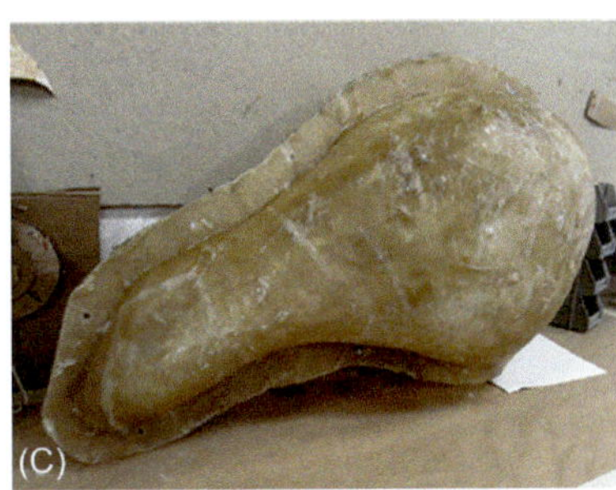

FIGURE 6-31C *Finished fiber glass mold*

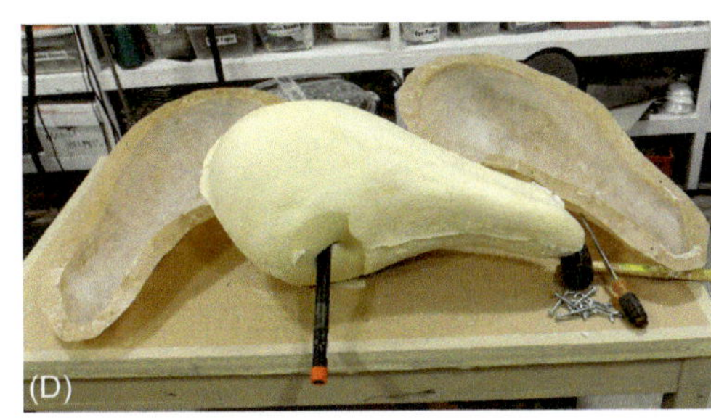

FIGURE 6-31D *Finished urethane foam cast*

17. Add the release agent to the flange – the exposed edge of the mold. The metal shim needs to be removed, and the built-up fiberglass flange is then exposed. If the release agent is not applied, then the new layer of *glass* will bond to itself.

18. Repeat the previous steps as before and cast the second half of the shape.
19. Dremel, sand, and refine sharp and uneven edges as needed.
20. Predrill holes for bolting together (no holes are needed if you are clamping the halves together).
21. Patiently pry apart the mold halves.
22. Again Dremel, sand, and refine sharp and uneven edges as needed.
23. Clean out the clay.
24. Add the release agent to the inside and flange edges of the mold.
25. Assemble the mold (by bolting or clamping) and pour the foam.
26. While foaming, add threaded pipe. This will allow the positive to be mounted to a stand.
27. When the foam has expanded and cooled, pop out of the mold.

If there is damage to the surface, use extra foam, Bondo, or epoxy putty to patch. Cut off any extra expansion with a hand saw. Then sand as needed.

28. Attach the inserted rod into the prepared metal socket and wooden stand.

CHAPTER 7

COMMON MASK MAKING MATERIALS

There are endless possibilities when it comes to materials for building masks. The choice may depend on the time budgeted for construction, the durability, the weight, the design, and even personal preference. It is possible to create many different designs with the same material, but it is also very helpful to know the resources available so that you may pick the material that best satisfies the need.

PAPIER AND FABRIC MÂCHÉ

Forms of papier and fabric mâché have been around for as long as humans have been making paper and fabric. Early Asian culture developed lacquerware and papermaking; the Egyptians used scrap papyrus, linen, and resins for cartonnage coverings; and the Greeks made armor out of layers of linen and rabbit hide glue. Papier mâché is very tough, nontoxic (depending on the glue), cheap, and one of the most lightweight materials for making masks. It may be used for any size of mask if built on a form/armature and/or it may also be used as a "finish surface" for other materials. Using fabric instead of paper may make the mask even tougher, and if the fabric has a distinct texture (cheesecloth, burlap, or erosion cloth), the end result may be uniquely expressive (see Figure 7-1).

There are many different traditional recipes for papier mâché glue. You can mix your own glue/paste with water and wheat paste or flour, and with a few other nontraditional additives, custom variations may be achieved. Papier mâché artists such as Jonnigood (ultimatepapermache.com) and Dan Reeder (Gourmetpapermache.com) offer many suggestions for papier mâché techniques and recipes on their sites.

DOI: 10.4324/9781003343264-7

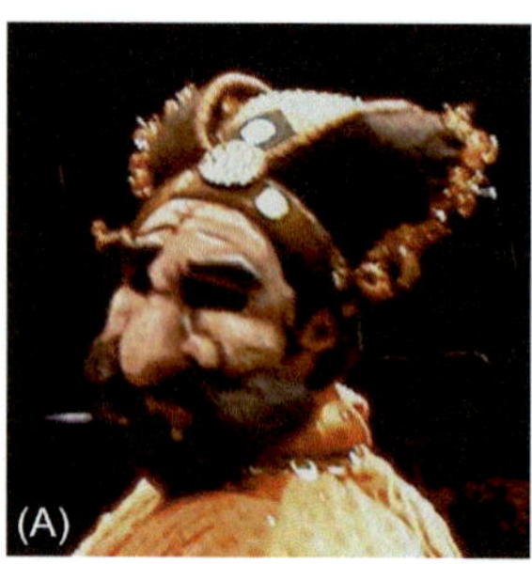

FIGURE 7-1 *Fabric and papier mâché masks from West Virginia University's mainstage productions: A) the "fat prince" from* The Caucasian Chalk Circle *(2008); B) "the priest" and "the mayor" from* The Visit *(2012)*

TIP BOX

Papier Mâché Recipes

A. **Basic:**
   a. Plain flour (no whole wheat).
   b. Hot water.
   c. Paper of choice.
B. **Mod Podge and Paper:**
   (no mixing of water required).
C. **Carpenter's Glue** (yellow or white) **and Water** (3:1 ratio)

Safety Note: If using a craft or wood glue, wear gloves because some of these may contain formaldehyde.

Celluclay is a form of prepared dry paper and glue ground into a powder. It comes in rectangular plastic-wrapped brick. When water is added, it expands and is similar to lumpy clay, which may be thinned with more water as needed. Unless pressed into a mold, it does not smooth as easily as clay, and when dry it can be deceivingly heavy, so use thin layers. It is incredibly tough when dry. It can be sanded and cut with a Dremel tool, but again it is tough, and it may take a long time to modify (see Chapter 12, "Horns").

BLOCK FOAM

Foam is a valuable material for building masks. It can be glued into layers and carved or flat patterned to create hollow shapes. It is very lightweight.

EVA Foam

This (Figure 7-2) is a type of closed-cell foam that comes in different densities and colors. It can be patterned, carved, sanded, glued, painted (airbrushed or painted by hand), and even bolted and hand-sewn if the proper washers are used. Because it is slightly less flexible and soft than urethane foam, flat patterns should be cut into more sections and/or the foam pieces may be precurved with a little heat to hold curved shapes.

Urethane Foam

This is a type of open-cell foam that is commonly used for upholstery because of its flexibility and drainage abilities (Figure 7-3). There are two varieties: polyether and reticulated. *Polyether* is a very soft small-celled foam

FIGURE 7-2 *EVA foam mask painted with acrylic paint. From* Foam Patterning and Construction Techniques. *Designed and constructed by the author*

FIGURE 7-3 *Dyed and airbrushed reticulated foam mask for the Dallas Children's Theatre production of* The Big Friendly Giant. *Designed and constructed by the author*

for interior upholstery. *Reticulated* foam is a large-cell variety that is tougher than polyether. Both foams may be patterned, carved, dyed, bolted, and hand or machine sewn with ease. It may also be airbrushed or spray painted. One drawback is that urethane foam is slightly heavier than EVA foam.

Safety Note: There are some inhalation concerns with this material. As the cells of the foam are cut, they may release small amounts of uncured gas. Constant exposure could affect the brain, lungs, and nervous system. If possible, lay out the foam for a day before using to help gas off and always try to work in a ventilated area.

Foam Putty

This is a sculptable air-drying product that has a closed-cell, foam-like consistency (Figure 7-4). Crayola's Model Magic and Calpalmy's Foam Clay are examples (see Figure 7-4). When dry, it is flexible. It can be used to make details such as teeth and horns as well as lightweight masks. It can also be pressed into molds and takes paint well. Rubberized coatings such as Flex Seal or Plasti-Dip may be applied as a finish before and after painting.

FIGURE 7-4 Crayola's *model magic and* Calpalmy's *foam clay are examples of foam putty*

FIGURE 7-5 *Foundation mask for University of Mississippi's Production of* A Christmas Carol. *Designed and constructed by the author*

LATEX

Latex or latex rubber is a naturally occurring material harvested from trees (Figure 7-5). Its actual color is light tan, but it can be tinted any color to some degree with acrylic/latex paint. When dry, it is flexible. There are lattices sold specifically for masks that are slightly less flexible than the latex used for makeup. To some extent, *mask making latex* can provide more structure so that the mask will not collapse and will hold its shape when upright (additional structure such as polyfoam should be added to help support larger latex masks). Depending on the mask design, a more flexible latex might be desired, so it is important to test which material is correct for the project. If a thinner consistency is required, natural latex may be thinned with distilled water.

Safety Note: Because latex is produced by trees as a self-defense and to heal wounds in the bark, many people also have reactions to it. There may be severe responses to latex in its wet or dry form, and sometimes even the smell (ammonia) and the talcum powder can cause a reaction (talc has been known to cause a separate set of problems!). When using different materials that might contact the skin, always ask if the actor has any known allergies. It may also be prudent (but perhaps risky) to have the subject put on a latex glove or to dab a small dot of latex on the skin. I have seen reactions range from redness and burning to swelling around the area where latex has been applied. Anaphylaxis shock has also been associated with exposure to latex, so caution is advised.

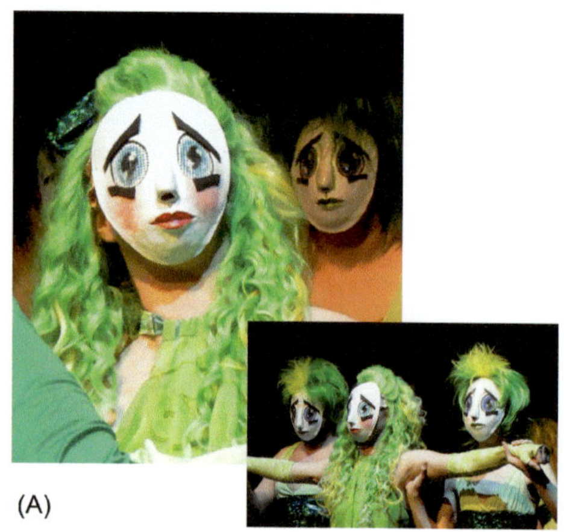

(A) (B)

FIGURE 7-6 *A) A princess and slaves from* Pericles *(2015), designed and constructed by the author; B)* commedia *masks constructed by undergraduate students during WVU mask making class*

Natural latex has a strong smell of ammonia, so ventilation is suggested. However, there are now lattices available that reduce the ammonia smell.

NEOPRENE

Neoprene (Figure 7-6) is a man-made rubber (the flexible variety may be used as a replacement for latex for some projects). It can be purchased in three consistencies: flexible, semirigid, and rigid. Each company has different consistencies, so before ordering ask for a small sample to test. All these forms may be used for masks. Again, testing the cured body or "hand" of the material is suggested before choosing a type at random. This material is slightly different from latex; even its *flexibility* is not as wobbly as the very flexible natural latex.

THERMOPLASTICS (CRAFT VARIETY)

Most plastics are somewhat malleable with heat but are not meant for heat manipulation There are industrial thermoplastics that are used for construction materials, such as polyvinyl chloride (PVC), the melting point of which is 212–500°F. Craft *thermoplastics* are designed to become pliable at 150°F. A heat gun, hair dryer, steam, or boiling water may be used. Craft thermoplastics come in a variety of forms: small pellets; thin, multicolored flat planks; solid plastic sheets; sheets infused with webbing or netting; finely spun, matted sheets with the texture of felt; and more. Depending on the vendor, different names for thermoplastics include Friendly Plastic (is there really such a plastic?), Worbla, Thibra, Altraform, Veraform, Fosshape, and so on (Figure 7-7).

Worbla

This material comes in plastic sheets in light brown, white, clear, and black. It is great for making any shape. When overlapping the material, the edges may be blended fairly easily. It cuts, sands, and paints well. One of the material claims is that small scraps can be reused, so save all the pieces.

Thibra

This material is similar to Worbla but is more malleable and less gritty. It is gooey and sticky when molten and can be shaped into anything. Seams are easy to blend.

Veraform

This thermoplastic comes in two weights: light- and heavyweight. I find the heavier gauge is best, especially for bigger shapes. Veraform is a fabulous material for making porous, rigid net-like masks and skull caps to anchor hair materials. It can be cut with metal snips or heavy scissors. Use Krylon Fusion spray paint and Design Master paints for big spray accents and finish with airbrushed or hand-painted acrylic paint for any details. This material may start to lose some of its ability to adhere to itself after being melded and pulled apart repeatedly, so use the material decisively. The scraps may also be used, so save everything. It can get heavy.

FIGURE 7-7 *Masks from West Virginia University's Mainstage Productions: A)* The Love of the Nightingale *(2009), designed and constructed by the author; B) "Zeke" from the West Virginia Public Theatre Production of* The Unlucky Princess Battles the Goblins *(2014) (Zeke's eyeballs move and are removable), designed by the author; C) an ensemble mask from the West Virginia Public Theatre Production of* The Visit *(2012), Built on a glasses frame, designed and constructed by the author*

Fosshape/Fuzzform

When in its raw state, this material feels like thin, dense quilt batting or felt, but when fused and contracted/shrunken with heat and pressure (hand iron or heat press), it becomes less fuzzy and more stiff. It may also be fused with a hand steamer. Fosshape can be further finished and sealed with multiple layers of wood glue and/or clear acrylic mediums such as Sculpt or Coat, Mod Podge, or Rosco's Gel Coat. I prefer to drape this material over complex shapes, adding sewn darts to aid with shaping when fusing with heat. After several dried coats of craft or wood glue, seams may be patched (Extra-Fast-Setting Drywall Spackle, epoxy putty, or Bondo), sanded, then sealed with several more layers of glue or other PVA materials described in this chapter.

Thermoplastics for Vacuum Forming

ABS, Styrene, and Vivac (plexiglass) are all forms of plastics that can be used in vacuform machines. This process requires the use of a positive mold or "buck." The plastic is heated to flexibility and, with the help of a vacuum, is pulled or sucked over the buck. Masks, props, armor, prosthetic dentures, and more may be made with this machine. It is also possible to use a heat gun to form these plastics, but without the even pressure of the vacuum, some shapes might be irregular.

Safety Note: A ventilated area is recommended when melting any plastic, even craft thermoplastics, as there are fumes created during the process because the plastics are being slightly burned to reach molten temperature. The exception is when using steam or hot water.

FIBERGLASS

Fiberglass (Figure 7-8) is a material that uses glass fiber to reinforce a liquid resin. When the glass fibers are added in conjunction with layers of resin, the final cured material can be lightweight and very tough and will reflect whatever finish is desired. It may be used in many forms, such as a brushable paste or layered in precut sheets. When it is important to capture the detail of a sculpture, a resin "gel coat" (lacking a fiber filler) is commonly recommended for the first layer. This provides a smooth "skin" to capture all the detail of the sculpture without having any of the fiber showing through. It still needs to be backed with two or three successive layers of fiberglass to be structural. Resin with nylon or plastic fibers may also be very structural – test

FIGURE 7-8 *Fiberglass masks mounted on welding foundations for the University of Dallas Production of* The Great God Brown *(2003), designed and constructed by the author*

before moving ahead with the final product. Fiberglass is also a very effective mold material. Use a silicone "glove mold" to capture the detail of the sculpture, and then use fiberglass as a "mother mold" or "blanket mold" to support the flexible silicone material.

Safety Note: Both polyester and epoxy resins have toxic fumes. When working with these materials, make sure to wear a respirator that fits your face with the proper filters. Use it outside or in a ventilation booth.

The glass fiber will infiltrate porous clothing, eyes, and skin, so wear vinyl or neoprene gloves, goggles, a plastic or rubber apron, and protective lower arm sleeves. I have even wrapped my arms with plastic bags and masking tape as a substitute when I run out of disposable sleeves.

LIQUID PLASTICS

Liquid plastic, which is actually an opaque epoxy, is a two-part material process. These are ideally designed for rotocasting, that is, rotating the mold continuously while the material coats the walls until it cures. This material can be quick to cure, so it must be used with a mold that is light enough to rotate and can be controlled by hand. The trick is to try to get an even coating and to not let it build up, or it can become very thick and heavy. Tint every other layer with a compatible pigment to determine the coverage of each coat.

This material can also be used as mother mold material. Artcast, a type of casting plastic, is perfect for this application.

Safety Note: Liquid plastics should be used in a ventilated area with a respirator, as the fumes are somewhat strong. Gloves, an apron, and protective sleeves are recommended.

EXPANDABLE COLD FOAM

Cold foam is a type of polyurethane foam that comes in liquid form (see Figure 7-9). This is the same foam that is used for upholstery but at smaller scale. A two-part material, cold foam has a short working time and, depending on the density and expansion amount, it can produce a great deal of foam. Though it does have a warm exothermic reaction when it is curing, it is called cold foam because it does not need an oven to cure. This contrasts with "hot foam" or foam latex, which requires a low-temperature oven to cure. For easy demolding, molds should be coated with mold soap. Latex can also be used as a skin for this material, but again, mold soaps (such as Murphy's Oil Soap) are still needed to help with demolding. Tint any soap with a little food coloring to help determine the coverage area in the molds. This material may be rigid or soft, depending on the product.

Safety Note: When using this material, wear a respirator and use it in a ventilated area, as the fumes are toxic but do not have a strong odor. Also wear gloves, an apron, and protective sleeves, because this foam in its liquid form is very sticky.

SILICONE

Silicone (see Figure 7-10) has multiple uses and can make very realistic movable masks that seemingly bond with the face as well as molds for capturing fine detail. The best silicone material for making masks is platinum, translucent, and very flexible. It can be tinted intrinsically with silicone pigment. Flocking fibers may also be added to create the effect of veining. The process requires the use of a core mold and a rigid outer mold. The silicone is then injected into the space left between the two molds. Some of the most wonderful silicone masks are those built by a company called Immortal Masks.

(A)

(B)

(C)

FIGURE 7-9 *Examples of cold foam masks: A) reproduction of an animated character, constructed by the author; B) the "Mooncalf," designed by the author and constructed by undergraduate student Zack White; C) "Pedro" from the WVU Production of* The Visit, *with hair augmented with EVA Foam, designed and constructed by the author*

FIGURE 7-10 *A silicone goblin mask made by immortal masks*

Safety Note: Molds built for this process are generally fiberglass or epoxy resin, so the fumes are strong (see section on "Fiberglass"). Silicone itself is not toxic (though not edible), but any topical painting requires a toxic solvent to adhere to the surface. A respirator, gloves, goggles, apron, disposable sleeves, and a well-ventilated workroom are all recommended.

MIXED MEDIA

To some extent, all masks may be considered "mixed media." However, true mixed media, such as masks made from recycled plastics, woven sticks, paper bags, cardboard boxes, and balloons, can make remarkable looking stylized masks. The important idea when using alternative materials is to let the material(s) show through – embrace and don't fight the look of what you choose.

NATURAL MATERIALS FOR MASK MAKING

Note: Some forms of papier mâché might fall under this heading.

Leather

This is a traditional material for mask making (Figure 7-11). It is still popular for commedia, cosplay, neutral, and acting masks as well as in non-Western cultures. This material is very lightweight and durable. It can be as labor intensive as some of the more complicated masks mentioned previously. Leather is commonly made of cowhide, and the process involves creating a positive sculpt (generally out of wood, but these may be made from plaster), soaking the three-to-four-ounce leather in warm/hot water until it is pliable, then stretching and pinning the leather in place over the buck until it dries. It may be pigmented with oil-based leather stains and paints, then a shellac is commonly used to seal the front and back.

FIGURE 7-11 *Leather mask from the West Virginia University Production of* Pericles, *designed by the author and created by WVU students*

Wood

It has been used in mask making in many forms, and wooden masks have probably been created in every culture at some point in history. Masks made from wood may currently be found created by native tribes in North and South America, Africa, Indonesia, etc. Some of these masks are made to support native customs and practices, and some are for the tourist trade. Wood may also be used to make a positive mold or buck for creating masks.

Natural Fibers

Natural fibers such as grasses and reeds, along with leather and wood, may also be used to construct masks (Figure 7-12). These may be woven like baskets,

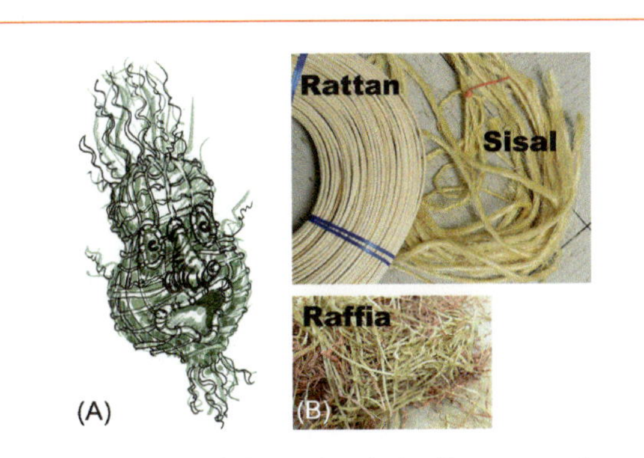

FIGURE 7-12 *A) Design for a basket-like rattan mask; B) rattan, sisal, and rafia*

FIGURE 7-13 *A) Sketch of gourds stacked, cut, and arranged; B) gourds ready to be transformed*

tied in bundles to a frame, or used as an understructure for other materials. Soak rattan, grapevine, or stiff reeds in warm water until pliable, then shape the mask by hand or over a form as desired. These may be pre-dyed with natural pigments or with Rit dyes before being shaped.

Gourds

Gourds come in many varieties that have structures that make them a perfect medium to stack, cut, and glue to be used as full or partials masks (Figure 7-13). Depending on the shape and size, some metal or plastic supports might need to be added as an armature or joint.

CHAPTER 8

CLAYS AND PLASTERS

MODELING CLAYS

There are many kinds of clays available to use as foundation sculpts for casting. Each might look the same when sitting side by side, but the "hand" of the clays can be very different (Figure 8-1). The determination of which to use can depend on 1) the speed at which you work; 2) the material that will be cast; 3) budget; 4) availability; and 5) sometimes all four of these.

Water-Based Clay

Water-based clay, sometimes called *pottery clay*, is very inexpensive (as long as it is not shipped) and can be found at schools that have pottery programs, art stores, and ceramics supply stores. Water-based clay is mixed with water and many different dry ingredients to create a "clay body" (it may also be dug straight out of the ground). A clay body can be mixed specifically for making different kinds of fired pottery or sculpture, or it could be mixed to contribute to a part of a process wherein the clay is taken only as far as the wet stage, cast, and then discarded.

Some clay bodies contain larger ingredients that support big sculptures, and these particles may be detrimental to fine sculpting, so ask questions when buying to make certain what the texture will be. Sometimes ceramics suppliers have extra custom mixes or junk batches that cannot be sold as regular inventory and thus might be sold for less.

This clay can dry out fast, so if care is not taken a lot of work may be lost. If a sculpt is in "process," it is important to wrap it with damp towels and layers of plastic that are sealed at the bottom. Any airflow will accelerate drying. Extra clay should be stored in sealed plastic bags with damp towels kept on top.

DOI: 10.4324/9781003343264-8

FIGURE 8-1 *Kind of clays: A) water-based pottery clay is inexpensive and comes in any earth tone color and texture depending on the ingredients; B) monster clay; and C) plasticine*

Besides expense, there are other advantages to this clay:

1. It is nontoxic and is biodegradable. However, if the workspace is not kept clean and there is a lot of dust particulate from dried clay, then there is a danger of inhalation.
2. Blending and smoothing with a tool, brush, or sponge and water works well.
3. Adding detail is very easy.
4. Tools clean well with water.

The following are the disadvantages of clay:

1. If the mask maker is not careful, clay can dry out fast.
2. It may contain sulfur, which can inhibit silicone from curing. I have never experienced this problem, perhaps because I coat this clay with several layers of *crystal-clear varnish* or I could have inadvertently used non-sulfur-based clay bodies.
3. If paper or tape is being used for a fast foundation understructure, moisture from this clay may make it collapse. If there is concern, then wrap the understructure with plastic and move forward with the clay covering.

WED (Walter E. Disney) Clay

WED (Walter E. Disney) clay is also water-based and is relatively cheap (25 pounds on Amazon is currently $33.24). Though it will eventually dry out, it has additional ingredients such as glycerin, which slows down the drying time. It still needs to be wrapped with plastic and kept moist. This clay may contain sulfur, so this should be a consideration when working with silicone.

Oil-Based Clay

Oil-based clay (such as Chavant, Plasticine, or Plastilina) contains oil as opposed to water. It comes in two pound bricks, though it is possible to buy "logs" or cases in bulk. The prices may go back to a more reasonable range but at present (2022), the current pricing ranges from $11.00 to $29.00 a brick, depending on shipping. This clay is very popular for prosthetics, art projects, and industrial sculpting. Because silicone will not cure when in contact with sulfur (a textural ingredient), Chavant, Inc., for example, offers clays with no sulfur (NSP). Depending on the sculptural need, there are many different varieties of smoothness, waxiness, sticking quality (sticky to nonsticky), and flexibility (ranging from soft to hard) and melting point. It can be smoothed with naphtha and a variety of other surprising and less toxic materials. Check Chavant's website (https://chavant.com/) for more details. It can be softened by using a double boiler, a heat gun, or a hot hair dryer. I once worked with an artist who melted huge chunks of plasticine in a pot floating in an electric skillet filled with water (homemade double boiler), and when it was reduced to a molten slurry, she would pour it out (just like fudge) on a marble slab and work it with a metal scrapper until it was cool enough to handle.

Monster Clay

Monster clay is a wax- and oil-based clay that is very popular with special effects sculptors. It claims to be made of "food-grade materials" and is therefore nontoxic. It also is half the price of plasticine oil-based clay, as it is not as dense, so you get more for the price. It too can be heated and made softer even using a microwave.

PLASTERS AND STONES

Right or wrong, the generic term *plaster* can refer to any calcium-based, Portland cement-based, or gypsum-based casting material. This material ranges from the softest, porous, pottery plaster to the hardest, least porous stones. All go through a curing process when water is added. The chemical reaction, or *curing*, is only about the *hardening of the material*; it is not about the loss of water. Any water that was added is still in the mold and takes time to evaporate – so you can have a cured mold that is damp. While curing, the material produces heat called an *exothermic reaction*. The reason for the reaction is the ingredient Portland cement or gypsum (depending on the material), which is heated to dehydrate all the molecular moisture. The exothermic reaction occurs when the material is rapidly rehydrated (molecularly) – the energy released with the rush of the reaction produces heat. It is very dangerous to cast a hand, for example, in a thick bucket of plaster: A) plaster that thick would cause an extreme exothermic reaction and would be especially hot, resulting in burns; and/or B) the hand would need to be cut or broken out of the material. There have been reports of lost fingers due to poor circulation.

The variations in setting time, density, and hardness are due mostly to the additives and to some degree on how finely the particles are milled. Companies such as Capital Ceramics have a formula for their casting materials.

Safety Notes:

1. All plasters and stones contain silica, so wearing a dust mask is recommended.
2. Most of these materials are very absorbent and will suck the moisture out of human skin. If you are planning on mixing multiple batches, wear safety gloves and/or moisturize regularly.
3. *Do not pore wet plaster down the sink drain or toilet.* It will cure in the pipes and permanently clog. Instead, let the unused plaster set up or cure in the bucket or bowl and scrape into the trash. Use Vaseline to line containers, and cured plaster will come out easily.

TIP BOX

Repeated Use of Plaster Molds

The best thing about using a mold is that multiples (around 12–15 depending on the material) might be made before the mold starts losing most of its detail. The loss of detail is a gradual process. Because of friction and heat, over time most plaster molds will start to lose definition.

Pottery Plaster

Pottery plaster has the least amount of Portland cement of all the plasters and is therefore softer when cured. It is also the most absorbent of all the plaster materials. Often you can find thick plaster table tops in ceramic shops covered with canvas made for wedging wet clay, that is, kneading clay to reduce moisture and eliminate air bubbles. It can also be used for slip casting clay. Pottery plaster may be used during many procedures during the mask making process, especially if you don't have hydrocal.

Hydrocal gypsum cement and hydrostone are similar materials (hydrostone is the stronger of the two). These are the perfect plasters/stones for single primary molds or

TIP BOX

What to Use: Rigid or Flexible Molds?"

As a rule, when casting rigid materials, use a soft mold, and when casting soft materials, use a rigid mold (see Figure 8-2). The soft *glove mold* with a rigid *mother mold* (a matrix mold) is the best of both worlds when casting a rigid object. This can also save money by using less silicone.

When using plasters for casting negative mold, always use the softer material on items that might be damaged, and when casting with plaster to create a positive, use the more rigid material for those items that are precious; for example, for a one-of-a-kind *positive cast* or duplicate of a rare fruit, use the hardest material – ultracal or resin. For a cast creating a negative mold of a sculpt on top of the fruit's positive cast, use a softer material such as pottery plaster – if it breaks, you can always make another negative mold but not another original copy.

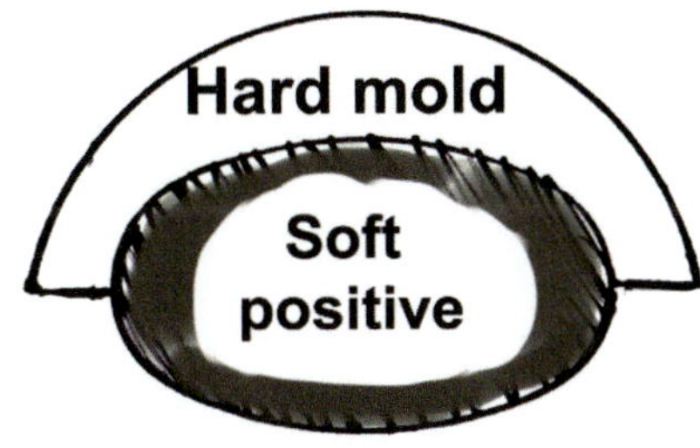

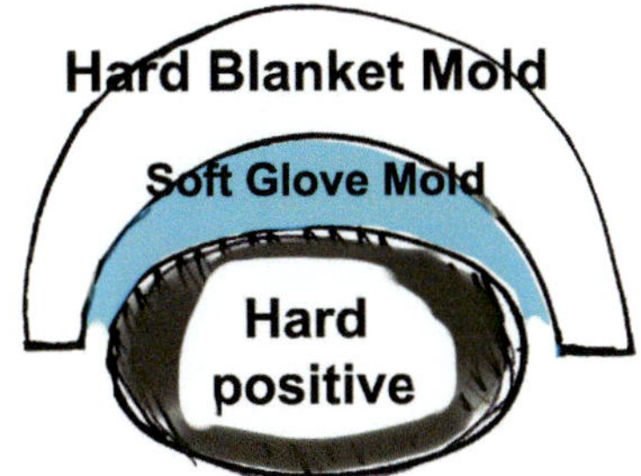

FIGURE 8-2 *Diagram of casting hard and soft materials*

secondary mother or blanket molds. I have also used them for making life positives. Like plaster, it can be sanded or carved, and it is good for making hollow casts. The cure time is a bit slower than that of plaster.

Ultracal 30 Gypsum Cement

Ultracal 30 gypsum cement is a very hard, dense material that is best for making solid or hollow casts. This would be the material to use to cast that special one-of-a-kind positive. It is a little trickier to work with than hydrocal or plaster, as it can cure fast all at once, so small batches used for hollow casts or poured casts are best. Its cure time is longer than that of hydrocal.

Dental Stones

Dental stones are the most finely milled and densest of this family of casting materials used for making very fine positives that need to pick up tiny details. This material is commonly used by dentists to make positive casts of teeth and in the prosthetics industry.

Mixing

Mixing the different plasters and stones is not complicated, but there is sometimes confusion when first learning the technique.

1. Pregrease the bowl or bucket with Vaseline before mixing. The residual hardened plaster will pop out cleanly (depending on the texture of the sides of the bowl or bucket).
2. Fill the container with warm water. The amount of water needed is based on an estimate of the amount of liquid needed to fill a mold or cover the item to be cast.
   Tip: Heat will help make the material set up faster, so be wary of hot water with plaster, as it already sets up relatively fast. Warm/hot water is helpful when working with hydrocal and ultracal. Reportedly, using a hair dryer to heat up the liquid plaster may help accelerate curing. Also, when using ultracal, if a little is left in the bottom of the bucket from a previous batch, it can act as a starter for the next batch.
3. Begin sprinkling cups of the plaster material all over the surface of the water (not just in the center). Continue to do this until the plaster stops sinking into the water. It will begin to peak or accumulate on the surface like an island – some call it a "dry cracked creek bed" (Figure 8-3).

FIGURE 8-3 *The "dry cracked creek bed" technique used to identify when enough plaster has been added to water*

TIP BOX

Mold-Making Terminology

1. *Positive sculpt* – the sculpt itself or an actual item.
2. *Negative mold* – a hollow mold taken from the positive sculpt.
3. *Positive cast* – when a material is poured into a negative mold, the item that comes out is the positive cast. A copy of the positive sculpt or original item.
4. *Mother mold or blanket mold* – one part of a matrix mold. The outer mold is commonly made of resin or plaster that supports the flexible glove mold. These can be very thin and lightweight when using resins (fiberglass).
5. *Glove mold* – the second part of a matrix mold. The soft interior negative mold commonly made of silicone used for casting rigid objects or delicate, detailed sculpts.
6. *Matrix mold* – a mold that has a mother or blanket mold outer layer (made of plaster, stones, or resins) covering a flexible inner mold (made of silicone or rubber).
7. *Undercut* – An area that travels the "downside" of a peak or a curve. When casting, it is a concern because a mold can get locked onto a positive or to itself if it is allowed to go over the halfway point (Figure 8-4).
   Solutions to working with undercuts:
   - Use a matrix mold with a soft glove mold material.
   - Use a multiple part mold. A two-to-three-part mold will generally help.
   - Divide the sculpt carefully.

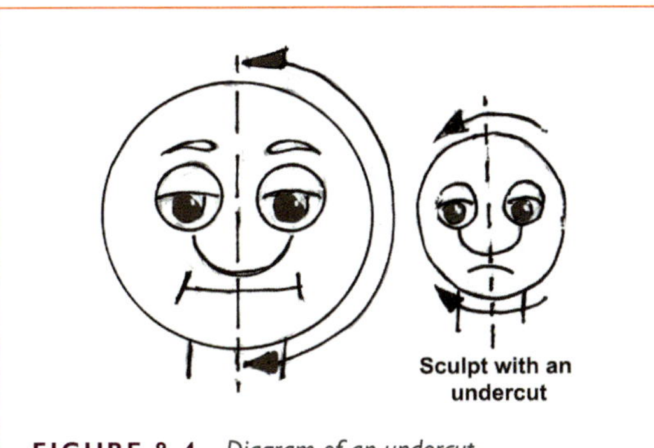

FIGURE 8-4 *Diagram of an undercut*

8. *Core Mold* – An "interior positive" mold used on the inside *of certain matrix molds to help create a custom skin or hollow prosthetic pieces. Common used with foam latex, silicone and cold foam appliances and masks.*

TIP BOX

Containers and Chip Brushes

I hate to waste things. I save bulletin board mylar displays, the giant rolls of stained paper backdrops from our photo lab, cardboard boxes, three-ring binders, aluminum can pull tabs, printer paper that has one side blank, and so on. Some of the images in this book might include occasional glimpses of familiar plastic containers. I reuse as many plastic food containers as possible for mixing plasters and other materials: yogurt cups, cheese containers, the big white "to-go" containers with lids (love those for storing and mixing paint), Nestle's Quik containers, etc. Just make sure to label them when using and dispose of them if permanently gooey. When used for plaster, chip brushes can be reused sometimes as many as three times if the bristles are greased with Vaseline. Tap the bristles with a hammer on a hard surface, then continue to work and brush out with a wire brush.

CHAPTER 9

FABRICS AND FUR COVERINGS

Depending on the mask, some sort of fabric might be used as a covering. This could be fur, antron fleece, or any number of stretch fabrics.

FUR FABRIC

Fur fabric is a great choice for covering a mask. The length and movement, not to mention the color, can add many nuances to the character that is being created (Figure 9-1).

Another aspect to consider is the direction of the *nap* (Figure 9-2). The *nap* or *fibers* can go in any combination of directions. If the nap goes downward, the fur will generally compress and may not look as fluffy – like the direction on a dog's back. However, if patterned so that it is upside down, gravity will make it fluff out and look full and on end.

Fur may be dyed, painted with an airbrush, colored with Preval sprayers or color hair spray, or tinted with inks or brushed-in acrylics.

Dyeing Fur Fabric

When dyeing fur, generally disperse dyes for polyester, acetate, and synthetics must be used. To dye a man-made fur of natural fibers such as cotton, bamboo, or linen, then union or fiber reactive dyes could be used. But generally (and unfortunately), fur fabric is made of plastics. This means a dye bath of high, consistent heat, with the fur being moved constantly around in the pot or dye vat. If the temperature is too high or if the fur sits on the bottom of the pot or dye vat, it will scorch, resulting in matted clumps. After dyeing, the fur should be put in the washer with a small amount of detergent. When finished, take it out of the washer and shake it vigorously upside down to loosen and fluff the fibers – finger combing will help as well. Hang to dry fur side up on a table, pinned to a clothesline, or over metal clothes rack so the fibers don't compress. I don't use real animal fur in my mask making, though there are techniques and dyes available for dyeing fur still on the hide.

DOI: 10.4324/9781003343264-9

FIGURE 9-1 *The "Ass" from the Colorado Shakespeare Festival's Production of* A Midsummer Night's Dream *(2002). This mask had a moving mouth and a lip that raised up to reveal big donkey teeth. Designed and constructed by the author*

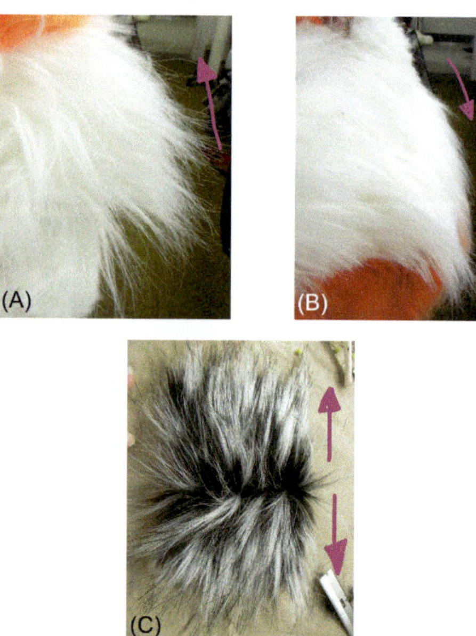

FIGURE 9-2 *Fur direction: A) fur is upside – against the nap. It will stay fluffy and full if cut to lay this way; B) Fur aiming down in the "growing direction" – with the nap – is smooth and controlled; C) fur sewn in opposite directions. This may be used if there is a part designed into the fur*

Cutting and Sewing Fur Fabric

When cutting fur fabric, the only rule is do not cut the loose fur fibers. If this happens, the organic quality is lost, and the seams will not be able to be disguised. It is possible to cut fur carefully with scissors, but the best tool to use is a single-edged razor blade (Figure 9-3). Cut the back of the fur fabric, that is, the foundation of the fur.

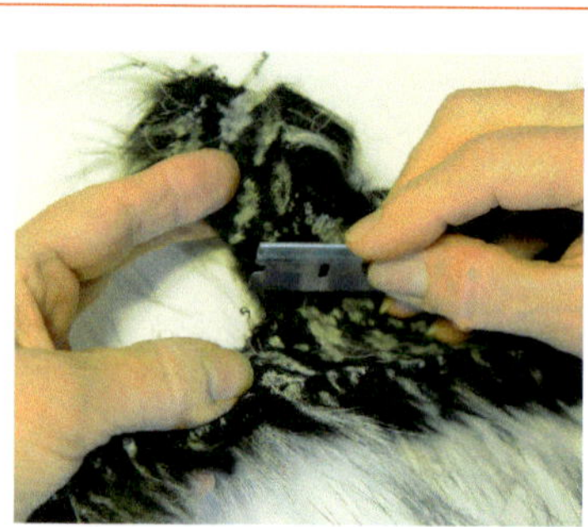

FIGURE 9-3 *How to cut fur*

Sewing techniques include machine serging, zigzag, and straight stitching as well as hand sewing (Figure 9-4). When sewing, the key is to keep the fiber tucked in. When finished sewing, carefully comb and tease the fiber out of the seam.

Though expensive, furs woven on stretch fabric foundations are also available at special vendors. These are

FIGURE 9-4 *Fur sewing techniques: A) Using a zigzag stitch; B) straight stitch with small seam allowance; C) serging edge. Note that the fibers are tucked back from the stitching edge*

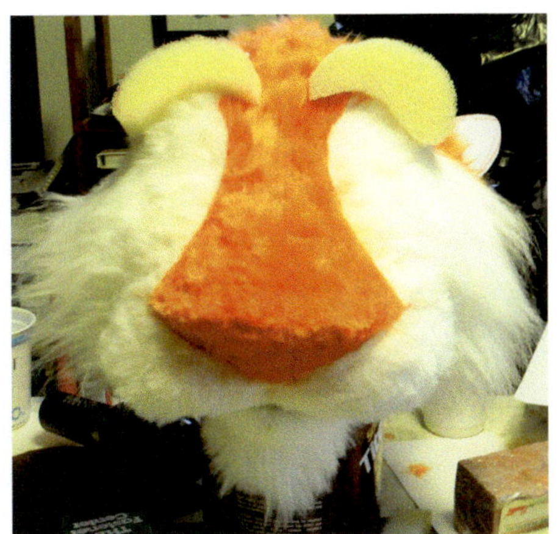

FIGURE 9-5 *Sculpting fur with scissors*

very convenient, because little darting is needed to contour onto and over a shape. Extremely long hair/fur lengths may also be purchased.

FIGURE 9-6 *Images of materials for coloring fur and other fabrics including plastic wig hair*

Trimming and Sculpting Fur

Long pile fur or fur with long fibers may be contoured and shaped to accentuate areas such as eyes, cheeks, and mouths. Use small sharp scissors and or shears to carefully contour the areas. Test with a sample piece of fur before jumping in on the real thing (Figure 9-5).

Painting Fur Fabric

When adding shadows and color contouring to fur with an airbrush or Preval sprayer or colored hair spray, it is helpful to style and set the fur with a stiff hairspray or workable fixative. The downside is that the fur will lose its loose, wispy quality. However, the results, whether subtle or dramatic, will add depth that can contribute greatly to the finished design.

Inks may also be used and will not weigh down the fibers as much as acrylic paints. Make your own tints with sharpies and alcohol or use diluted artist inks. Color may also be brushed into fur fibers with a toothbrush or a stiff hog's hair paint brush (Figure 9-6).

FIGURE 9-7 *Sample images of the same fabric with different names: nylafleece, antron fleece, or muppet fleece. The brilliant colors are achieved using rit and acid dyes*

ANTRON FLEECE

Antron fleece, sometimes called "muppet fleece," is now only available at the vendor Georgia Stage, which refers to its product as *nylafleece* (Figure 9-7). It is a unique fabric,

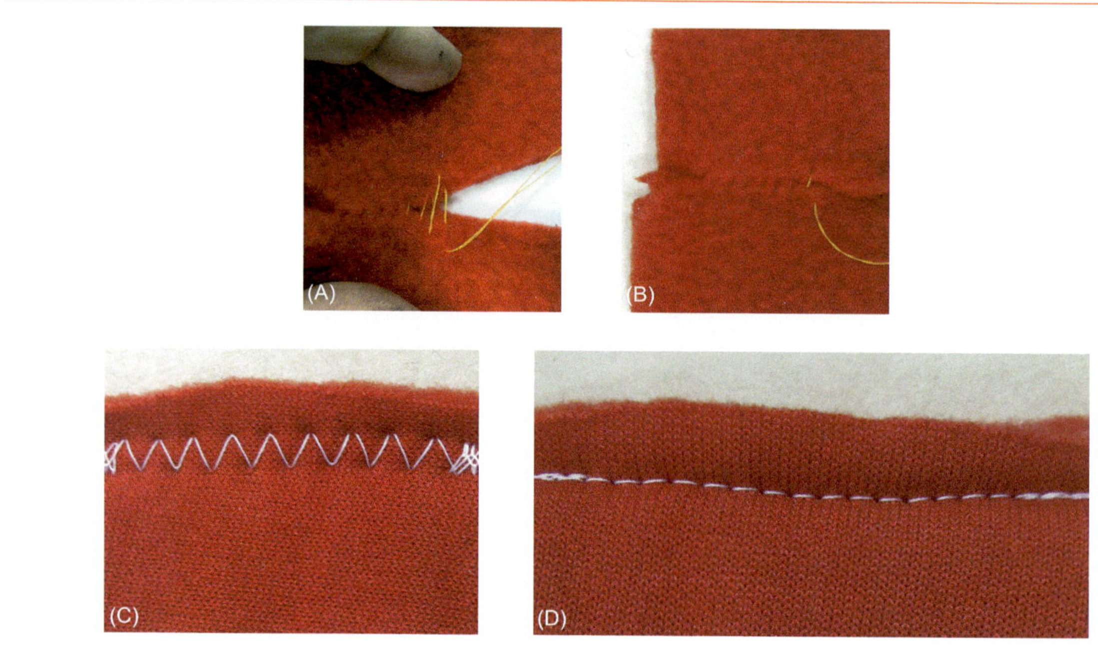

FIGURE 9-8 *Examples of stitches for fleece: A) Hand stitching with yellow thread. if a matching color is used, the seam is invisible; B) when stitches are pulled together and "picked out," they can be invisible; C) a zigzag stitch. this is often preferred as this fleece stretches; D) a machine straight stitch*

as the matted fiber allows for seams to become invisible after sewing, enabling the user to "pick out the seams." Therefore, antron fleece is extremely useful for puppets and masks.

Dyeing and Painting Fleece

Because of the molecular formula of nylon, *nylafleece* (made of nylon) is therefore easily dyeable with union dyes such as Rit or acid dyes. Prewet the fabric uniformly and use vinegar in a hot bath (making the fibers more pliable and open). The vinegar allows for the acid dye to absorb into the fabric by changing the pH of the water.

This material may be airbrushed, painted with a brush, spray painted with floral sprays, or brushed/dusted with pastels to add subtle color effects. It is a stretch fabric.

Sewing Fleece

Stitching antron fleece may be done with machine zigzag, stretch, or straight stitches (straight stitches will break when stretched, so be aware of the direction of stretch). Hand stitches include the famous "Henson stitch" and the baseball stitch, both of which are great for hiding seams. The advantage again is that after it is sewn, the seams may be picked or brushed out to create the illusion of unstitched skin (Figure 9-8).

SPANDEX AND OTHER STRETCH FABRICS

Spandex comes in a variety of thicknesses, stretch directions, and a surprising variety of design motifs (Figure 9-9). There are many stores dedicated to the sale of this special fabric with hundreds of options. It can be used as a "skin" covering for masks or for covering individual features and may also be used as a foundation for adding texture and paint. It generally comes in 60 inch widths and can have a two- or four-way stretch.

FIGURE 9-9 *A small example of the variety of stretch fabrics offered at spandex house*

Other stretch fabrics, such as velour, pleather, and sequined fabrics, may also be used as coverings.

Sewing Spandex

Like antron fleece, spandex is a stretch fabric, so a machine zigzag and stretch stitches are preferred (straight stitches will break if stretched, so be aware of the direction of stretch).

When sewn, however, the seams will show, so it is important to try and position any distracting seams toward the back away from the face, under headpieces and wigs, or under attached facial features.

Dyeing and Painting Spandex

One hundred percent spandex will dye well with acid dyes and unions dyes with the addition of vinegar. Be mindful that there are spandex-like fabrics that are polyester and will not take dye well. Check the fiber content before purchasing. If the fiber content is 50% or less of spandex or nylon, the fabric will only take half of the desired color. Dye testing is always recommended!

Spandex may be airbrushed, spray painted with floral sprays, or even painted with a brush (in a painterly style).

Using Spandex and Other Stretch Materials as Foundation Fabrics for Texture

Spandex as well as other smooth stretch fabrics can be used as a foundation for surfaces that will be coated and layered with texture and paint. The reason to use stretch fabrics is so that there will be no wrinkles (see the section "Mask Project 3: Orange Dog," in Chapter 14). Acrylic coatings such as Rosco clear gel coat and Liquitex acrylic mediums are wonderful when layered and stippled with a porous sponge.

NETTING

Depending on the mask, stretch netting such as *power net* and even those nets that don't stretch, such as tuille or cheese cloth, may be useful for skins and vision ports. A mask built with rattan or varaform could benefit from a skin of draped and stiffened netting – it maintains the porosity and airflow of the foundation mask while also providing a recognizable skin that reacts to the materials underneath.

Simple masks made with stretch netting made like a contoured sock can also give a blurred, dreamy effect (Figure 9-10).

FIGURE 9-10 *Images of net masks from West Virginia University production of* Mud. *Faces appear blurred and indistinct by the netting. Designed by the author*

HEAT-MANIPULATED FABRICS

Another effective finish may be achieved with a heat gun and different plastic-based fabrics. Depending on the thickness of the fabric, when heated, it will crinkle and retract or burn, creating a wonderfully organic texture. Don't leave the heat gun on the fabric for too long or it will burn. Try crystal organza. (This fabric printed with an intrinsic pattern is amazing when heat hits it. Then try hitting it with a dry brush paint accent. Wow!) Even craft felt can work well. So many fabrics are made with plastics (unfortunately) that there are endless varieties of textures just waiting to be discovered (Figure 9-11).

Safety Note: Any burning or heating of plastics with a heat gun should be done outside or in a well-ventilated area as melted plastics produce toxic fumes.

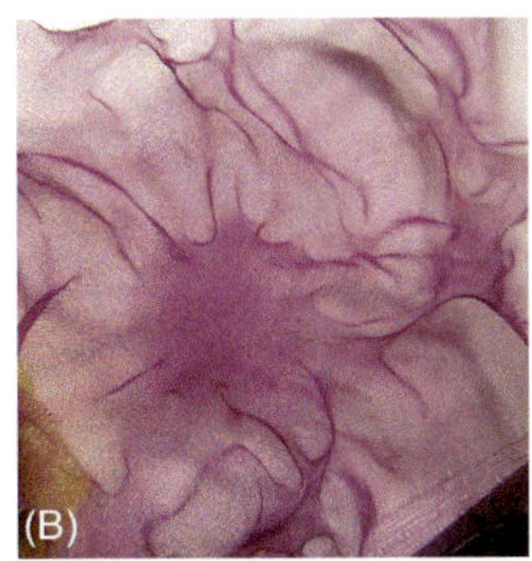

FIGURE 9-11 *An example of heat-manipulated fabrics: A) crystal organza melted with a heat gun then dry-brushed with glitter paint. B) organza unpainted. Note: the fumes when melting this plastic fabric are particularly powerful. Wear a respirator, use a ventilation booth, or do this process outside*

CHAPTER 10

PAINTING

In terms of adding color and painting a mask (refer to Chapter 9 on painting coverings/fabrics), there are some considerations to be made before plowing ahead. Some basic questions are as follows:

1. At what point in the construction process are colorants and/or paints added?
2. What kind of paint should be used?
3. What is the best tool to get the desired effect?

WHEN TO ADD COLOR?

If the mask project is very involved, then a plan is often helpful. Take the time to make a punch list with categories to help prioritize what needs to be done first before moving on the next step. This will help with ordering supplies and multitasking the construction of parts as the mask is being built. Some materials such as latex and silicone may have colorants intrinsically added to provide an overall hue, whereas others may wait until the final steps to be painted.

Considerations for use of certain materials such as feathers, gemstones, and sequins will be affected by whether spray paint and varnishes will be used. Ostrich feathers will weigh down and lose their fluff, and gemstones and sequins might be dulled.

TIP BOX

Dyeing Feathers

Just as with silk and wool, feathers are a protein-based natural item. Acid dyes are used for protein-based textiles and can also be used for dyeing feathers.

1. Heat the water until it is hot. It is too hot if it is steaming (212°F).
2. Add approximately one teaspoon of dye to a gallon pot of water.

DOI: 10.4324/9781003343264-10

3. Add half a cup of vinegar to the pot and mix until all the dye lumps are gone. (Tip: Mix with a small strainer. The metal mesh will easily help diffuse and break up dye clumps.)
4. Hold onto the quill end of the feather and dip it into the dye. Hold it in the dye until the desired color is reached. If the color is not what you want, then repeat the process and add more dye.
5. Rinse the feather with warm water and hang it upside down to dry.
6. Using a cool and low air setting on a blow dryer, apply until the feather is fluffy and dry.

WHAT KIND OF PAINT TO USE?

The type of paint or colorant may depend on the foundation medium of the mask as well as the desired effect.

Kinds of Paints

Acrylic/latex are interchangeable terms. There is no latex in "latex paint"; unless otherwise specified, they are all acrylic based. This paint dries fast and is compatible with many acrylic mediums. It can be used on many surfaces and textures – wood, plastic, or paper – and it dries fast. There are many grades available from the very inexpensive low-end *Apple Barrel* to midgrade *Liquitex* and the higher-end *Winsor Newton*. Find the brand and quality of paint that is right for you and fits the budget of the project. I use whatever is at hand, even house paints, and am always open to trying new products.

Oil paint is composed of dry pigments and oil (generally linseed oil). It is a very slow drying paint unless a solvent such as turpentine is added.

Rub N' Buff is sold in a tube. This wax and oil-based product is combined with metallic powders to create a material that can be used to add metallic sheens to masks. It is especially good for the finishing touches.

Fingernail polish comes in a variety of colors and can often be inexpensive. It is good for small detail painting such as eyes and jewelry. It can be applied with fine brushes.

Spray paint comes in dozens of brands, and some are specifically made to bond with plastics. Graffiti artists have been using this paint to create intricate highlights and shadows and subtle blends of colors. It is an indispensable paint for mask artists. Use it for priming, for foundations colors, or for painting the entire mask. There is also a new collection of translucent colors for clear plastics. Krylon is the brand that I lean toward, as it is fast drying and the nozzles (for the most part) do not clog. Note: Save the nozzles when throwing away empty cans; they may come in handy if a nozzle breaks on another can of the same brand.

Floral sprays are a type of spray paint intended to be used for adding tints and shades on faux silk flowers. This paint is perfect for adding translucent tones to fabrics and plastics – there are a huge range of subtle colors too. One manufacturer for this line of sprays is Design Master, which also has a line of translucent spray paints for clear plastics – perfect for clear Worbla and plastic hemispheres used as eyes.

Colored inks are great for tinting fur, resins, and clear Worbla. Apply with an airbrush, paintbrush, or toothbrush. Note: Wear a respirator when doing this!

Puff paint is commonly associated with clothing: decorating t-shirts, tennis shoes, and canvas handbags. But it may also be used to create custom texture on mask surfaces and fabrics.

French enamel varnish (FEV) is created using lacquer, pigment (such as metal powders, oil paints or wood stains), and denatured alcohol. It can be used as a glaze on metal or painted plastic to add a patina of age or translucent color.

Foil effects are not technically paint, but the adhesive for this process is painted onto the surface and dried, and then the foil is rubbed on like a temporary tattoo. It will work on any surface – not just clothing.

TIP BOX

What Is a "Glaze"?

A glaze is a mixture of paint and clear medium that appears translucent when applied. Water may be used as the clear medium for acrylic paints, but there are many other materials available, including acrylic and oil mediums in matte and gloss finishes. A series of glazes can add subtle layers of color and depth to the look of a mask.

COATINGS AND SEALANTS

After painting is complete, consider sealing with a clear coating to protect and to add a gloss or matte finish (see Figure 10-1). Some of these may be used as a *primer* before painting. A primer is a material that is applied to an object before painting (1) to help visually detect any flaws on the surface; (2) to create a foundation color to build on; and (3) to prevent the paint from absorbing into the surface.

Clear spray varnishes – Krylon makes fast-drying, quality products. The new *Crystal-Clear Glaze* is like painting two coats at one time. Be careful when using it around feathers and resin gemstones, as the coating will weigh down the feathers and may eat into resin stones, dulling them.

Clear PVA varnishes and coatings – Rosco, Mod Podge, Liquitex, Minwax, etc., have developed a series of water-based varnishes that vary from gloss to matte. A lot of these are great for building up textured layers and using as a sealant or finish – these may also be used for glazes. Sculpt or Coat is a thicker material that is also for stiffening, sealing, and building up layers for texturizing surfaces.

Rubberized coatings – Flex Seal and Plasti Dip are rubberized coatings in spray and paste forms, which means they mix the solvents with the synthetic rubber. It comes in black, white, and clear. It may be used as a coating for latex, paper, fabric mâché, and thermoplastics. It also comes in thick consistencies that can be used in molds. Test materials before applying these coatings and also before troweling them into your mold, because they may react badly to the foundation and mold material or your chosen release agent.

FIGURE 10-1 *A variety of coatings and sealants*

Safety Note: Some of these materials have fumes that are strong and harmful. Use with a respirator and/or outside.

PAINTING LATEX

When using latex for masks, it may be tinted (intrinsically colored) before pouring. In fact, if it is pink, then it has already been tinted; natural latex is a light tan color. Remember also that acrylic paints will dry darker, so pigments might seem a little milky when added to uncured latex.

By itself, acrylic paint often flakes or peels off latex. One reason for this is that there is no way for the paint to merge or bite into the cured surface; and the second is that latex rubber is flexible, and though acrylic paint has some flexibility, it does not flex enough. There are three techniques for painting latex that I use, though there may be more out there!

1. *Pax paint.* Invented by Dick Smith, pax paint is a combination of Pros-Aide adhesive and acrylic paint. Pros-Aide is an acrylic-based adhesive used in the medical and special effects industry. Because it stays sticky and flexible after it dries, it is perfect for latex appliances and human skin. If mixed with acrylic paint, it can make a very sticky paint (a *contact cement* paint) that will adhere well to flexible latex surfaces. When the paint dries, it remains sticky until powdered. That said, it will stay gummy under the powder and

TIP BOX

Painting with Pax Paint

a. Before painting a latex mask, use a sponge to stipple a layer of Pro's-Aide onto the surface and let it dry. The surface will be more receptive to pax paint with an additional sticky foundation.

b. Add approximately 15% Pro's-Aide to the paint. If the paint is not sticky when dried, then add more Pro's-Aide.

c. It is also better to apply thin layers of paint than thick paste-like layers.

d. After paint is dry, powder with baby powder or corn starch, then lightly brush away excess. If there is a dusty look to the surface, dampen a tissue and dab (don't rub) the surface to collect the remaining powder. A spritz of water might also help.

TIP BOX

Painting with Lacryl

1. Use one part latex to one part paint. If it needs to be diluted or brushes need cleaning, use distilled water.
2. Paint the surface of the latex mask and let it dry.
3. Paint successive layers as normal.

therefore might need to be touched up periodically. This is because it does not bond intrinsically with the latex surface – friction will wear it off. Additional sealing methods include a light coating of crystal clear or a light airbrushed coat of Mod Podge or Rosco's crystal gel coat. Also try clear Flex Seal. These will help, but again, with friction the paint will most likely wear off.

2. *Lacryl.* I learned this technique from the good people at OrganicArmor.com. Their work is fabulous! Anyone who has worked with latex knows that latex loves to stick to itself. That said, to help acrylic paint stick to latex, mix latex into the paint. If the paint needs to be diluted, use only *distilled water*. The latex acts as a bridge between the colorant and the mask – magic happens, and the paint sticks wonderfully (the same technique may be used when painting neoprene, but use neoprene as a paint additive). After the foundation layer of lacryl paint has dried, paint as you would normally, but again keep the layers thin instead of thick. Seal with a *light* coating of Crystal Clear, clear Flex Seal, or flexible Mod Podge.
3. *RCP* (rubber cement, oil paint and naptha) – this recipe has been modified and adapted by many amazing artisans in the special effects industry. The idea is that the chemical naptha will bite into the latex by lightly dissolving the surface and, with the addition of rubber cement, the paint will stick. Check the Monster Makers website (www.monstermakes.com) for helpful tips and supplies.

Safety Note: This is an *extremely toxic paint*, especially when used with an airbrush. If you use this paint, do it outside or use a paint booth. Wear a respirator, goggles, and gloves.

TIP BOX

Painting with RCP

1. Prep the surface of a latex mask by wiping it down with a cloth and lacquer thinner.
2. In a glass container, mix rubber cement and naptha until the cement is diluted to the consistency of paint (if airbrushing, it should be diluted additionally). You can prepare this medium in a larger batch to add to multiple oil paint colors.
3. Add this mixture to oil paint, then redilute to the method of painting; that is, if it is brushed, then make it thicker, and if it is airbrushed, make it thinner. The paint method should be in thin layers.
4. A hair dryer may be used to speed up drying time.

Note: Wear appropriate protective gear, and use RCP in a ventilated space.

PAINTING SILICONE

Silicone rubber is a unique material because of its flexibility, translucency, and the fact that it only sticks to itself. For that reason, it may be tinted intrinsically (meaning add pigments to one part of the silicone body) and/or painted only with silicone pigments. This includes floating flocking fibers and powdered materials such as glitter, powdered makeup, mesh fabrics, and so on. As with latex, to paint silicone topically, additional silicone is needed as a part of the painting

TIP BOX

How to Paint Silicone

1. To remove any oils or release agent, wipe off the surface with acetone or 99% alcohol.
2. Measure out small amount of clear silicone (part A and B) and mix both parts thoroughly.
3. Add naptha or a solvent of choice to the silicone to thin and extend working time.
4. Add silicone pigments in the color of choice.
5. Airbrush or paint in thin layers. Note: This is a toxic paint. Wear a respirator, goggles, and gloves and work in a well-ventilated area.
6. Accelerate drying time with a hair dryer.
7. Repeat layers of paint as needed.

medium, as well as silicone pigment and a solvent that will turn the paint into a *glaze* (this paint is toxic, so again, wear the appropriate protective gear and use the paint in a well-ventilated area). As one of the main reasons to use this material is its translucency, it is important not to paint silicone opaquely. *Brick in the Yard Mold Supply*, https://www.brickintheyard.com/ (free videos) and *Stan Winston School*, https://www.stanwinstonschool.com/?utm_source=Adwords&utm_medium=Search&gclid=Cj0KCQiAjbagBhD3ARIsANRrqEuUa581dQDThtBSroJaXBL8SQ4R9LQH6e9eN8DqWU7dnVpv4dXY9wlaAk39EALw_wcB, both have great YouTube tutorials on how to paint silicone.

PAINTING OTHER SURFACES

Materials such as papier and fabric mâché, plastic, and fiberglass may be painted with spray and/or acrylic paint. It is possible to lay on a foundation coat of spray paint and then add acrylic paint details. Add a gloss urethane or acrylic varnish to seal.

WHAT IS THE BEST PAINTING TOOL TO USE?

Brush bristle/hairs. Beware the bristle! A bad brush is one that loses its hair, that has an overly soft bristle, or that will not make a point when moistened. A bristle that is so soft with no "spring back" will make you fight to load the brush and get paint on the surface. I have seen students try to paint with the ferule as the bristles drag behind the brush. White or light-brown taklon is a good bristle material, as is the more expensive sable (made from squirrel hair). If you can, try to feel the bristles before you buy.

There are also very cheap brushes with plastic handles that come with plastic model kits. Those drove me crazy as a child. The bristles were blunt and chunky. Makes me wonder why I ever pursued art!

Rounds are those brushes with a round ferule (a ferule is the metal part of the brush) (see Figure 10-2). The bristles should be able to make a point with moisture, and the better-quality brushes should not lose as much hair. *Flats* are those brushes with a flat ferule. There is also the *cat's tongue* or *filbert* brush in this style but in multiple sizes. Brushes made with stiff hog's hair are generally used for thicker paints such as oil or acrylic painting to be used on big canvases, but you can pretty much use any brush with any medium as long as it is not too thick and doesn't dissolve the bristles. *Chip brushes* are all purpose, cheap, and known for being disposable. These are commonly used with mold making for plaster, resin, and silicone molds. Chip brushes may lose a hair or two, but they are also good for painting as well.

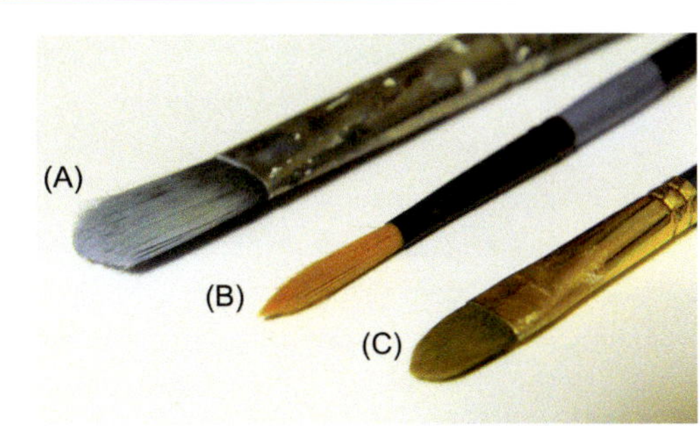

FIGURE 10-2 *Types of brushes: A) a flat; B) a round; and C) a cat's tongue or filbert*

Sponges. Natural sponges are perfect for adding organic painting effects to surfaces such as faux skin and pock-marked fabrics. Other sponges and drain-dry foam may be torn to get an irregular painting edge.

Airbrush. It's amazing what the right combination of paint particulate and air can do. A *single-action* airbrush is one that only allows control of the amount of paint. A *dual-action* airbrush allows the user to control the airflow and the amount of paint (see Figure 10-3). There are many brands. I have used the same Pasche dual-action airbrush for over 20 years. The kit includes three sizes of needles, replacement nose cones, as well as other handy items. The key to good airbrush ownership is proper cleaning of the parts. During painting and after, occasionally spray a little 99% alcohol (do this in a ventilated area). I also use the mall wire found inside in a baggy tie to run through the tiny air holes in the nose area. A small wire brush and a piece of steel wool are also helpful for cleaning off excess paint. If the airbrush gets clogged, take it apart and soak the

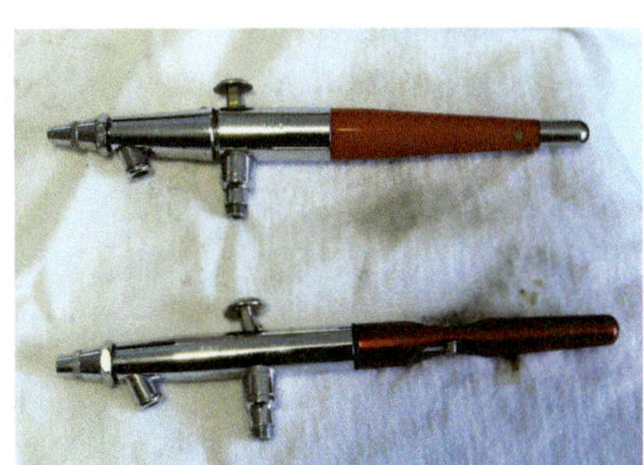

FIGURE 10-3 *A double-action and a single-action airbrush*

metal parts overnight in a glass jar (with a lid) filled with naptha, then reassemble and spray 99% alcohol through it and clean it with the baggy tie. Do not let the naptha evaporate and the "goo" dry inside the airbrush, or you will need to start over.

Preval sprayer. This is a disposable can of compressed air that comes attached to a glass bottle, which you then fill with whatever you want to spray. It can be used with dye and paint, but as with an airbrush the particulate must be the right size to go through the nozzle.

Rigid tools. It is possible to paint tiny veins and achieve a sgraffito technique (that of scratching away a paint color to reveal another below) with straight pins or an awl. It is time consuming, but the effects when painting small striations in eyes is wonderful.

PAINTING TECHNIQUES

Spattering. This refers to a random array of tiny droplets of pant achieved with a bristle brush, such as a toothbrush, airbrush, or hog's hair paintbrush. The airbrush will nullify the organic quality you can get with a paintbrush unless the paint is too thick to go through the nozzle evenly.

Stippling. This technique is achieved by using a small brush or a brush with separated bristles, dabbing the brush in paint, then lightly dotting the desired surface with the loaded brush (see Figure 10-4).

Dry brush. To use paint that has little water to light high-dimensional areas by dragging the brush or sponge over the top. This technique is especially useful for wrinkles, pustules, and cracked surfaces.

Wet blending. Just as its name implies, with this technique the paint is almost mixed on the surface of the object. It is great for shading and adding color accents. This is a good technique when working with acrylic paint, as it tends to dry swiftly.

Stencils and stamp painting. Stencils and stamps may be helpful to use on masks if there are repeated graphics, tattoos, or textures.

Capillary Technique

This is one of my favorite techniques for renderings, masks, makeup, and eyes, and for paint treatments on walls and furniture (see Figure 10-5). This technique adds an organic "cellular quality" surface treatment.

FIGURE 10-4 *Examples of different painting techniques: A) stippling; B) dry brush; and C) an example of custom creation of a large stamp with pieces of bubble wrap cut and glued to a rectangle of plexiglass*

FIGURE 10-5 *Capillary technique: close-up of an eye that has been glazed and wrapped with soft plastic until dry. When the plastic is removed, the impressions of the folds and creases are left behind*

Follow these steps for the capillary technique:

1. Paint the surface with a foundation color and let it dry.
2. Mix a glaze of the color of choice, then paint it over the foundation color. It does not need to cover the surface completely.
3. While the glaze is still wet, lay a piece of soft plastic (such as plastic wrap, dry cleaner bags, or grocery store veggie bags) on the surface and crumple it so that the paint concentrates in the folds of the plastic.
4. Let it dry for a few hours or overnight.
5. Remove plastic and *witness the coolness*!
6. Additional softening of the cellular quality may be achieved with additional glaze colors or spattering.

CHAPTER 11

HORNS, ANTENNAE, AND EARS

"Art is all in the Details."

– *Christian Marclay*

Never was a truer word spoken. Protruding exterior shapes and details are those that help bring together the whole look of a mask; it is the final definition of positive and negative space of a design. The success of communicating the *attitude or emotion* of a design is also often dependent on the final choices for features such as a set of ears (Figure 11-1). The shape, direction, choice of covering/finish, and placement can all be crucial.

Faux horns, antlers, eye stalks, and other protuberances can have different connotations depending on the intent of the design. Those designs with pointy or sharp horns that are coated with a dark, shiny finish may seem completely different if they are covered with stretch velvet or made of ruched, fluffy materials such as stacked tissue flowers or tinsel (Figure 11-2). What conveys the emotional attitude of the mask can be emphasized by these particular choices.

DOI: 10.4324/9781003343264-11

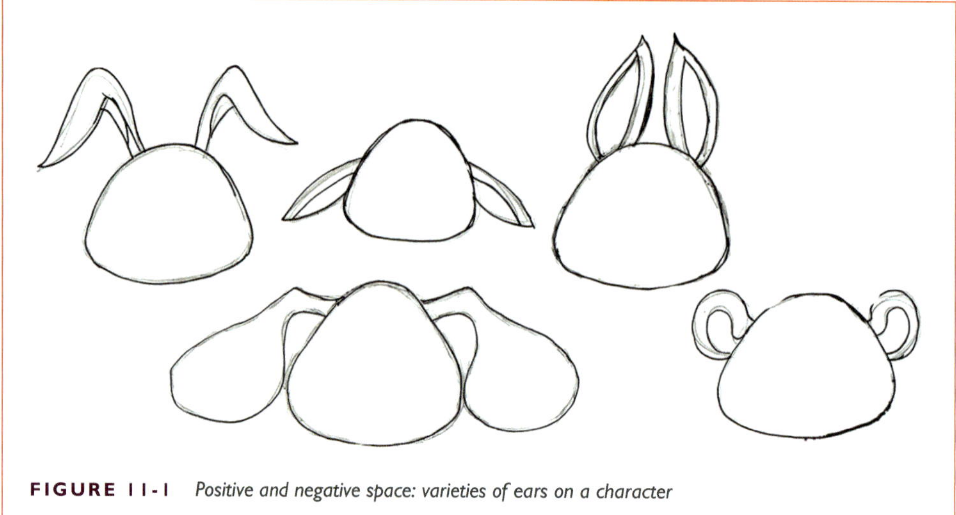

FIGURE 11-1 *Positive and negative space: varieties of ears on a character*

FIGURE 11-2 *Examples of different texture on the same object*

TIP BOX

The Steps for Creating an Exterior Feature

1. Consult the design – what is the scale?
2. Make a mockup to determine the scale needed.
3. Create a version (in partial or full scale) of the desired form by:
   a. Sculpting and creating a mold.
   b. Sculpting and draping a pattern for foam.
   c. Creating a flat pattern for foam.
4. Create the full-scale shape by:
   a. Casting the foundation piece with preferred material.
   b. Cutting, sewing, or gluing together the parts to make the foundation.
5. Add structures needed for attachment to the mask, such as struts and interior armatures.
6. Finish the external feature with a soft (fabrics) or hard (paints and varnishes) surface.
7. Attach the feature to the mask by bolting, gluing, stitching, using zip ties, etc.
8. Add painted and additional details as needed to meld it to the rest of the mask.

SCULPTING

When sculpting, it is possible to use different clays (water, oil, or wax based), paper and masking tape, EPS or XPS foam, aluminum foil and hot glue, etc. (Figure 11-3). Even if they will eventually be covered with a soft material, if the interiors are rigid, they will need to be sculpted and sometimes cast.

SCULPT ONE OR TWO?

If a pair of horns or ears are a generic shape, that is, it does not favor toward the right or left, then only create one pattern or sculpt. But if there is specificity to the right or left, then two sculpts or patterns will need to be completed (Figure 11-3).

As a rule, rigid molds are used for soft casting materials, and soft molds (with or without mother molds) are used for rigid casting materials. The reason is that a cured, rigid material with undercuts will get locked in a rigid mold. The exceptions to this rule include (1) neoprene, which is pulled out of the rigid mold before it completely cures, but would otherwise lock in and break the mold when being removed;

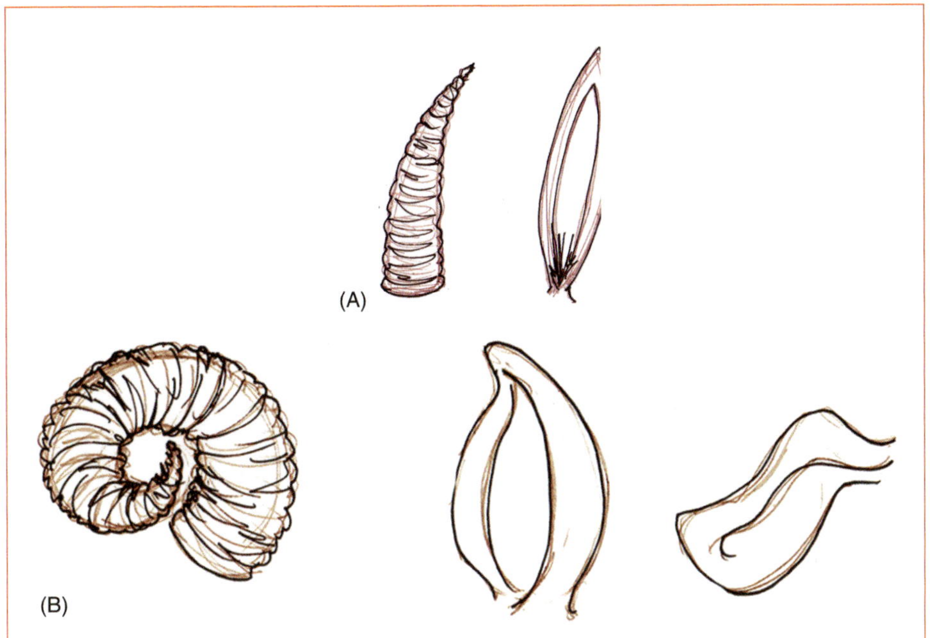

FIGURE 11-3 *A) Examples of ears and horns that may be duplicated for two sides; B) Examples of ears and horns that may be used for only one side*

and (2) rigid materials such as papier mâché, fiberglass resin, or rigid foam, which can be used in a rigid mold *only if there are no undercuts.*

HOW TO SCULPT AND CAST A WATER-BASED CLAY HORN

This horn sculpt (Figure 11-4) is not specific for right or left and can work for both sides, so only one was sculpted.

1. Figure 11.4A–C: Sculpt on a foam foundation out of any clay. Water-based clay was used.
2. Figure 11.4D–G: This sculpt was cast with two different mold materials: (1) a single hydrocal plaster mold; and (2) a matrix mold made with a silicone glove mold and a hydrocal plaster mother mold (see Figure 11.5). This provided the option to experiment with different casting materials.
3. Figure 11.4H–J: The hydrocal plaster mold was used for this set of horns. Each side is cast separately with three layers of plaster. Then the horn was popped out of the mold halves.

   One horn was cast using papier mâché with a fabric interior, and for the other only paper was used. Before adding papier mâché to the molds, thoroughly coat them with Vaseline. *Be warned*: without this release agent, both casting materials would permanently adhere to the molds.
4. Figure 11.4K–N: When the cast is dry, carefully lift/pry it out of the mold halves using a butter knife, a popsicle stick, or a flat head screwdriver. Trim edges with a Dremel, scissors, or sharp-bladed tool. Glue the halves together. Hot glue may be used (without cardboard tabs on the inside) to temporarily hold the halves together, while celluclay or epoxy putty is used to patch and hold the outside together (Figure 11-6).
5. Figure 11.4O: Let the halves dry, then sand and prime them with a base coat before painting them with the final color.

TIP BOX

Attachment Strategies for Different Shapes

Figure 7-11 presents diagrams of attachment strategies for the following structures.

a. Hollow horn structure.
b. Pointy ear frame structure. Depending on the size of the ear, aluminum or steel might be substituted for nylon rod.
c. Solid round ear structure.
d. Antennae.

FIGURE 11-4 *A–O) Casting horns with two kinds of molds*

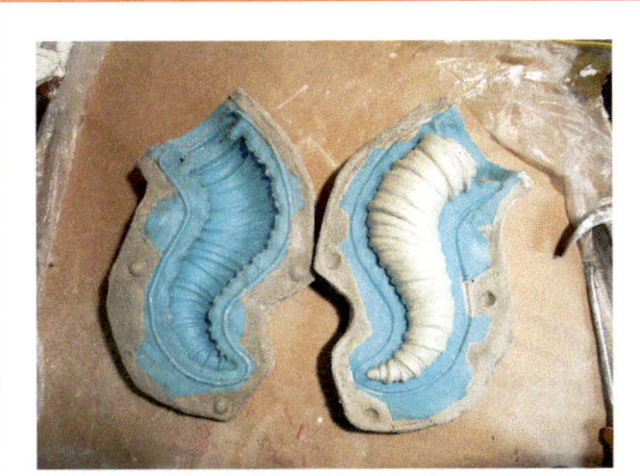

FIGURE 11-5 *Image of the finished matrix mold of the previous horn sculpture*

FIGURE 11-6 *A) A whole untrimmed neoprene; B) half using celluclay; C) finished papier mâché; and D) half of a liquid plastic (epoxy)*

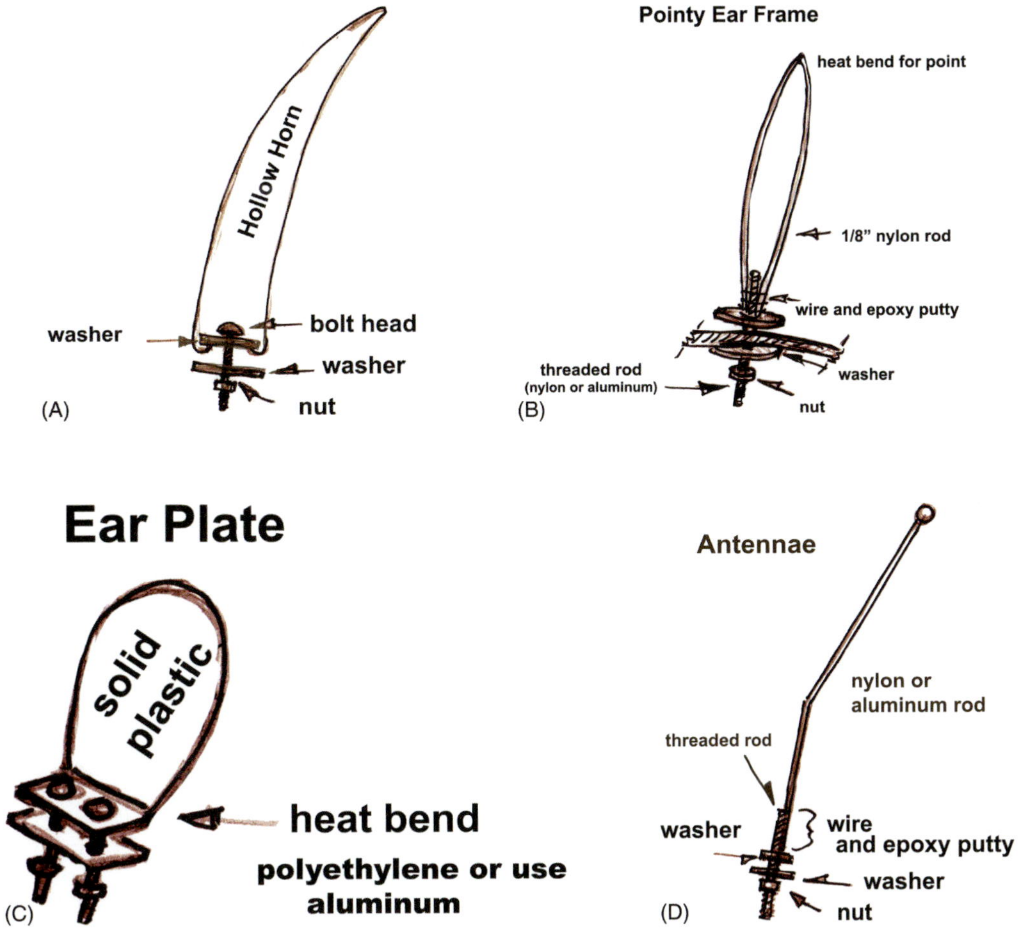

FIGURE 11-7 *A–D) Diagrams of attachment strategies for different structures*

CHAPTER 12

EYES

DESIGN: WITH EYES OR WITHOUT?

Just like a puppet, to some degree, there is an expectation that a mask will have eyes. However, it does depend on the intent of the design. Some of the most horrifying masks and makeup are those without eyes or even indentations where eyes should be. A part of the horror is that humans and many other animals read body language and take visual cues from eyes and the muscles/expressions surrounding eyes. Eyes are also sensitive receptors easily damaged, and over time we learn to regard them with respect. A poster designer once told me that some of the best marquees are those with faces and eyes, whether they be masks or human; people seem to want to connect with faces, and a big part of that are the eyes. As designers, it is important to stay open and explore possibilities; if the design needs to make a connection, then include eyes or sockets of some sort; if the design lends itself to disconnection and perhaps chaos, then consider the option of no eyes. Conversely, try turning the tables and see what happens (Figure 12-1).

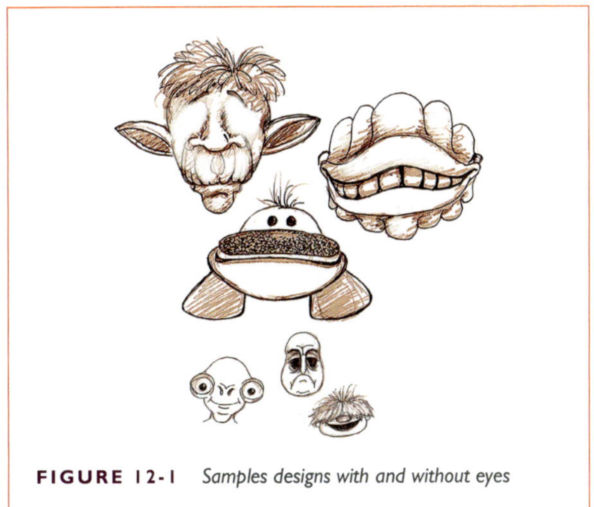

FIGURE 12-1 *Samples designs with and without eyes*

SHAPES AND ORIENTATION

There are as many options for eye shape and orientation as there are grains of sand. One of the best ways to determine this is to draw sample shapes digitally or by hand (see Figure 12-2).

DOI: 10.4324/9781003343264-12

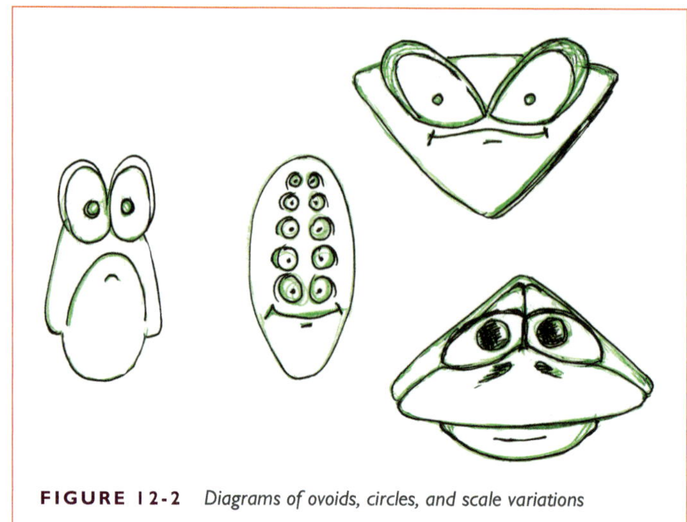

FIGURE 12-2 *Diagrams of ovoids, circles, and scale variations*

Sometimes a quarter-inch decrease in size or move in proximity to the other eye or placement on the mask can make a huge difference. Make sure to take the time to play with options.

CONSTRUCTION OPTIONS

1. *Realistic eyes.* These may be custom made with resin or can be purchased from taxidermy companies. Glass eyes are often sold for taxidermist projects but may be used on masks as well. The only issue might be variation in size.
2. *Premade and vacuform hemispheres.* One option for eyes is clear hemispheres sold in different sizes of ovals and circles. These might be found in bulk on arts and crafts websites and can often be found in local hobby store chains. Easter and Christmas are good holidays to stock up on different sizes. Another option is using a vacuform machine to make your own plastic shapes. The last option is to sculpt your own shapes, then rotocast them with opaque resin in a silicone mold.
3. *Nonconventional.* The normal human eye has a sclera, an iris, and a pupil, therefore nonconventional is anything that challenges the normal shape and configuration. This might be achieved by stacking the iris and pupil and using different shapes, sizes, and colors (Figure 12-3).

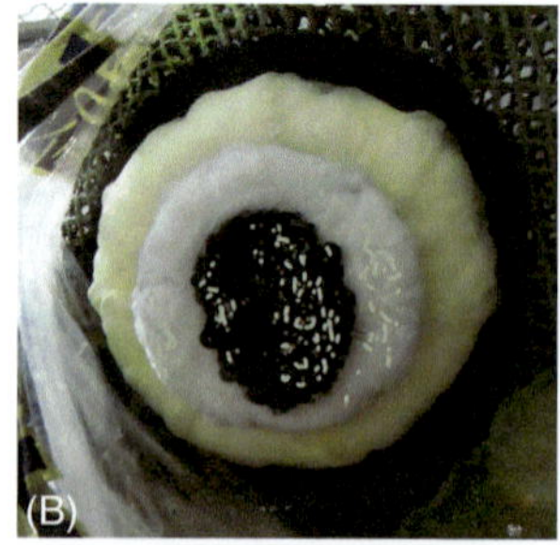

FIGURE 12-3 *Examples of different interpretations of eyes. A) Silver beads in an open eye socket to catch the light; B) the eye for "Earth" from* The Elementals *project (see Chapter 14). stacked layers of foam covered with organza to give the eye dimension. Pupils are clusters of black sequins; C) large dragon eye. sequin fabric covers the sclera; D) the moon from* The Elementals *project (see Chapter 14-128A to 14–134E). Thick white felt sclera with a black sequin pupil mirrors the same shape; E) stacked layers of foam with bead eyes. This is a puppet, but it could also be effective on a mask; F) vacuform sclera with another layer cut for the iris and pupil. Hand painted with acrylic; G) same style of eye with three stacked individually cut pieces (sclera, iris, and pupil). The iris and pupil are painted with fingernail polish; H) dark sclera with rhinestone pupils; I) single layer of foam with a button; J) wooden ball painted with acrylics, then coated with two-part epoxy; K) similar style to C) without sequins on the sclera. The sclera was painted with blacklight paint (Continued)*

FIGURE 12-3 *(Continued)*

TOPICAL AND INTERIOR PAINTING

Topical painting deals with the outside surface of the eye shape. It can be done on any shape.

Interior painting involves painting backward, starting with the most forward colors and details and then layering backward to the final base coat (see Chapter 14, "Mask Project 2: The Alien").

RESIN EYES

The art of resin eye making has exploded in popularity because of special effects and cosplay. With the help of wonderfully detailed photographed eyes of birds, reptiles, and other animals, there are many realistic and fantasy interpretations readily available.

TIP BOX

The Pros and Cons of Resin Eyes

There are a couple of reasons for using resin eyes:

1. Realism. They can look incredibly real. The layers of paint and resin adds depth – some eyes even seem to travel and watch the observer.
2. Options. A variety of custom options can be created, which could include tinting the resin different colors and adding floating elements, such as glitter, and small fiber veins.

The negative aspects of resin eyes include the following:

1. Weight. Some finished eyes can be heavy.
2. Cost. Because resin is a petroleum product, prices can be in the high $20s and $30s for a small can of material. Remember it is a two-part process, so don't forget to buy both.
3. Toxicity. Look for those resins that note that they are "low VOC." But even those will have some fumes. Always work in a well-ventilated area with a respirator and wear gloves.
4. Time. Many resins take 24 hours to set up, so painted layers take a long time to achieve.
5. Mistakes. Potential for mistakes, such as air bubbles, can ruin eyes that have taken a long time to create.

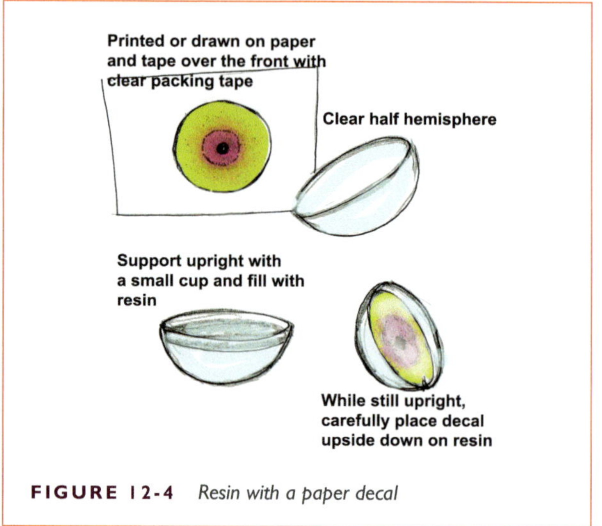

FIGURE 12-4 *Resin with a paper decal*

Techniques for Constructing Resin Eyes: Three Techniques

1. **Printed 2-D paper decal with resin filler** (Figure 12-4):
   a. Hand draw or digitally design and print out a clear image of an iris and pupil. Note: Make sure the circumference matches the depth to which you want the image to sink into the shape and connect with the resin.
   b. Cover with clear packing tape and cut out the image.
   c. A silicone mold or a premade plastic dome can be used for the eye shape.

      Note: If you are using a plastic dome, to protect the outside, add painter's tape to the front surface.
   d. Place the dome upside down on a cup, then fill it slowly with resin to the depth matching the size of the printed image.
   e. Lay the image on top of the wet resin and smooth carefully outward from the center.
2. **Half hemisphere within another half hemisphere** (Figure 12-5):
   a. Find domes that fit inside each other – a larger and a slightly smaller one.
   b. Prepaint the interior dome with opaque color of choice and add details such as veins and irregularities to the sides.
   c. Paint the pupil or glue a button (or a black epoxy putty pupil) that matches the contour of the interior dome. Use a circle template to help with accuracy if you are drawing the pupil.

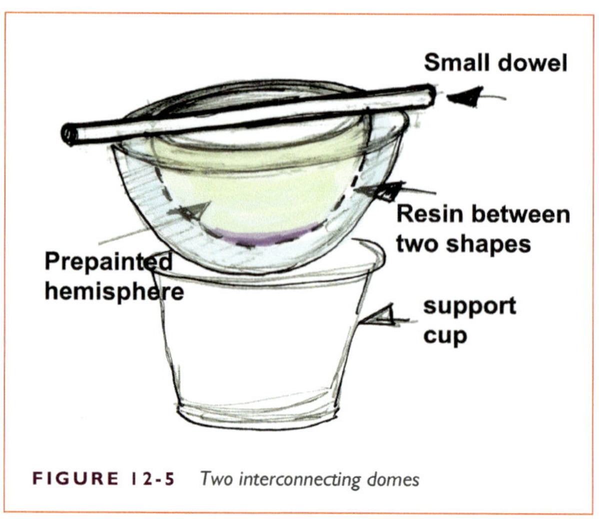

FIGURE 12-5 *Two interconnecting domes*

d. Temporary hot glue a small stick/dowel to the back/rim of the interior eye.
e. Rest the larger clear dome on a cup or, if using a larger silicone mold, place it on a level surface.
f. Fill the mold or the larger clear dome about half full of clear resin, then drop the interior eye down into the resin. Rest on the inside dome a weight just heavy enough to push it down in the outer resin-filled dome. If the resin doesn't reach the top of the outside edges, then top off the dome with more resin.

   Note: The closer the interior dome comes to the outside larger dome, the clearer the eye will look. The look of cataracts or milky eyes may be achieved by distancing the interior dome from the outer dome and enhancing this by adding powdered pigments to the clear resin.
g. Let the resin stand until cured.

3. **Painted layers** (Figure 12-6)
This technique is based on Yvonne William's YouTube demonstration (https://www.youtube.com/watch?v=rs_eJr9z8PI) of painting glass cabochons with an awl and fingernail polish – beautiful work! In the video, she advises using glass (because resin will eventually yellow) and fingernail polish, but try experiments with different resins, paints, and layering (see Figure 12-6).

   Using a plastic eye mold (or you can make your own), either cast yourself some clear custom resin cabochons or buy premade cabochons. You may also use a clear dome to house the resin.

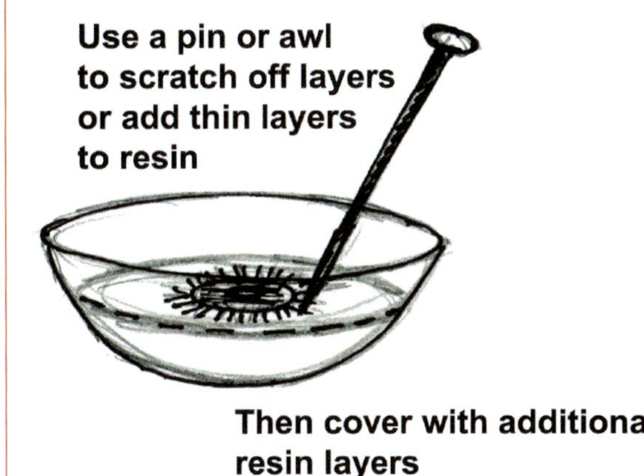

FIGURE 12-6 *Painting layers on a clear cabochon or resin*

a. Use grid paper or create your own grid with a ruler and cover with plexiglass.
b. Pop out clear resin eye shapes, or the clear partially filled plastic domes, and using the grid as a guide, dab some acrylic paint (use the thicker variety such as Liquitex or Winsor Newton) onto the center to represent the pupil with an awl, a needle tool, or a toothpick. With scratching motions, pull the color outward. You might also be able to do some of this with a paint brush.

   Note: Test fingernail polish with the resin you are casting, and if it doesn't dissolve the resin, then use it.
c. Slowly build up layers according to your design.

   Note: If the color scratches off, paint on a small amount of the resin with cardboard tab or Q-Tip.

CHAPTER 13

HAIR

Hair is an essential part of finishing for many styles of masks. Like features such as horns and antenna, hair can emphasize character/attitude, accentuate the silhouette, and draw attention to movement. This chapter explores the many choices available for hair and hair-like materials.

CHOICES FOR HAIR AND HAIR LIKE MATERIALS

Foam

EVA foam. Quarter-inch and one-eighth-inch EVA foam can make styles that are wavy, spiked, patterned, or carved (see Figure 13-1). It can be rolled onto a paper tube or dowel rod and with a little heat and will remain curled. The one-eighth-inch variety comes in a variety of colors (and may be ordered in big sheets), and the quarter-inch foam comes in black or white. It can be primed with spray Plastic Dip or Flex Seal and painted, then sealed again. Attach the foam with contact cement to a fabric foundation or use fabric washers (on the inside and outside, or fasteners will rip through) dyed or painted to match and stitch, wire, or zip tie it through the mask surface.

Urethane foam (drain dry, Scot). This porous foam comes in thin widths and can be dyed any color. Try carving, patterning, and braiding this foam. It can be glued, stitched, or attached with zip ties.

Thermoplastics

Wigs. The plastic fibers in wigs are basically thermoplastic. With the addition of steam, about any shape can be produced. Like human hair, it may be rolled, teased, and braided. Materials such as PVA glues, gelatin, and conventional hair products can help set styles (see Figure 13-2). Additional materials such as wire frames and tuille, other stiffened thermoplastics, rope, faux plants, and shredded fabrics may be used for the hair itself. These may also painted or dyed to match the wig hair or left unpainted to add visual texture.

DOI: 10.4324/9781003343264-13

FIGURE 13-1 *Queen from the West Virginia University Production of* Pericles. *One-eighth-inch and quarter-inch EVA foam was heated and rolled on dowels to form curls. Designed and co-constructed with undergraduate student William Wrightstone*

Worbla and varaform. Both of these plastics can be rolled on a long cone, paper tube, PVC pipe, or dowel rods to make curls. Using corrugated cardboard (the big sheets used to mail foam), laid over different sizes of cardboard and PVC tubing starting from big to small, is a great technique to create fluid rolling locks of hair with thin sheets of thermoplastic.

Plastics

Faux plants and flowers. Depending on the mask theme/style, these can create unique stylized hair, not to mention an entire mask! Attach the plants to a separate foundation with zip ties and then attach them to the mask.

Conventional acrylic and chenille yarn. Such yarn can be used for a shaggy sheep dog, a spaghetti monster, or as hair for giant doll mask. Sew the yarn directly to the mask or attach it to a net or fabric foundation like a conventional wig, then zip tie the yarn to the head.

Tubbing. Depending on the tubbing (the less weight, the better), this can be used in its natural state or primed with the right material, and it may be painted. Polyethylene tubbing comes in a variety of colors. Flexible, corrugated tubbing can be great for tentacle hair!

Note: *Poly horse-hair tubing* is a lightweight mesh material, comes in many colors, and has bounce to it. It can be stitched on glued. Make sure to fuse the ends with heat or stitch – otherwise, it will unravel.

Nylon ties (zip ties). Either short or long, these are made to attach! The short ties make great bristles, especially if cut and split carefully. The longer ties can create a spikey collection of hair. Though it looks great, too many applied together could also be heavy!

Plastic box strapping. Love this stuff! It is the strapping that holds printer paper boxes closed. I have only seen it in white, yellow, and light green. It can be split with scissors and also by tearing, then glued or zip-tied into the mask head.

Plastic rope. Some of this looks like faux hair extensions, but there are many colors and textures.

FIGURE 13-2 *Thermoplastics used for stylized hair. A) Masks from the WVU production of* The Visit. *Wig hair is steamed and fixed with PVA glue. The mask with a top hat has fosshape foundations for each tuft, painted black. The hair is styled over the shape with PVA glue. B–C) Varaform mask from the WVU production of* The Love of the Nightingale. *Strips of varaform are curled around a dowel and paper tube to get different sized curls, then painted with Krylon fusion and design master spray paints*

Water bottles. For a nonconventional mask made of recycled plastics, use water bottles on their ends all over the mask head. Add in some box strapping too.

Natural Fibers

Sisal, raffia, and jute. These fibers are often found in rope and can be shredded and stiffened with PVA glue. Jute soaked in glue, wrapped around a dowel (coat with plastic wrap), and dried makes great ringlets.

Goat and sheep woo. Long goat wool (mohair) can make dyeable, fluffy hair. It may be purchased as a part of a hide (still attached to the skin) or as loose fibers.

Both sheep and goat hair can also be crudely felted with other porous fabrics to create an unusual skin texture. Though hot and perhaps itchy without a backing, it is even possible to *felt* a mask.

Feathers and feather boas. Feathers are perfect for "sympathetic movement," a term pertaining to a movement that echoes the previous movement of an object. Use a complete feather boa (this especially works well with ostrich and turkey feather marabou) and coil it over the top of a costume character or full head mask. Attach with zip ties or stitch. The individual *barbules* on ostrich plumes may be plucked and glued between fur fibers with small dabs of hot glue. This gives a wispy, layered visual effect.

Note: Like chickens and turkeys, ostriches are butchered for meat, skin (to make leather), and feathers. Male peacocks naturally shed their long plumes once a year.

Check out the *Cornel University's Cornel Lab, BirdAcademy* website (https://academy.allaboutbirds.org/?gclid=Cj0KCQiAjbagBhD3ARIsANRrqEsnRoF6Dp9-jtx6-wYJb5tUJ4w6Xgf8Q54FIFJQrfnzQqqiCY-lpD6AaAjy5EALw_wcB) for more information about feathers … and birds!

Fabrics

Fabric strips. Many fabrics can be cut into strips as is or shredded to add a frizzy, more chaotic appearance. T-shirt-grade *stretch knit* may be cut and then stretched to form long, wavy strips. These can be dyed before cutting or dyed in a batch of strips with union dyes or fiber-reactive dyes.

Gathered fabrics. If gathered densely, lightweight fabrics such as tuille and organza can be attached to a foundation strip. This can then be sewn to a rigid, painted skull cap made of a material such as variform and then attached to the mask. The fabrics such as muslin and cheese cloth may also be soaked in PVA glue or other fabric stiffeners, then dried hanging upside down.

Braided fabrics. Fabrics and rope may be twisted and braided in small three-strand braids to wide braids resembling basket weaves. Not only would this make an interesting technique for a mask, but the potential for the visual of woven hair on a mask is very exciting. Test the weight of the materials before jumping in – some fabrics may end up being heavy.

Metals

Wire. Old springs and wire coiled on dowels make a unique wiggly hair display. It could be attached to a skull cap made from an old colander or a piece of wire screen.

Note: If you are using long strands of stiffer, straight wire (or plastic tubing), consider making a small crushed loop at the end of each wire or adding tips with small beads attached with epoxy. Wire can get out of control and easily jab into unprotected eyes.

Chicken wire. I have made several wigs with chicken wire and fine it exciting to use this and other wire fencing for masks. It can be sculpted into many tall and wide shapes, is not extremely heavy (especially if you add small weights for balancing the mask), and different materials may be woven through and tied into it. It may also be used for draping thin fabrics such as dry cheese cloth or cheese cloth soaked in PVA glue.

Paper

Gathered and shredded paper. Tissue and brown craft paper both can be used not only for making a complete mask but also for hair. Both may be shredded or folded, tied at the center, and finessed into big or small paper pompoms that can then be zip-tied to a skull cap or directly to the mask. Check out YouTube videos on "making paper flowers."

Cardboard. Cardboard tubes, boxes, and corrugated shipping materials may be stacked, patterned, and finessed into large shapes. Even small boxes can be stylized, stacked hair.

CHAPTER 14

MASK PROJECTS

MASK PROJECT 1: THE OX

Papier mâché

The design was an emotional response to a large, forceful animal. The fanciful long mane could enhance big gestural movements or act as sympathetic movement for a dance piece (Figure 14-1). Figure 14-2 shows the final design.

1. First decide how the mask should be approached in sections or in one piece. The Ox was divided into 1) the foundation mask and 2) the horns (Figure 14-3).

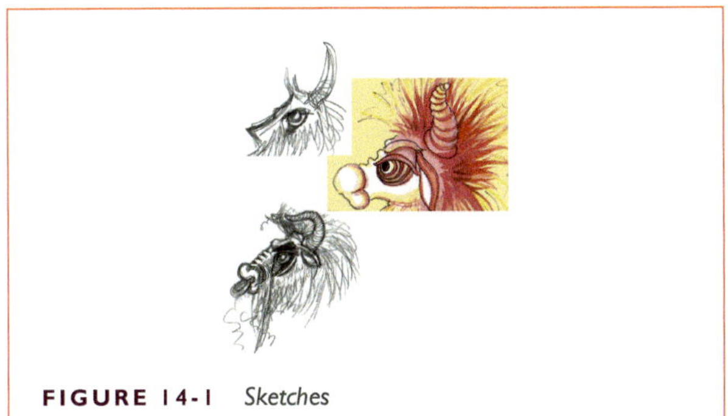

FIGURE 14-1 *Sketches*

FIGURE 14-2 *Final design*

2. The foundation mask is sculpted in water-based clay over a plaster head form (see the example of how to make this in Chapter 8.
3. Slowly build up layers of clay until the desired shape is achieved (Figure 14-4). I chose to use water-based clay because I work fast, and it was available.
4. When finished sculpting, wrap the sculpture in lightweight plastic such as grocery store vegetable bags or plastic wrap/cling film. This will make it easier to remove the mâché shell from the clay sculpt (Figure 14-5).
5. The next step is adding the layers of papier mâché. I prefer to lay on a foundation layer of fabric mâché to give the overall piece a fibrous strength; however, this is not mandatory, and many artists do not employ this

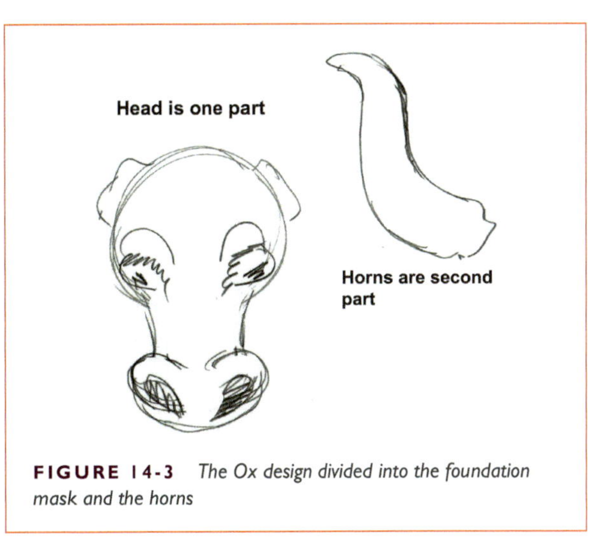

FIGURE 14-3 *The Ox design divided into the foundation mask and the horns*

DOI: 10.4324/9781003343264-14

FIGURE 14-4 *A–D) Slowly building up layers*

FIGURE 14-5 *Removing the mâché shell from the clay sculpt*

step. Cut the pieces of muslin into irregular squares, soak in PVA glue and water mixture, then smooth onto the plastic-covered sculpt until it is covered (Figure 14-6).

6. After the fabric layer is dry, begin adding two or three torn layers of paper. Alternate kinds of paper so you can tell if you missed a spot (Figure 14-7).
7. When the last layer is dry, draw a dotted line for a cutting guide. Use a carpet/utility knife, a Dremel with a wide cutting disk, a sharp knife, etc., to cut the mask shell off the clay form (Figure 14-8).
8. To reassemble the mask, tape the mask/shell foundation together on the inside and outside, then add temporary hot-glued cardboard tabs about every six inches to the inside seam.
9. Add several layers of papier mâché over the outside seam. When this is dry, repeat the process on the inside with fabric mâché (Figure 14-9).
10. Cover entire mask with layer of blue toweling (Figure 14-10).
11. When the mask is dry, decide if the mask needs to be trimmed. By using a cord, the trim line is

FIGURE 14-6 *A–B) Fabric layer*

FIGURE 14-7 *A–B. Two primary paper layers added*

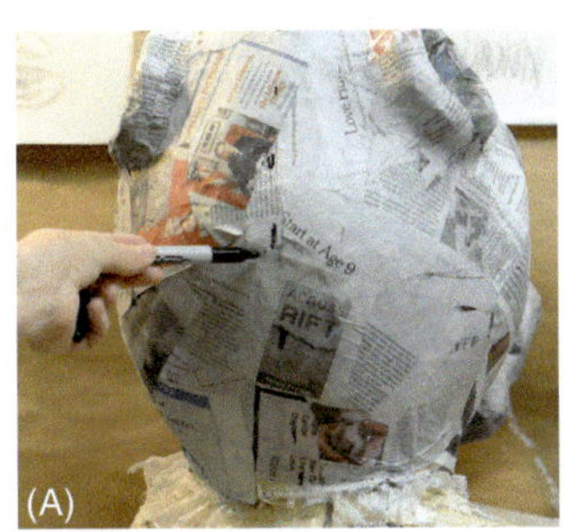

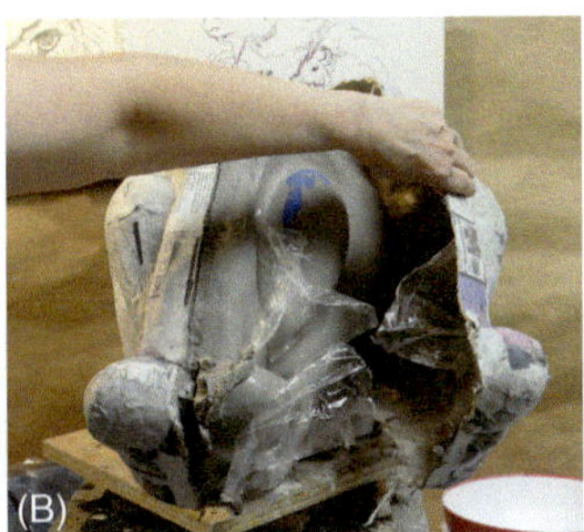

FIGURE 14-8 *A–C. Marking and cutting off the shell*

FIGURE 14-9 *A–B) Attaching halves together*

FIGURE 14-10 *Covering the mask with blue toweling – the final layer of paper*

visually stronger. **Tip:** Save the scraps to make ears (Figure 14-11).

12. Sketch the vision port areas and cut them open. Put the mask on to help determine what might need to be removed. Remember this opening could be for ventilation as well as sight (Figure 14-12).
13. Using different sizes of piping cord or rope, outline significant areas to add depth (Figure 14-13). Hot glue the piping in place, then cover with blue toweling and glue.
14. Bovines generally don't have manes; however, this one does. Make a wire, veraform, or rattan grid and nylon tie or wire it to the head. Then tie sisal, ribbons, polytubing, or lengths of wig hair to it. Braided, sisal bailing twine soaked in pure PVA glue stiffens up well when dried upside down. Upright braids might also be supported by having a wire core. Whatever the grid is made of, add papier mâché over it for strength and to visually meld it to the head (Figure 14-14).

Horns (see Chapter 11 for more information on making horns).

FIGURE 14-11 *A–C) Trimming the bottom, then using the excess for ear foundation*

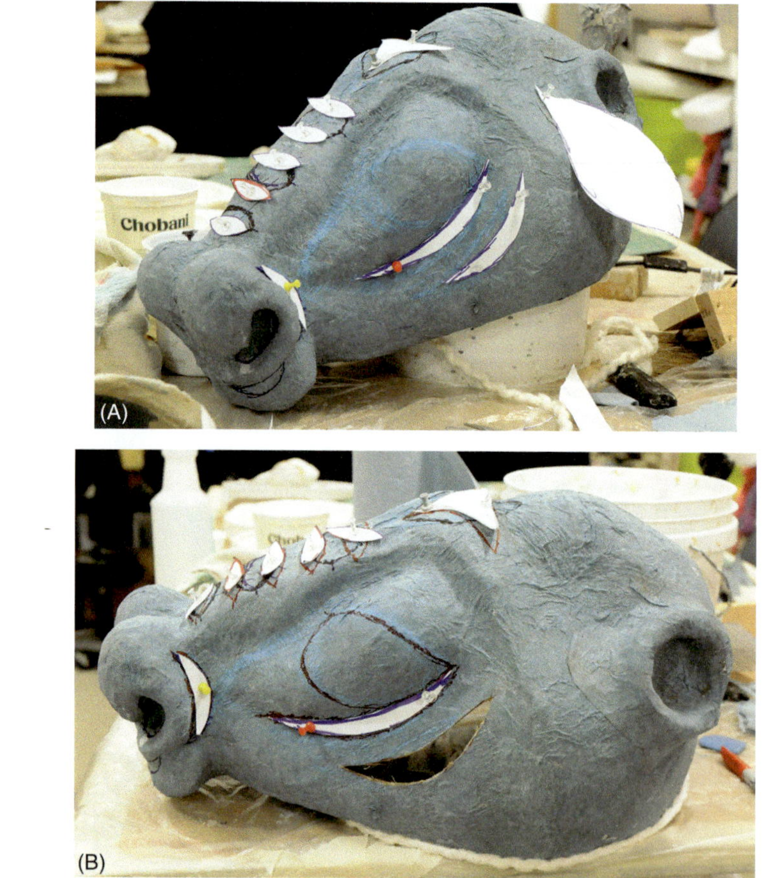

FIGURE 14-12 *A–B) Using paper patterns to determine the areas to cut out of the mask*

15. For this project, several sets of horns were sculpted until the desired size and shape were determined. The final horn positive sculpt was made of paper and tape (Figure 14-15).
16. Wrap the sculpt with thin plastic to seal the mold, then tape in place.

> **TIP BOX**
>
> When making a sculpt, take a plastic and packing tape pattern. Then you will have a pattern for foam as well.

FIGURE 14-13 *A) Using large piping on eyelids; B) Gluing piping on around all cut-out areas; C) Adding piping to ears; D) After adding blue toweling over the piping; E) Blue toweling added to ears; and F) Ears attached to the mask*

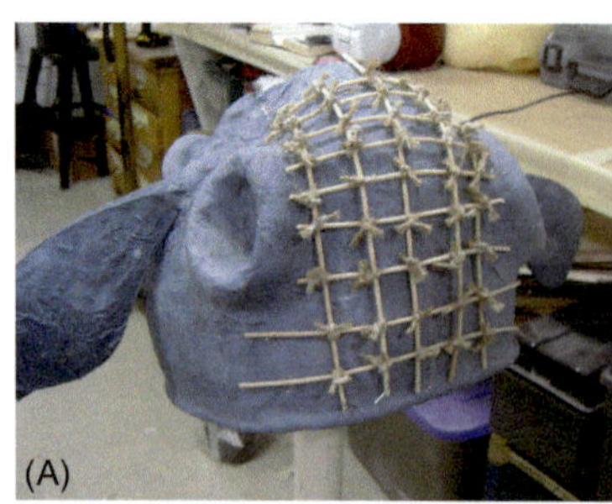

FIGURE 14-14 *A) Grid can be made of wire, rattan, or plastic; B) beginning attachment of sisal*

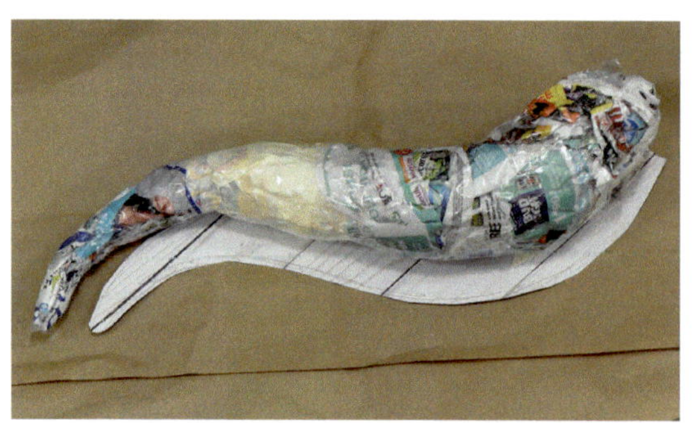

FIGURE 14-15 *Paper and tape positive sculpt of horn; it lays on its paper pattern*

FIGURE 14-17 *Mâché horns*

17. The first layer is muslin. After it dries, add two layers of papier mâché. Apply the mâché over the bottom about one inch (Figure 14-16).
18. When the mâché is dry, slice up the side of the horn carefully as much as you need to wiggle and pull the paper mold out. The positive mold might be destroyed, but you will still have your mâché horns (Figure 14-17). These horns are tough and very lightweight.

FIGURE 14-16 *First layer of fabric mâché over which is later added two more layers of paper*

Hot glue the paper tabs up the incision until cool. Then close the other side with the same technique.

19. These horns get deep ridges made with thick piping cord spiral-wrapped up to the tip. Make a rough measurement to estimate the amount needed. Wrap the cord around the horns with the desired spacing (Figure 14-18).
20. Make custom washers that match the diameter of the horn base using one-eighth-inch celtex/sentra or thin luan. Drill holes in the center of the disk and use either custom-made bolts (made with threaded nylon rod or use carriage bolts (Figure 14-19). Affix the heads of the bolts onto the washer with epoxy adhesive or epoxy putty.
21. Cut slashes in the end as needed to insert the washer, then two-part epoxy the mâché overlap on top of the washer unit (Figure 14-20).
22. On the mask head, drill a hole in the horn socket for the bolt and attach the bolt with another custom washer and a nut. On the inside, trim off any excess bolt length so it won't gouge the person wearing it. If the joint is

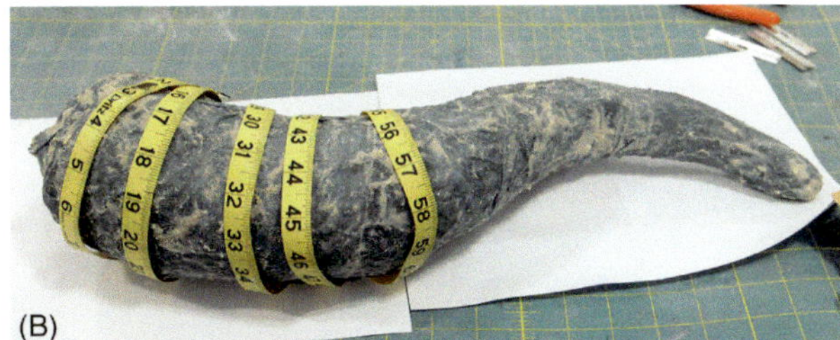

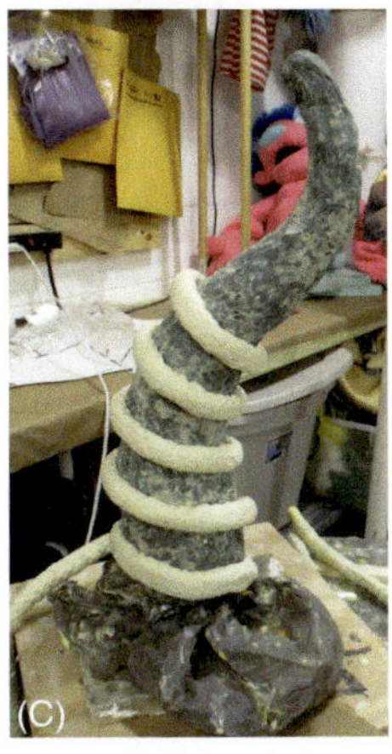

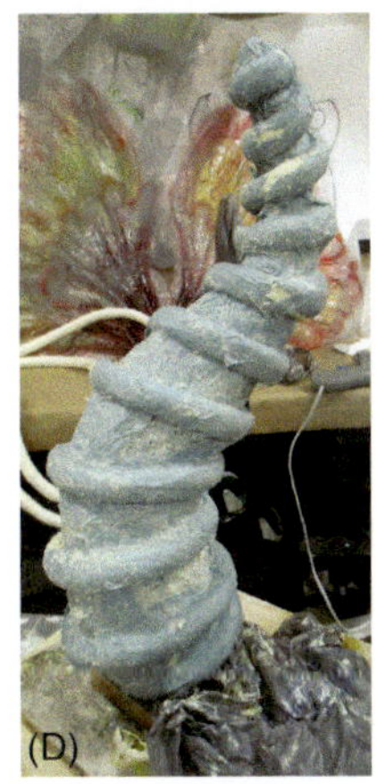

FIGURE 14-18 *A) Adding paper tabs to a foundation for gluing; B) measuring for piping cord; C) gluing piping cord around the horn shape; D) blue toweling over piping cord*

FIGURE 14-19 *Custom washers with nylon threaded rod inserted and glued with two-part epoxy*

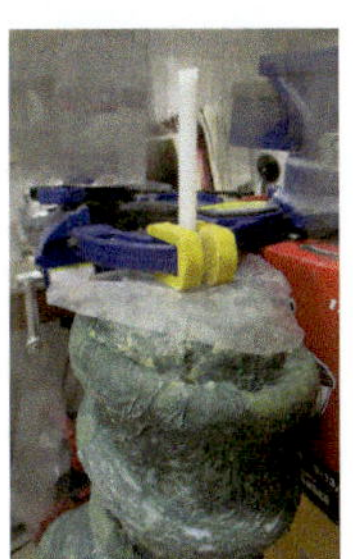

FIGURE 14-20 *The washer unit is clamped in place to allow the epoxy to cure wax paper is being used to keep it from sticking to the clamp*

visually rough, add more papier mâché between the mask head and the horn base (Figure 14-21).

23. Paint the inside of the mask black with acrylic paint and a brush or spray paint.

24. Attach the helmet liner or helmet inside the head using nylon ties or bolts (see Chapters 4 and 5 and Figure 14-22).

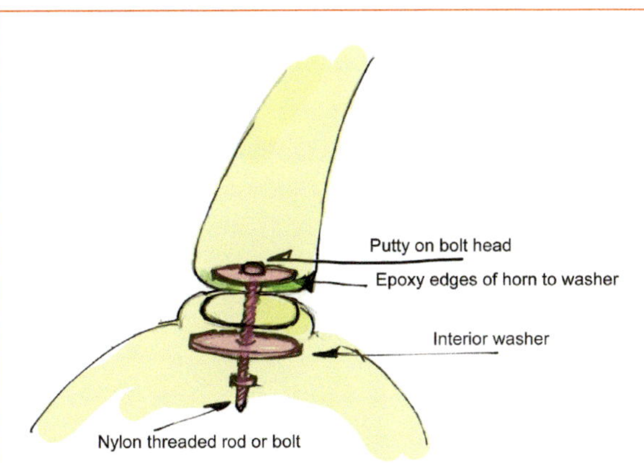

FIGURE 14-21 *Diagram of how the horn will attach to the mask*

FIGURE 14-22 *Sketch of the helmet liner attachment inside the mask; a rigid helmet may also be used*

25. After the helmet is inserted, cover any exterior screw heads or other hardware with epoxy putty or more mâché, then paint with a foundation coat over the entire mask surface.
26. Add finished paint details (Figure 14-23). Additional sisal was added to the front by punching holes and gluing.
27. Figure 14-24 shows the finished mask.

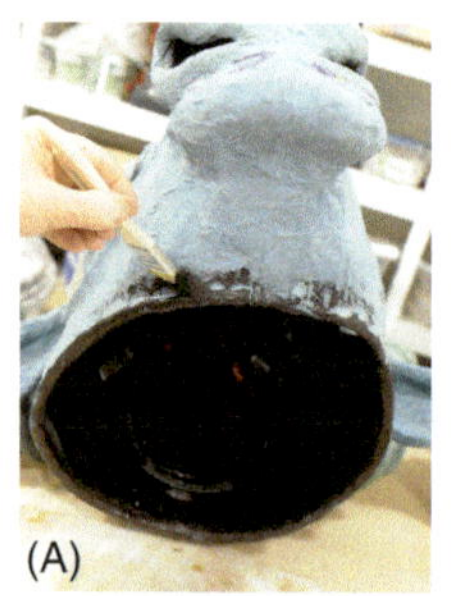

FIGURE 14-23 *A) Painting the inside black after the helmet is inserted; B) adding a brown foundation color with acrylic paint; C) underpainting the areas soon to be covered with bright red; D) adding red to the mask; E) another view of the process*

FIGURE 14-24 *A–B) The finished mask*

MASK PROJECT 2: THE ALIEN

Fabric mâché

The Alien is a spin on the stereotypical alien style – big head, large eyes – but I wanted this version to seem like a cartoon that is slightly stressed. The mesh of the cheesecloth softens the surface. It has an attached chin in the style of a traditional Balinese mask (see Figures 14-25 and 14-26).

1. First decide how the mask should be approached: in sections or in one piece. The Alien was built onto an existing vacuform mask with an attached domed head.
2. Trim the eyes and nose openings, making them larger for vision ports. The chin of the mask should also be cut away at this time (Figure 14-27).
3. A paper and masking tape positive sculpt was built up on a foam head form and covered with aluminum foil (Figure 14-28).
4. The pattern is then traced onto fosshape (also called *fuzzform*), being careful to note darts (Figure 14-29). If desired, fabric or papier mâché can be used in place of fosshape.
5. The darts are then sewn on a machine, trimmed down to a quarter inch, and placed over the paper sculpt (Figure 14-30).
6. With heat (steam) and pressure, the scupt shrinks and forms to take on the shape of the positive. Use an iron (place a piece of muslin between the fosshape and the iron) and an occasionally a clothing steamer (Figure 14-31).

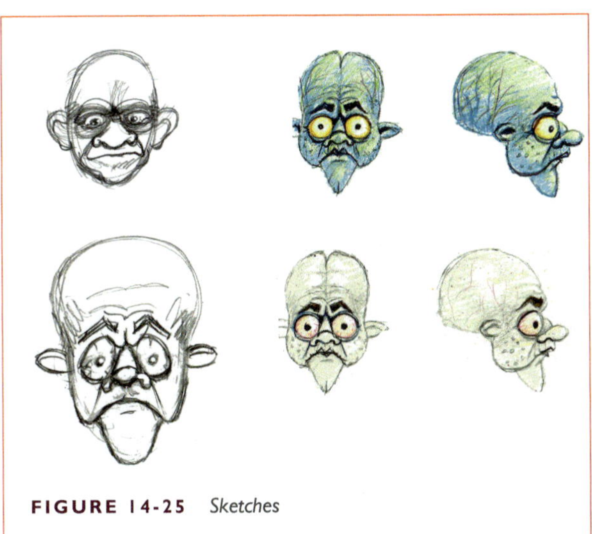

FIGURE 14-25 *Sketches*

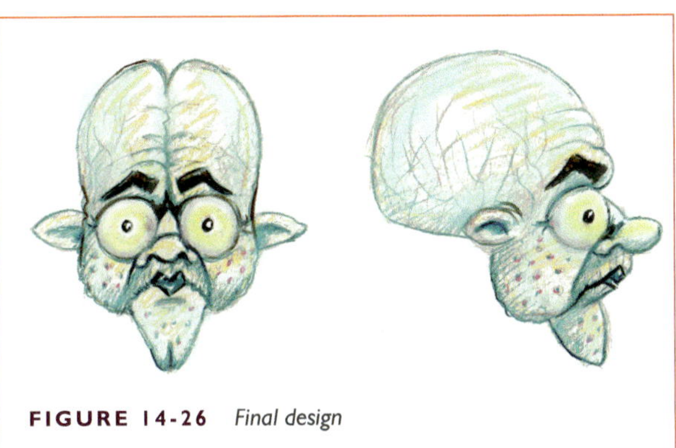

FIGURE 14-26 *Final design*

FIGURE 14-27 *Enlarging the eyes and nostrils and cutting away the chin*

FIGURE 14-28 *A) Building up paper foundation; B) adding aluminum foil over the paper sculpt*

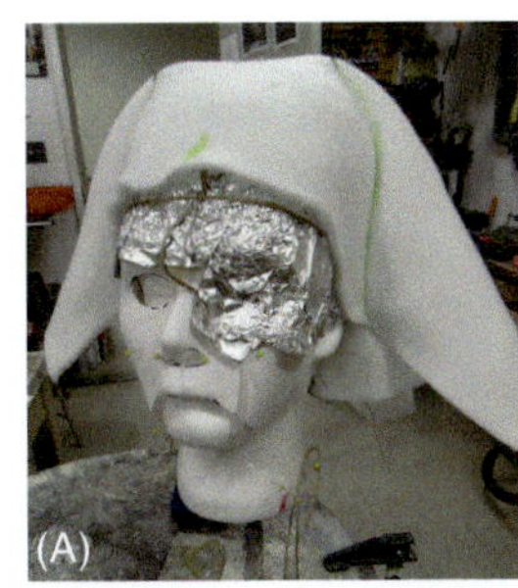

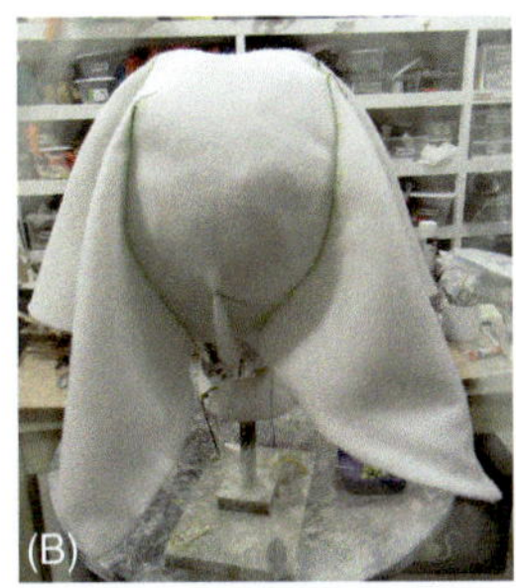

FIGURE 14-29 *A) Draping fosshape over the sculpt and adding darts; B) back view*

FIGURE 14-30 *Darts trimmed*

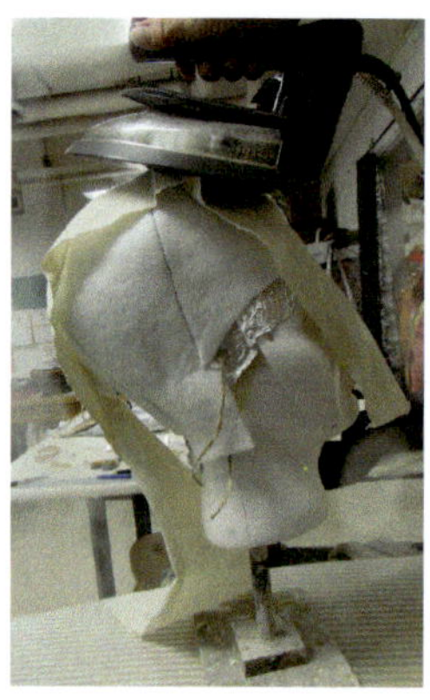

FIGURE 14-31 *Steaming the fosshape, using a hand iron for pressure and steam*

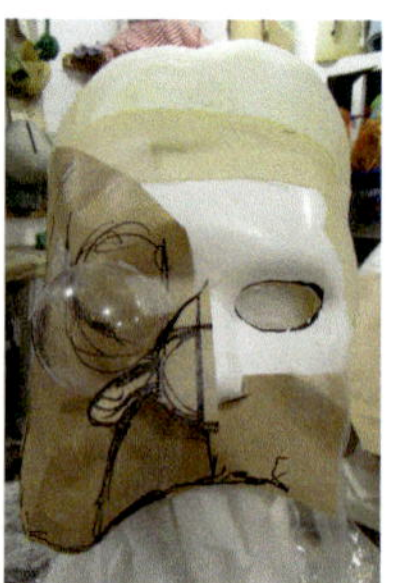

FIGURE 14-32 *Creating a rough paper pattern of facial shapes with the eye dome taped on.*

7. The vacuform mask is adhered temporarily to the fosshape dome with a small patch of hot glue. Then a few connecting pieces of fabric mâché are added to connect the mask and the fosshape dome.
8. Make small paper patterns for cheeks, forehead, nose, and brows out of muslin or paper and cut each out of polyether foam (upholstery foam). Then adhere them with cooled hot glue. The eye size can be estimated at this time as well. To help better judge the desired size, cut paper patterns (Figure 14-32).
9. With small sharp scissors and/or razor blades, round out the plains of the foam face and carve wrinkles or skin folds (Figure 14-33).

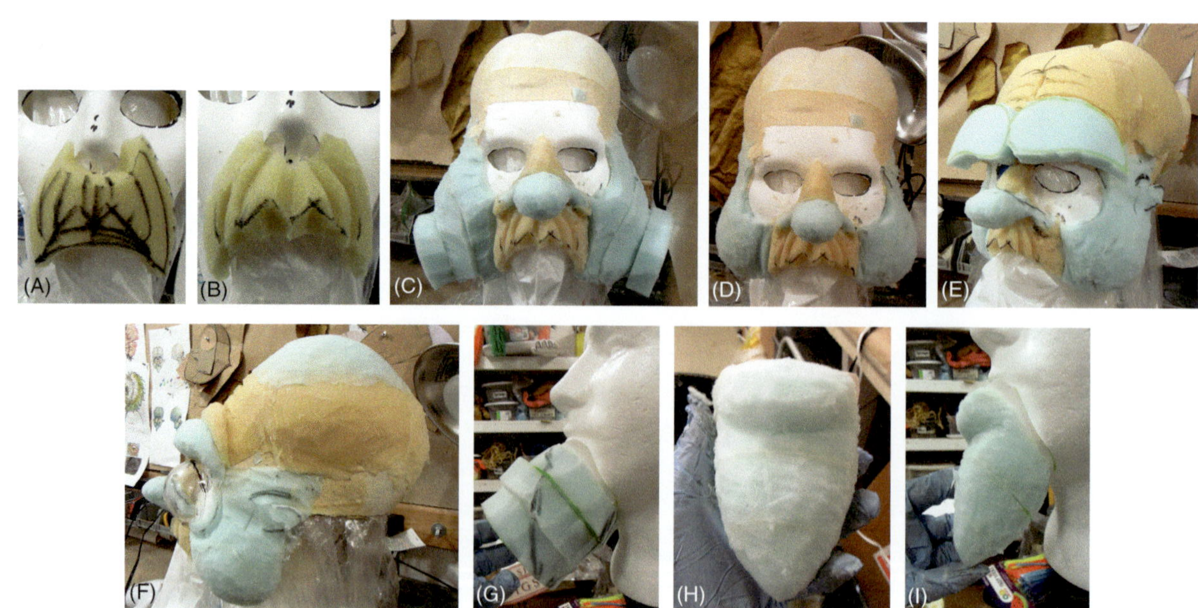

FIGURE 14-33 *A) Upper lip with half inch polyether foam, sketched out with a sharpie; B) lip carved with a razor blade; C) cheeks stacked and glued with neoprene contact cement; D) cheeks refined and carved down with razor blades and small scissors; E) adding brows; F) brows and the back of the head in process; G) setting up the chin for carving; H) carved chin with scissors; I) carved chin attached to the plastic chin foundation*

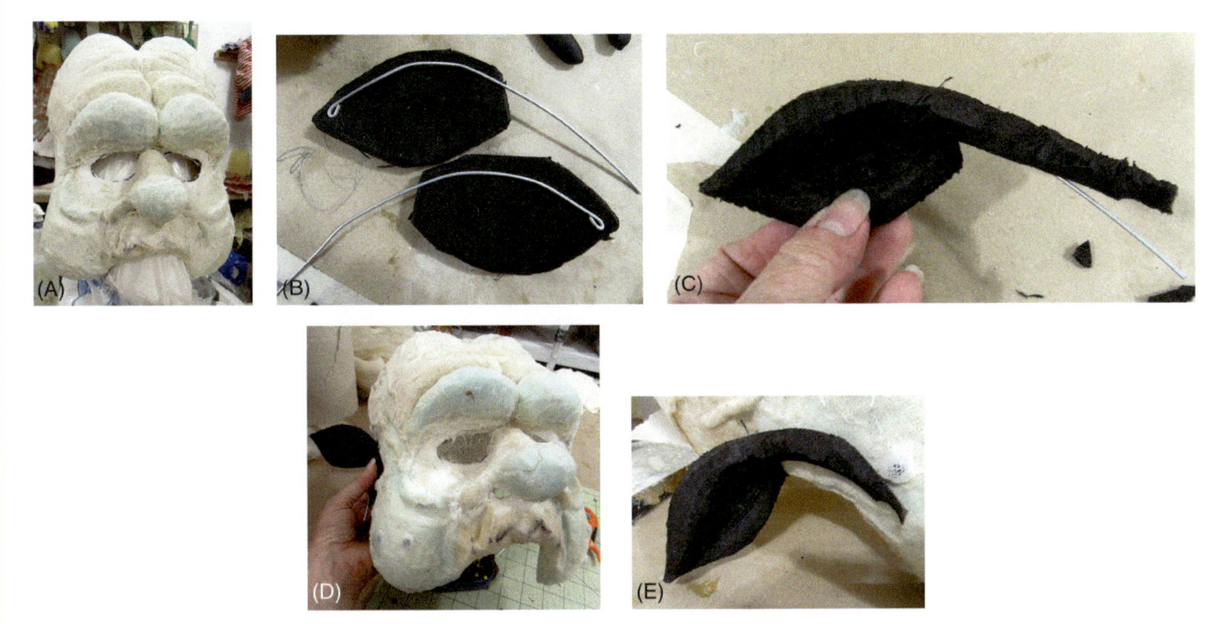

FIGURE 14-34 *A) Beginning to cover the mask with glue and cheesecloth; B) carved eva ears with wires attached; C) a small strip of eva is cut to cover the wire and also creates the top ear ridge; D) gluing ears on with contact cement; E) close-up of rough ear*

10. **Note:** Before adding mâché, remove the mask foundation and cover the foil and EPS foam mold with a plastic bag. Prepare the glue and water mix: 3 PVA glue to 1 water (Elmer's, white wood glue, or yellow wood glue). Store this in a container that can be covered because it will be used for successive layers.
11. To prepare the material, cut small irregular squares out of cheesecloth, scrim, or muslin. If muslin is used, feather the edges of the fabric (called the *Dutchman's Process*) so that the muslin pieces meld seamlessly.
12. Starting on the outside from top to bottom, paint an area with glue and then apply a square of cheesecloth. With the chip brush, paint on more glue (it can be thicker if needed) and press the cloth into the glue (Figure 14-34). Smaller pieces may be used to wrap around nostril holes.
13. Let each layer dry before adding successive layers (two to four layers as needed). Any excess that hangs past the mask edge should be softened and wrapped around the edges onto the inside of the mask. At this point, ears can be carved and attached to the sides of the mask.
14. On the second to the last layer, add textural details such as bumps and veins (Figure 14-35), then cover with the final layer of cheesecloth.
15. After the layers are dry, again dry-fit the eye domes. If the eyes are don't fit well, use an X-Acto knife to carve out the areas. Recover these with more cloth mâché (Figure 14-36).
16. At this point, fit the mask and determine if it needs to be padded. Because the Alien has a big cranium, it needs an interior foam structure as well as a t-head strap. The mask is so lightweight that it does not need a helmet.
17. The vision ports lie in the wells of the eyes and in the nostrils. The ports may be darkened with stretch black

FIGURE 14-35 *The third layer includes textural details such as veins and bumps. cover any 3-d additions with layers of fabrics and glue*

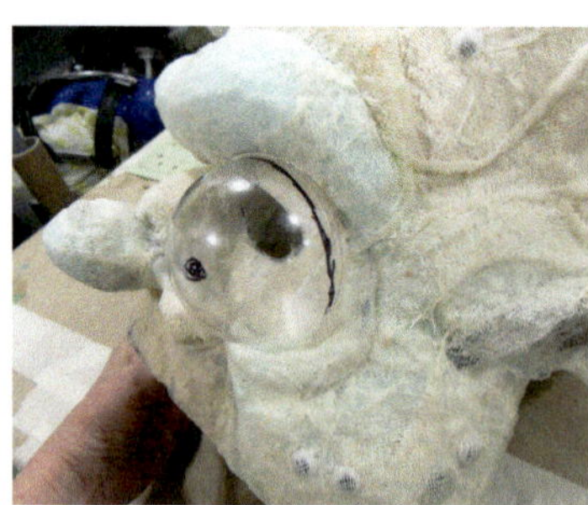

FIGURE 14-36 *Eye domes with pupils and trim lines sketched on the outside with a sharpie*

mesh or layers of black tulle. Apply inside with contact cement or (the dreaded) hot glue.

18. **The chin:** Bore two holes at the sides of the chin shape and sew on black elastic. Then fit and pad out the chin for desired movement. Tape or safety pin the elastic inside the mask before trying it on so that the correct tightness can be achieved. Glue or stitch through the mask sides to attach elastic.
19. Felt may be used to cover the foam, but chamois or soft suede is recommended in the chin cup or in areas where the face rests. It is much softer than felt (Figure 14-37).
20. **Painting:** Paint any exposed and unfinished areas inside the mask. Black is the preferred color as it visually disappears on stage and makes it easier for the actor to see out of the mask.
21. Follow through with painting the pits of the eyes and the deep creases of the face. Then dry brush and stipple the tones of aqua, turquoise, and pinks (Figure 14-38).

FIGURE 14-38 *A) Foundation of black in the eye sockets and in some of the wrinkles; B) lose fitting the painted eye before attaching; C) pattern of eyebrows as painting continues*

22. **Eyes:** If there is concern that the outside surface of the eye domes might be scratched, then cover this area with painter's tape. If the domes need to be shaped, trace the areas with a Sharpie and carefully Dremel off the excess. Sharpie marks may be removed by using 99% alcohol.
23. Pupils may be drawn on the outside of the domes to determine eye focus. These will be helpful when painting and gluing pupils on the inside.
24. Round flat pupil shapes found inside toy googly eyes were used to create the pupils (Figure 14-38). These may be glued carefully onto the inside of the dome following the Sharpie mark on the outside. To glue these in the exact spot, use 5-minute epoxy or Super Glue

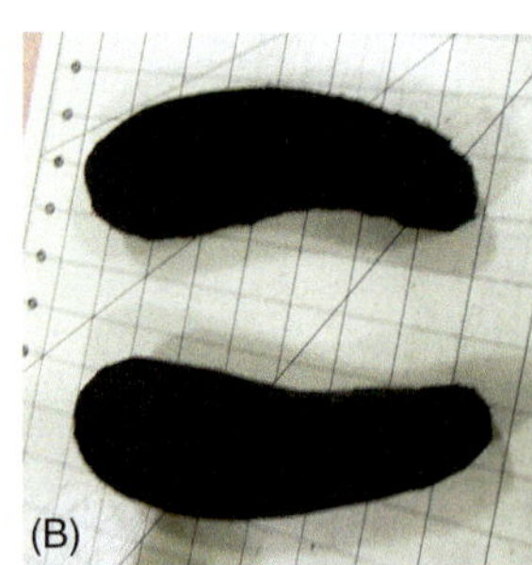

FIGURE 14-37 *A) Adding foam inside the prepainted mask. (make sure to mask any areas that might have glue applied, as paint will not allow glue to adhere properly); B) the shapes to be glued inside the mask to pad the top of the head; C) the chin (right) is attached to the inside of the mask with pieces of elastic glued in place with additional bands of elastic (notice that the chin and anything that contacts skin is covered with chamois)*

FIGURE 14-39 *Close-up of a painted eye inserted, glued, and melded with the socket using additional fabric mâché and putty*

FIGURE 14-40 *Most of the details painted and complete at this point*

Gel. Tweezers or a Q-Tip dabbed with honey, syrup, or thick PVA glue may be used to temporarily pick up the pupil for placement.

25. After the pupil has cured, paint successive layers backward (i.e., a decorative pupil outline, veins, and an accent color at the outside edge of the dome). Finish the painting process with a final coat of color. This process will produce a very lightweight eye. Resin eyes might also be created, but these can be heavy (Figure 14-39).
26. Glue the eyes into the sockets with 5-minute epoxy. Then frame the eyes with small pieces of cheesecloth, glue, and epoxy putty. Finesse the eyes into place with a small blunt tool such as a popsicle stick and let them dry.
27. Finish painting with a brush or airbrush (Figure 14-40).
28. **Brows:** The Alien has carved EVA foam brows covered with trimmed black fur. To take down the "black," these are finished with a dry brushed Prussian blue acrylic paint (applied with a toothbrush). Glue them into place with contact cement (Figure 14-41).
29. Figure 14-42 Shows the finished mask.

FIGURE 14-41 *A) One-inch fur glued to eva foam brows; B) brows trimmed with small scissors and dry brushed with blue paint to decrease the harshness of black*

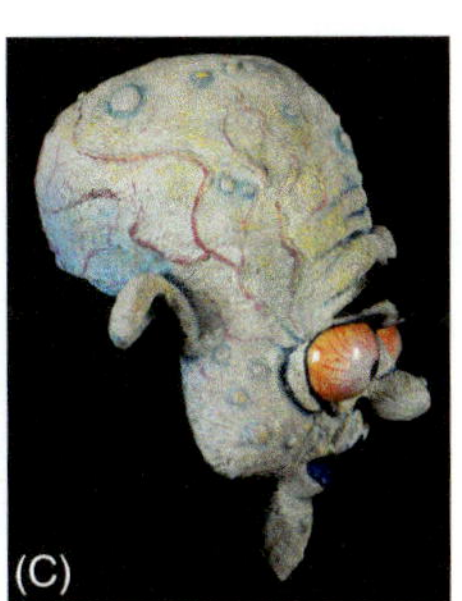

FIGURE 14-42 *A–C) The finished mask*

MASK PROJECT 3: THE ORANGE DOG

Block foam costume character head

The Orange Dog is a cartoon version of a big, goofy hound dog. The techniques for working with block foam are covered in more detail in my last book, *Foam Fabrication: Turning 2-D Designs into 3-D Objects*; however, this section deals specifically with all the steps needed to create a foam *mask*, which is not covered in that book (Figure 14-43).

30. For this project, I merged an existing muzzle pattern with a new head shape. The bean-shaped head was based on a paper and masking tape sculpt (Figure 14-44).
31. Cover the paper and tape sculpt, with thin plastic and tape (masking or clear). Then mark the pattern pieces symmetrically around the whole shape. Label the parts to remind yourself how they all go together (Figure 14-45).
32. Because it is sometimes extremely difficult to understand how the pieces reconnect when lying flat, the more notes added to the pattern pieces, the better (Figure 14-46).

FIGURE 14-43 *Sketches and final design*

FIGURE 14-44 *The bean-shaped head made with a masking tape and paper*

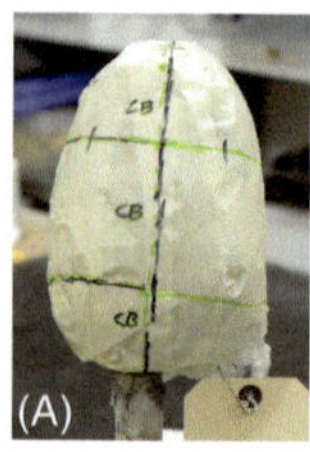

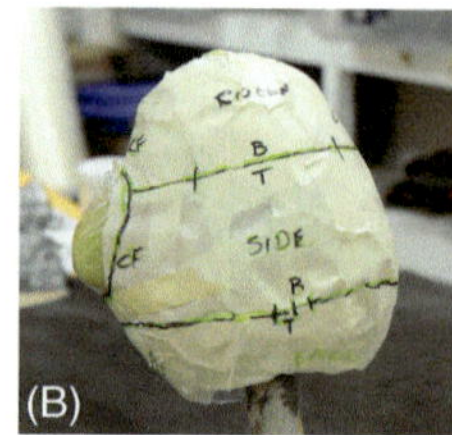

FIGURE 14-45 *A) Labeling the pieces after the head shape is divided into sections; B) side view*

FIGURE 14-46 *Example of a complicated latex chicken pattern with copious notes and notches. sculpted by undergraduate student Andrew Swisher*

33. Cut each pattern piece apart, then lay out each piece and add darts to help make the piece flatten out.
34. Tape sets of these pieces to a sheet of paper and *true up* the lines with a ruler and a pencil or extra fine point marker. Label each sheet carefully (see Figure 14-47).

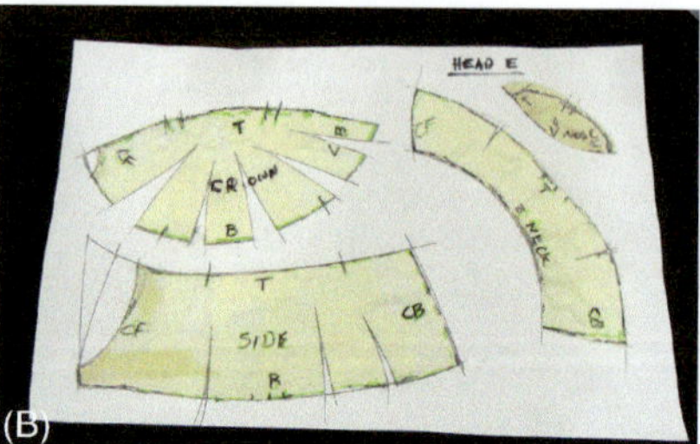

FIGURE 14-47 *A) The original foam dog head without bean shaped cranium added; B) patterns for the bean-shaped cranium, cut apart and taped to a sheet ready to enlarge*

TIP BOX

How to Determine Scale

a. Create a life-size drawing of the mask or object (Figure 14-48).

b. Because this is a mask, you want a human head to fit comfortably inside the mask. Measure the width and height. If the mask is too small in height or width to accommodate a human head wearing a helmet, then it will need to be enlarged.

c. When the drawing is complete, remeasure.

d. If you have a small-scale model of the mask head and you want to enlarge it, measure the height and width of it in the same areas as the life-size drawing.

e. Pick one measurement and divide the small measurement into the larger measurement:
   Life-size width/scale model width = Z.
   Z = how many times the small-scale model needs to be multiplied to get it to life size.
   Because a photocopier starts at 100%, you need to multiply Z × 100.
   Z × 100 = what you type on the photocopier's keypad.

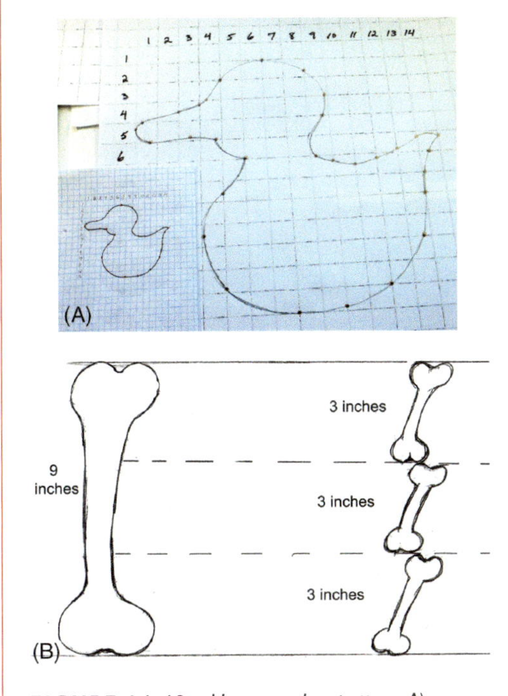

FIGURE 14-48 *How to scale a pattern: A) use a grid; B) divide the big object by the small-scale object*

FIGURE 14-49 *All the pieces enlarged to 100% create a sample head out of eva*

35. Scale the size of the pieces based on the human head. This pattern was scaled to approximately 100% (see Figure 14-49).

36. Enlarge on a photocopier. If the pieces are too big, then copy each part and tape them together until the piece is complete.

37. Lay out the pieces on foam and trace around each. This foam is half-inch black EVA. Make sure to flip each piece for the right and left side. Draw an "x" on the pattern-side-up-pieces. This small step will be very helpful when assembling the head (Figure 14-50).

38. Using a two-inch razor blade, cut the foam at the proper angle. If this is not done accurately, then the overall shape will be distorted (Figure 14-51). Hold the blade at a 90° angle for pieces that are joined to create straight sides. If beveled angles are desired, the blade should be held to cut the foam at different angles, dependent of course on the final shape. Practice and experimentation are the key. See *Foam Fabrication and Construction Techniques* for more details.

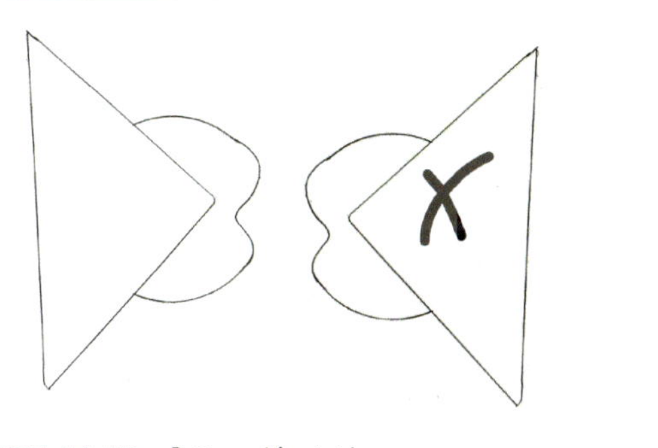

FIGURE 14-50 *Pattern-side-up pieces*

FIGURE 14-51 *All the pieces cut out for the mockup*

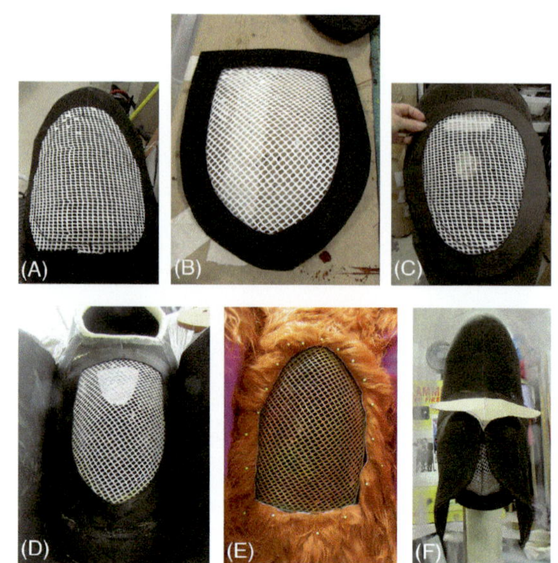

FIGURE 14-53 *A) Rough cut variform vision port; B) thin foam frame laid over the vision port; C) ready to glue to the back of the head with contact cement; D) glued to the bottom of the chin; E) prepainted with orange spray paint and floral spray to match the orange fur; F) insert in the mouth area*

39. Using the *correct* contact cement to hold the foam, glue the pieces together. If while gluing the process becomes confusing, refer to the full, half plastic skin remaining on the small-scale sculpt. Note: Add any additional foam to help with the shape as needed (Figure 14-52). For half-inch EVA and larger, use Barge Cement.
40. After the head is fully assembled, map out and install the vision and ventilation ports (Figure 14-53).
41. The ventilation and vision ports are cut in the back of the head, in the mouth, and on the bottom of the chin. More might be added as per the mask design and intention or need.
42. Varaform was used to make the vent and vision ports. It is a thermoplastic, so it can be shaped to match any contour. Pattern and glue in place with contact cement and foam. Paint the varaform with spray paint to match the fur color. *Optional step:* hand glue (with hot glue or contact cement) tufts of fur onto the varaform to allow maximum ventilation. This technique may also be used for vision ports.
43. If a fan is desired, this is the time to install it using plastic (Sintra/Celtex) washers and nylon ties. Place it so that it aims at the face and back of the neck. An additional fan could be situated in front of the ventilation port(s) to assist with circulation (see Chapter 4).
44. The helmet will be attached to the inside of the foam form with a one-eighth-inch polyethylene or 1/16-inch aluminum ring. Depending on the head shape, more rings or supports of varying thicknesses may be needed for stability. Measure the outside of the head to help determine the circumference of the ring.
45. To assemble the stabilizing ring as a part of the interior structure, put it inside the head form and mark it or subtract the thickness of the foam from the outside measurement, then clamp together the ring, drill holes and hold together with bolts, lock washers, and nuts.

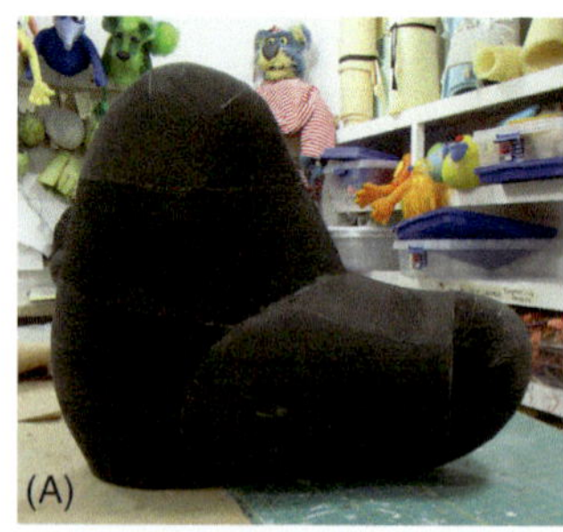

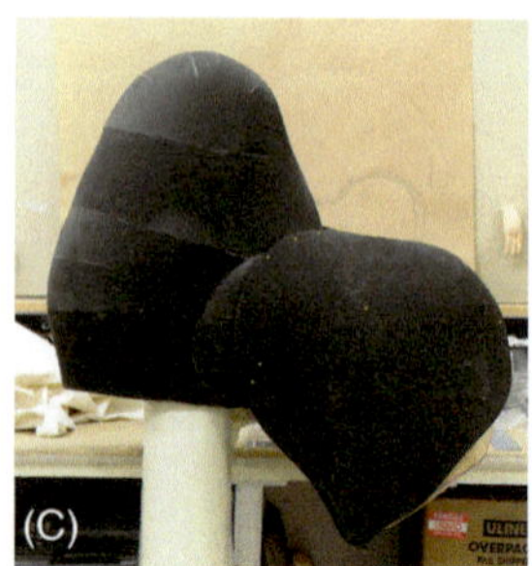

FIGURE 14-52 *A) The final size of the head; B) the final head with doggie chops added alongside the mockup; C) side view of the final head*

46. The struts are polyethylene. Countersink the bolts into the inside of the helmet foam. This will allow the bolts to extend farther out and keep the bolt heads from digging into your actor's scalp!

47. Depending on the character's head, it may be easier to attach the helmet to the ring, then install the whole unit inside the head, but it is also possible to attach the ring first with struts attached, then insert the helmet. Do whatever make the most sense for the project.

48. Attach the ring to the head with nylon bolts and plastic washers (Figure 14-54).

FIGURE 14-54 *A) measuring the outside to determine the rough measurement of the interior support structure; B) view of the polyethylene band before it is inserted permanently; C) the ring; D) a standard helmet; E) the ring attached to the helmet with cardboard struts; F) top view; G) heat bending polyethylene using a vice and a heat gun; have spray bottle with water handy to flash cool the plastic; H) a strut that was shaped with a heat gun; I) three struts ready to go; J) pushing the bolt through the helmet; use a spade bit to drill through the inside foam, thus countersinking the bolt into the helmet; K) after the struts have been attached, dremel down the ends of long screws as needed; L) custom made plastic washers; M) ring attached to the helmet and ready to install*

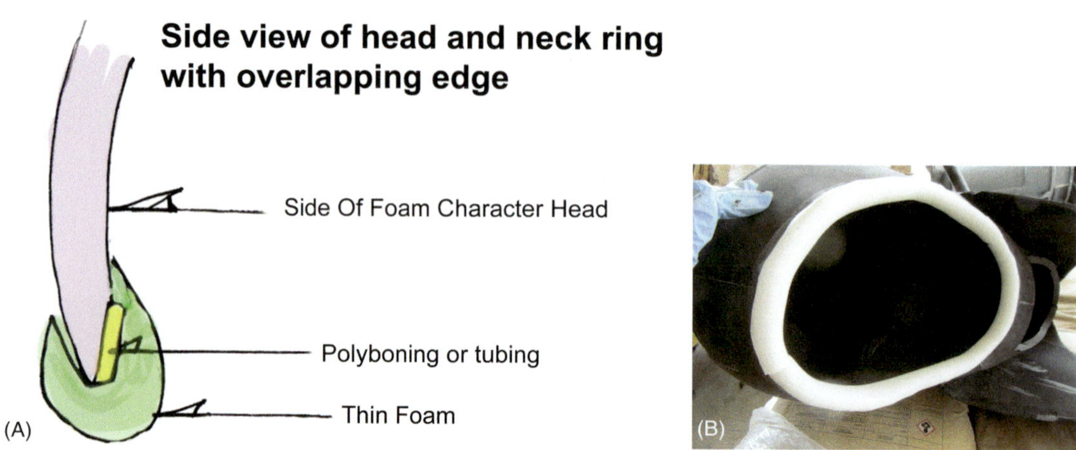

FIGURE 14-55 *A) Diagram of polyboning installed in the layers of the foam; B) the finished edge of the head with the ring installed, then wrapped with one-quarter-inch white eva foam*

> TIP BOX
>
> The Importance of the Neck Ring
>
> The neck ring is a structure that creates a support for foam seams that run perpendicular to it, that is, it prevents seams from splitting open at the bottom. The ring also helps form and support the shape of the head.

49. After the helmet is installed, add a plastic ring into the neck opening. Cut the foam at a 45° angle so it can easily wrap around the ring. The ring may be polyboning (rigilene) or polyethylene tubing (see Figure 14-55).

50. **Patterning fur:** drape the fur pattern with smooth fabric, preferably muslin. Divide it up into muzzle and head (Figure 14-56). Remember: you only need to drape half of the head. Indicate the direction of the fur with arrows and add plenty of notches with small notes.

51. The muslin pattern may be used as the primary pattern, or it may be transferred to paper. Here the pattern is transferred to paper. Trim the pattern and transfer it to fur. Before cutting, pay special attention to the direction of the arrows, which indicate the direction of the fur (Figure 14-57).

52. Except for the center back (CB) seam and the neck opening, the fur needs only a quarter-inch seam allowance. Add three to four inches to the neck opening and one inch to each side of the CB.

53. Cut out fur pieces with a razor blade or a carefully finessed pair of scissors. A razor blade is preferred

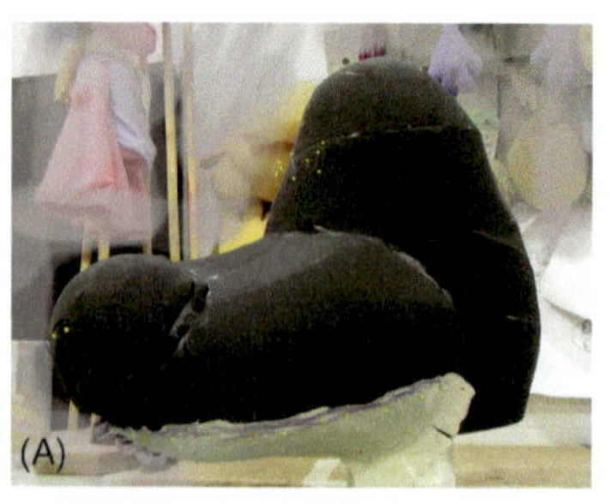

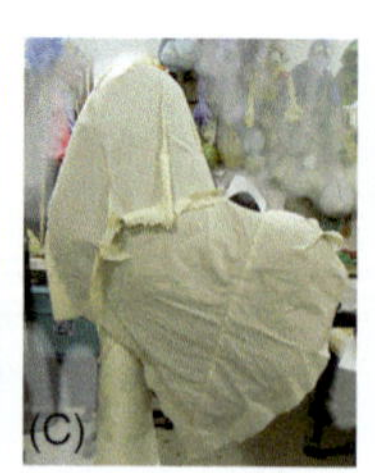

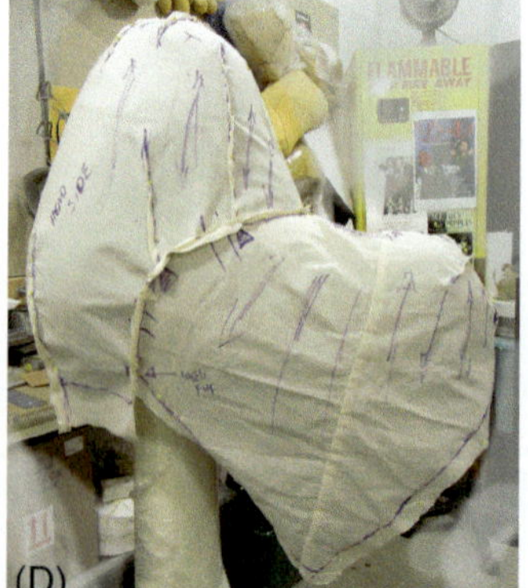

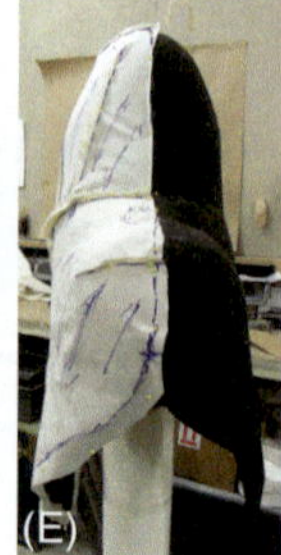

FIGURE 14-56 *A–E) Draping muslin on the chin (note: no doggie chops in this image)*

FIGURE 14-57 *A) "Truing up" the muslin pattern before transferring it to paper; B) all muslin pieces transferred to paper*

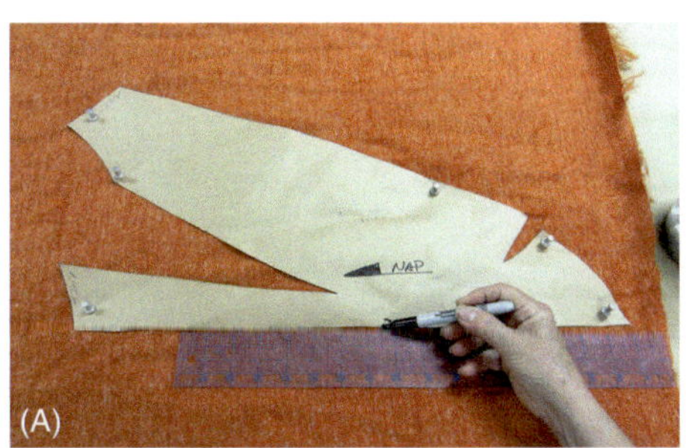

FIGURE 14-58 *A) Transferring the pattern to fur using a ruler as a guide; B) transferred (note that the pattern has been flipped); C) with the Fur panel cut out*

(Figure 14-58). It is especially important to only cut the fabric on the back of the fur and avoid cutting the long fur fibers as these will help hide the seams

54. Start by sewing the darts, then move on to the rest of the pieces (Figure 14-59) image of pinned dart (note: pink spandex was used to reflect the inside of the dog's chops)
55. Slide the fur skin over the foam shape and finesse it into place. Use T-pins to anchor the skin in place as needed, then sew the fur at the back of the head by hand.
56. At this point, it is possible to start teasing the fur out of the seams. Use a T-pin or a fine-toothed comb to carefully pull the fur trapped in the seams. This will make the back of the head look seamless. Continue all the way to the bottom of the neck fur.
57. After seams are teased and fluffed, glue the neck fur with contact cement to the inside of the head. If needed, the fur may also be stitched through the foam to itself to help augment the contact cement (Figure 14-60).
58. **Nose:** Study the paper patterns of the nose and eyes made earlier and make any final size decisions at this point (see Figure 14-61).

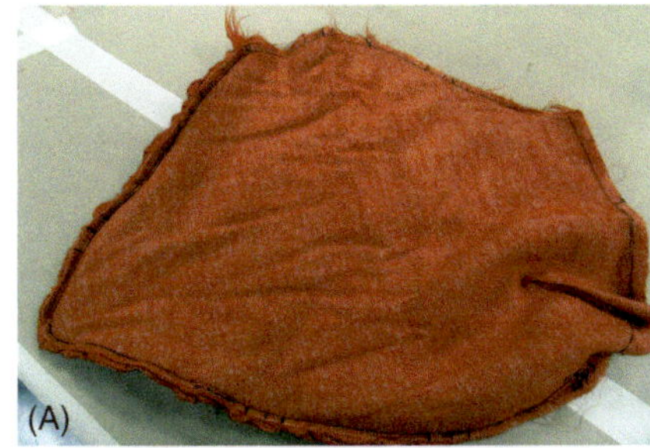

FIGURE 14-59 *A) Part of the muzzle with one dart sewn; B) I chose to add a panel of pink spandex inside the chops, so it needed to be sewn to the outer cheek fur*

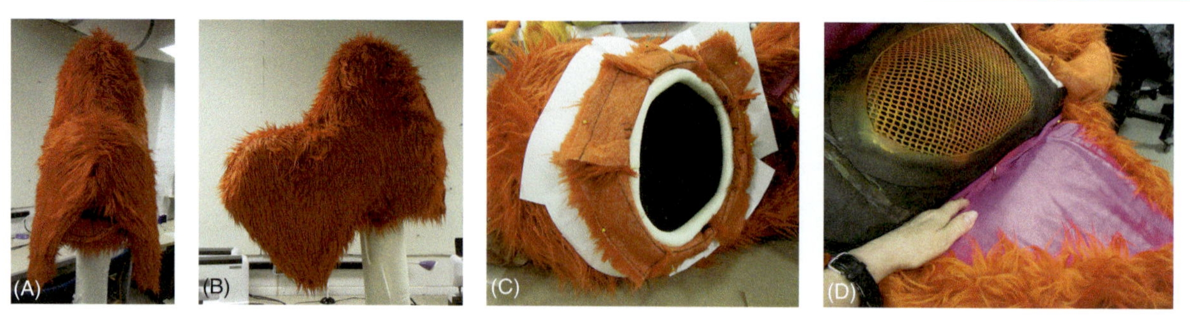

FIGURE 14-60 *A) The fur is on the head; B) side view; C) gluing the fur around the neck opening; D) an upside-down view of the underside of the head. the pink spandex cheek lining is glued onto the foam next to the chin*

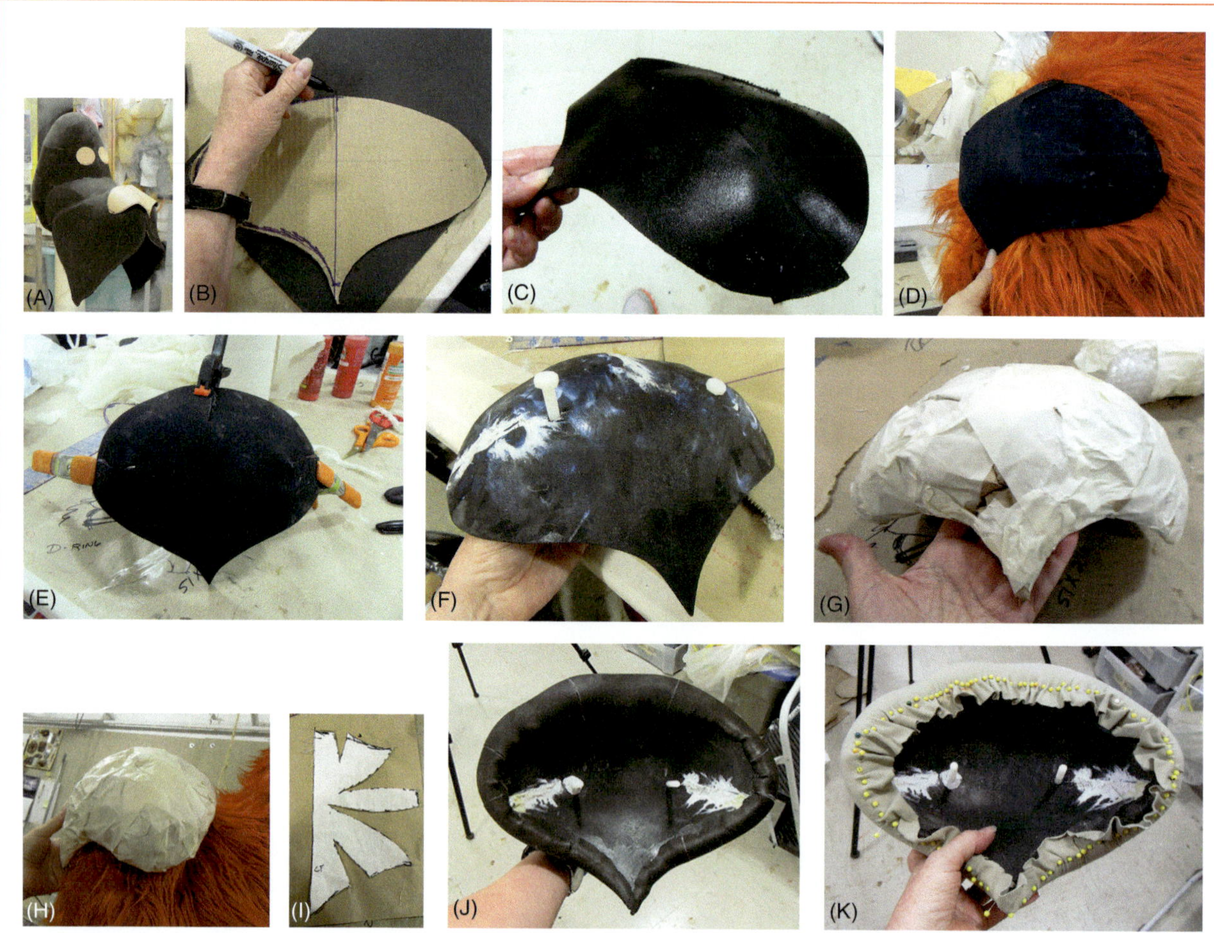

FIGURE 14-61 *A) A pre-scaling shapes for features before fur is applied; B) laying a symmetrical paper pattern onto sintra/celtex and tracing with a sharpie; C) the sintra/celtex piece heat bent with darts cut into the sides helps to create the shape; d) lose fitting the foundation; E) gluing the darts with epoxy; F) the darts were smoothed with putty (optional), then holes were drilled for the nylon bolts; G) sculpting a paper nose shape to create a foam pattern; H) testing the shape of the sculpt; I) half of the muslin pattern for foam; J) use black eva to make the nose bulb. cut the foam flat using the muslin pattern. the darts created the round bulbous shape. To attach the nose to the nose plate, bevel the edges of the foam and glue on the back side of the plate with contact cement. wrap the beveled edges around the plate edge; K) use stretch fabric to create a smooth surface on the nose. divide up all the wrinkles with pins. It helps distribute the wrinkles. glue edges of spandex with contact cement; L) the nose getting a second layer of rosco's acrylic medium. sculpt or coat and liquitex mediums also work well. stippled with porous foam scrap; M) surface is dried and ready to paint; N) begin by starting underneath and painting toward the front. build up layers of color (Continued)*

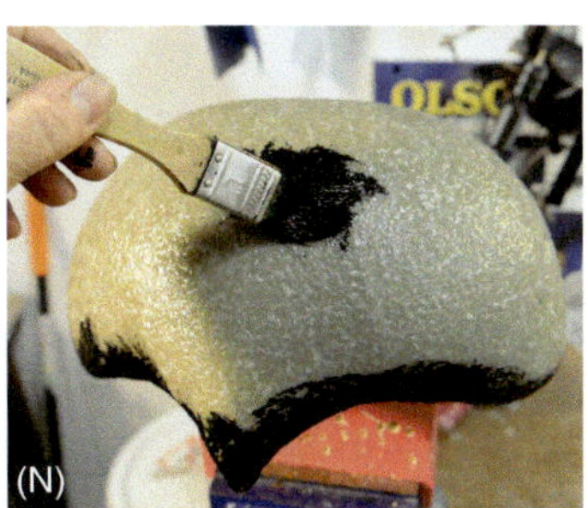

FIGURE 14-61 *(Continued)*

59. Use the paper pattern to cut the foundation for the nose. Heat-bend the foundation to hug the area as needed, then drill a hole at its center and glue a bolt (measured to the length needed to go through the foam layers) through this piece. **Note:** Make sure all the plastic is coarsely sanded to break up the surface for gluing.
60. Washers will also be needed inside to keep the nuts from tearing through the foam. Make these using a template, with the same plastic and cut on a bandsaw.
61. Pattern a dome of EVA (L-200) or carve ethafoam, construction Styrofoam, extruded foam, or even stacked EVA foam to achieve the desired shape. For this mask, I patterned a bulbous nose, then attached it with contact adhesive.
62. Cover the shape with spandex or any stretch fabric, then using contact cement adhere it to the back of the foundation plastic. The tension of the fabric will hold the shape onto the foundation.
63. Leave it unsealed; that is, use bare fabric such as a stretch velour or cover it with several layers of thick acrylic medium. To get a bumpy texture, stipple three to four layers with a porous sponge. Let it dry between layers.
64. When dry, paint the nose with acrylic paint and then seal it with another coat of clear acrylic medium.
65. To attach, bore a hole through fur and foam with an aw, an X-Acto, knife or a sharp pair of scissors, and with a washer and nut, find the bolt end inside the nose. This can be tricky because of the size of the head and human arm length, but be persistent. A nut driver is helpful to extend the reach.
66. **Eyes:** After the size of the eye is determined, create a custom vacuform shape or use a premade clear half hemisphere (Figure 14-62).

FIGURE 14-62 *A) Eye shape first cut on bandsaw, then sanded to form a dome; B) vacuforming four shapes, two of which are for pupils; C) shapes rough cut on a bandsaw; D) two pupils cut with a dremel tool*

FIGURE 14-63 *Nylon bolt glued into the eye shapes with epoxy*

67. After the desired eye size and shape has been achieved, sand the surface (inside and out) thoroughly with course sandpaper (60 or 80 grit), and then (on the outside only) with fine sandpaper. The goal is to score the surface and then to remove any deep groves on the outside that might mar the finish.
68. To remove dust and any oils, wipe the domes with 99% alcohol.
69. With the correct length of bolt (remember this will be going through the foam of the head area), epoxy the head into the inside of the sanded dome (Figure 14-63).

    Being careful not to damage the threads. Use masking or painter's tape to attach the ends of the bolts to dowel rods. This will add a longer rod to hold when spray painting (Figure 14-64).
70. Paint the eyes with several *thin* layers of paint, letting each layer dry before the next is applied. A spritz of pale blue just at the edges can provide a subtle contour. This may also be achieved with an airbrush.
71. Remove the rods from the eyes and attach to the mask head with washers and nuts.
72. An optional step is a layer of black or colored felt or foam behind the eyes. This will add a nice color break between the fur and the eyes, making them more pronounced.
73. Use gloss black spray paint, finished with two coats of gloss varnish.
74. To determine the placement of the pupils, use tape to temporarily adhere the pupils. Add a light pencil mark to indicate the placement, then glue with Super Glue Gel or epoxy. Note: Do not leave the pupils until the adhesive is cured, or they could slide out of focus.
75. **Ears:** This design features floppy, stylized ears that can move with the actor. These have an interior support and are hinged at the joint. Insert long bolts into the tubing and secure with epoxy putty. Then bolt into the head with a "joint" rectangular washer. This will keep the ears from sagging (Figure 14-65).
76. Contour trim the fur with small scissors or electric shears, then attach the eyebrows (Figure 14-66).
77. To style fur, use super hold hair spray or workable fixative.
78. Optional: airbrush any details such as whisker indentations and eye and lip shadows.
79. Optional: attach feathery tufts for sympathetic movement (Figure 14-67)
80. Figure 14-68 Shows the finished mask.

FIGURE 14-64 *A) Eye shapes sanded and attached to dowel rods; B) eyes painted with several layers of matte white spray paint. black felt or craft foam can be used to accent the eyes; C) pupils attached to white foundations and mounted to the head*

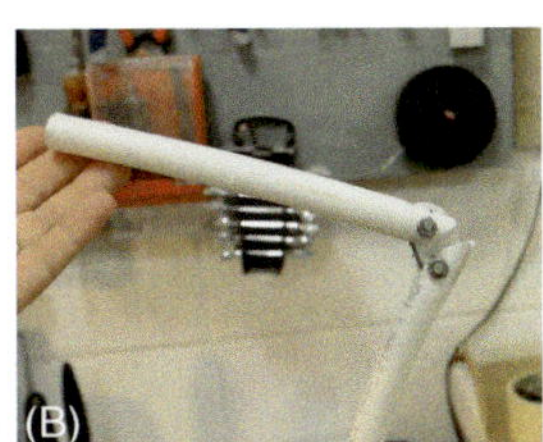
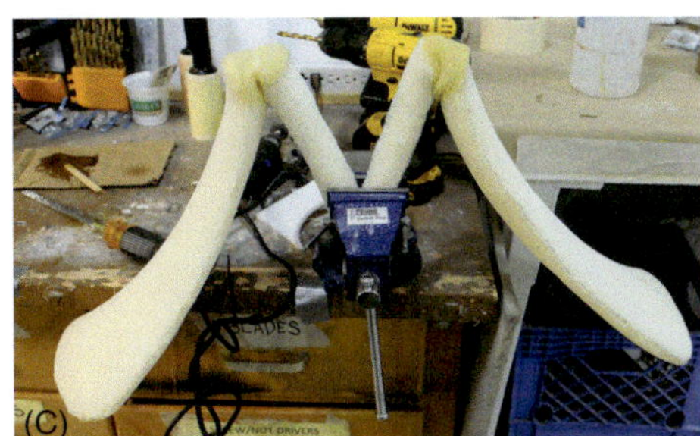
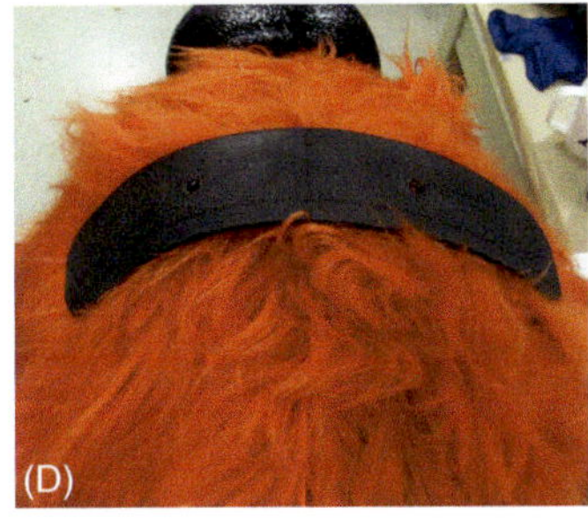
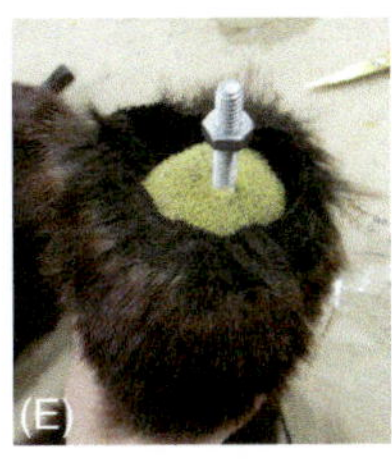
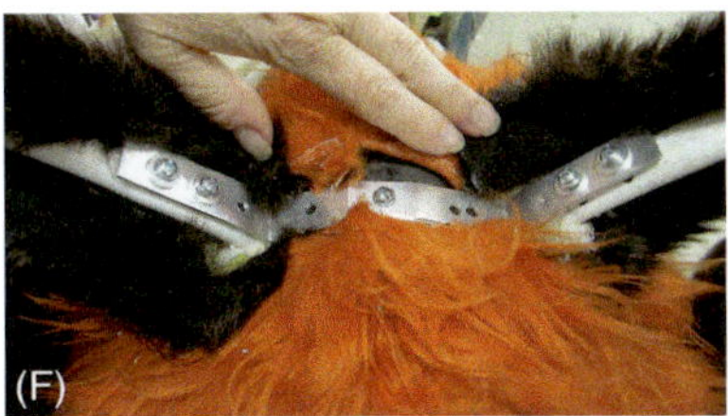

FIGURE 14-65 *A) Foundation for floppy ears; B) jointed with washers so ears will move freely; C) ears covered with foam; D) rectangular washer to support the ears. cut two; E) bolts inserted in foundation tubing, then foam is glued over the end. fur is then glued after that; F) use metal brackets or make your own out of one-eighth-inch aluminum. push bolts through outer washer plate through to the interior plate, then finish with lock nuts or lock washers and nuts. if the ears were heavier, then an interior support attached to the head ring, would be recommended*

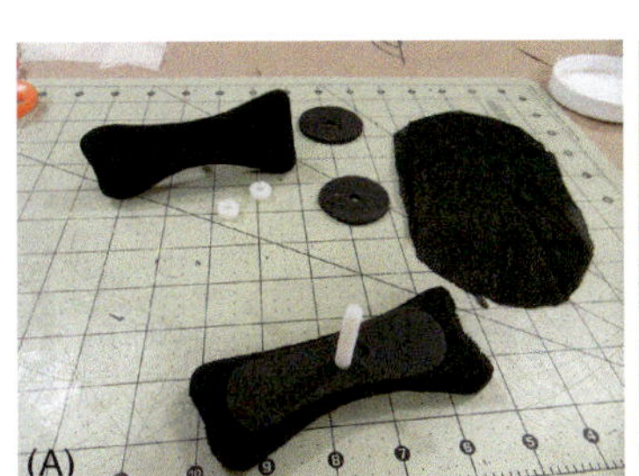

FIGURE 14-66 *A) Eva foam brows attached with sintra plates with preglued bolts. the brows are covered with stretch mesh; B) all parts attached*

FIGURE 14-68 *A and B) Finished mask*

FIGURE 14-67 *Sample of gluing individual feathers into fur*

MASK PROJECT 4: FOAM MARDI GRAS MASKS

Mixed-media Mardi Gras masks

These flat cartoon masks are easy to make and great fun (see Figure 14-69). These were used for a dance piece with black light costumes. These could be painted, or other foam could be used that might be dyed to show up in black light.

FIGURE 14-69 *Final designs*

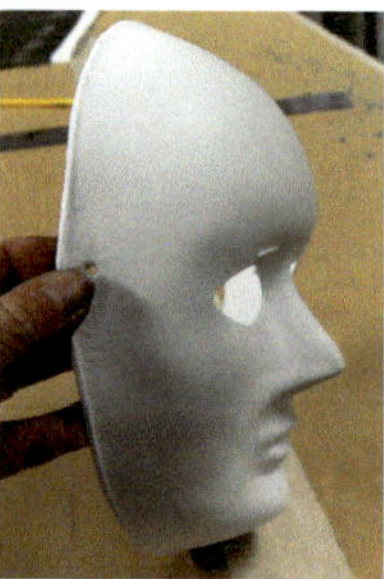

FIGURE 14-70 *Paper mask foundation*

1. Start with a mask foundation. This could be a vacuform plastic mask, a mask made from papier mâché, or a premade compressed paper mask (Figure 14-70).
2. Prefit the mask, trim, pad, and line with comfortable fabric as needed. The eyes and nose openings might need to be adjusted to the wearer's needs.
3. If you are using a plastic mask, lightly sand the surface and remove dust. Paint the foundation black using flat black acrylic or Krylon spray paint (see Figure 14-71).
4. Enlarge the mask designs on a photocopier or by hand to the scale to the desired size. **Note:** The bigger the enlargement, the more structure the mask will need to support the pieces.
5. Cut out the patterns and trace them onto the desired foam material. The foam used for these masks is one-eighth-inch EVA foam.
6. Cut one set of shapes out of the colored foam and another out of black foam. The black foam is to add structure the back of the colored foam. Adhere the shapes together using contact cement.
7. Using the facial features as a guide and being careful not to block the eye openings in the mask foundation, glue foam squares (they can range in thickness and size from half an inch up depending on the desired depth) to the mask, to visually distance the features from the foundation and to support the features.
8. Glue the facial features to the foam squares using contact cement.
9. To add additional visual depth, cut layers of black netting (three or four layers). The netting acts as a shadow between the black foundation and the colorful foam.
10. The netting is glued between the mask under the foam features.
11. To add extended eyebrows or antennae, using 20- or 18-gauge wire, make a small loop at one end and sandwich it between the colored foam and the other piece of black backing foam.
12. Thread the opposite end of the wire through the netting wreath and make a larger loop. Flatten the loop to lay flat against the foundation, then sandwich the flattened

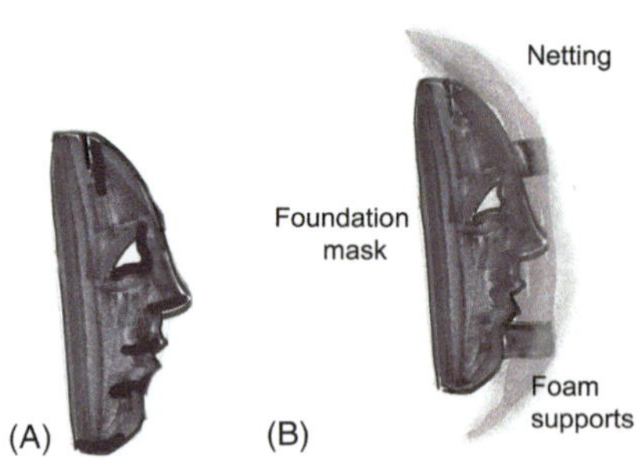

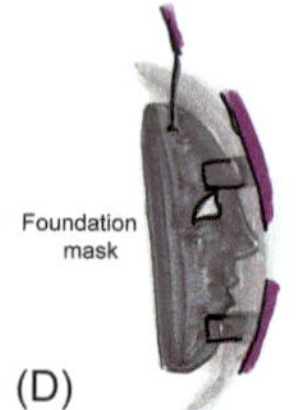

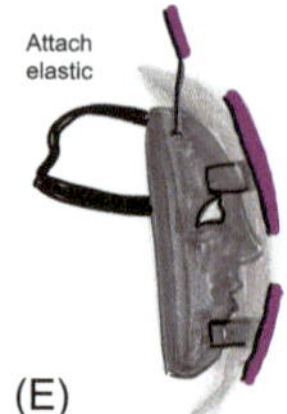

FIGURE 14-71 *A) Store purchased mask foundation painted black; B) diagram of beginning structures. The foam spacers/supports will need to be placed wherever the craft foam facial parts need to go; C) paper patterns taken from designs and enlarged to cut the foam; D) craft foam facial parts glued to spacers/supports with contact cement. note the eyebrow is supported with a black wire; E) attach black elastic as a strap around the head and one strap going down the center of the head*

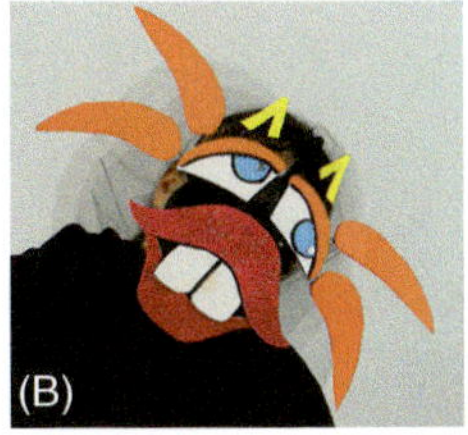

FIGURE 14-72 *A and B) Finished masks*

loop against the mask with a piece black foam. Fasten it in place with contact cement.

13. Figure 14-72 shows the finished masks.

MASK PROJECT 5: JACOB MARLEY

Latex

This was a recent design for West Virginia Public Theatre's *Christmas Carol*. We wanted a desiccated, scarry Jacob Marley. The mask had a lower chin attachment that allowed for movement. The design ended up being very zombie-like (Figures 14-73 and 14-74).

1. Construction on a latex mask needs to start with a foundation sculpt, and since this was for a series of future actors, I found a larger generic form. This mask had a separate chin attachment that was built later. Use makeup latex as opposed to mask latex because it allows more flexibility.
2. The design was sculpted in water-based clay, but any clay could have been used.
3. To provide a protective skin, it was coated with Crystal Clear Glaze.
4. Prepping the sculpt for a two-part hydrocal plaster (stone) mold. Plaster is the desired material because the process involves "slip-casting," that is, filling the mold and leaving it so that a skin forms as the moisture absorbs into the plaster (Figure 14-75).
5. Cast the clay sculpt front (Figure 14-76).
6. Prep the back for casting, then repeat the steps in Figure 14-77 to finish the mold.
7. Open mold and clean out the clay. Wash out mold halves with dish soap and water. Using a toothbrush and a one-inch chip brush may help to remove clay from small nooks and crannies. Let mold halves dry in front of a heater, a fan, in the sun, or, if the mold is small enough, in a low-temperature oven.
8. Surform any sharp edges.

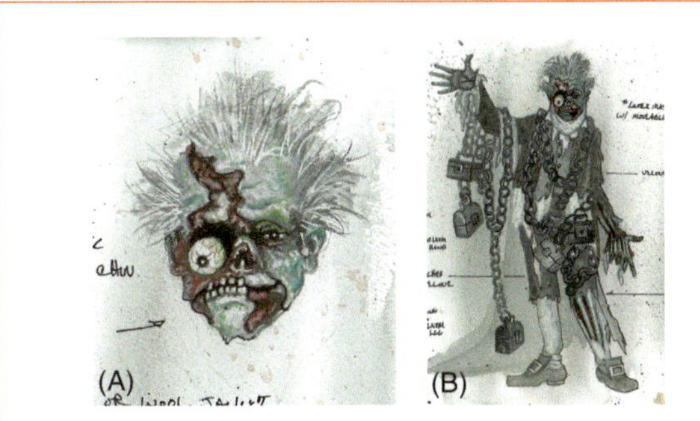

FIGURE 14-73 *A and B) Final mask with costume design*

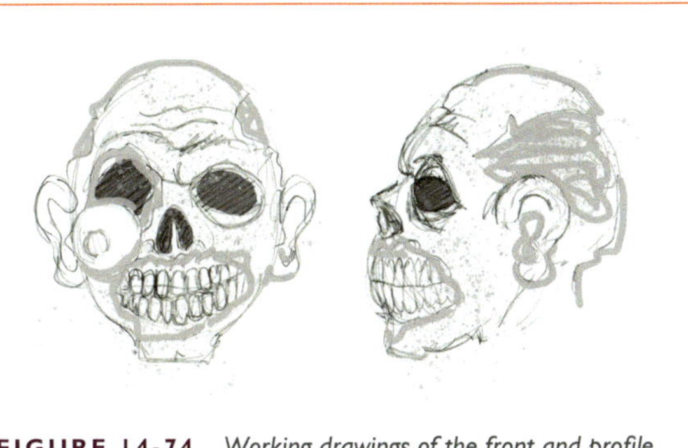

FIGURE 14-74 *Working drawings of the front and profile for sculpting reference*

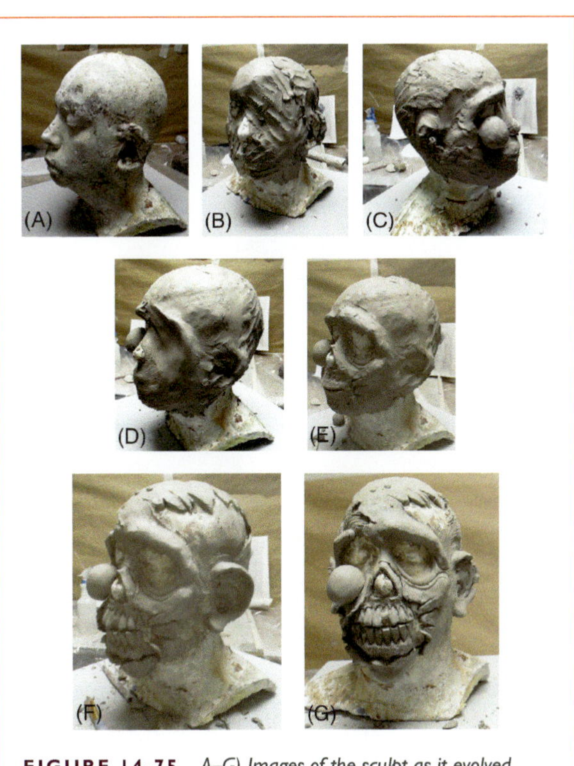

FIGURE 14-75 *A–G) Images of the sculpt as it evolved*

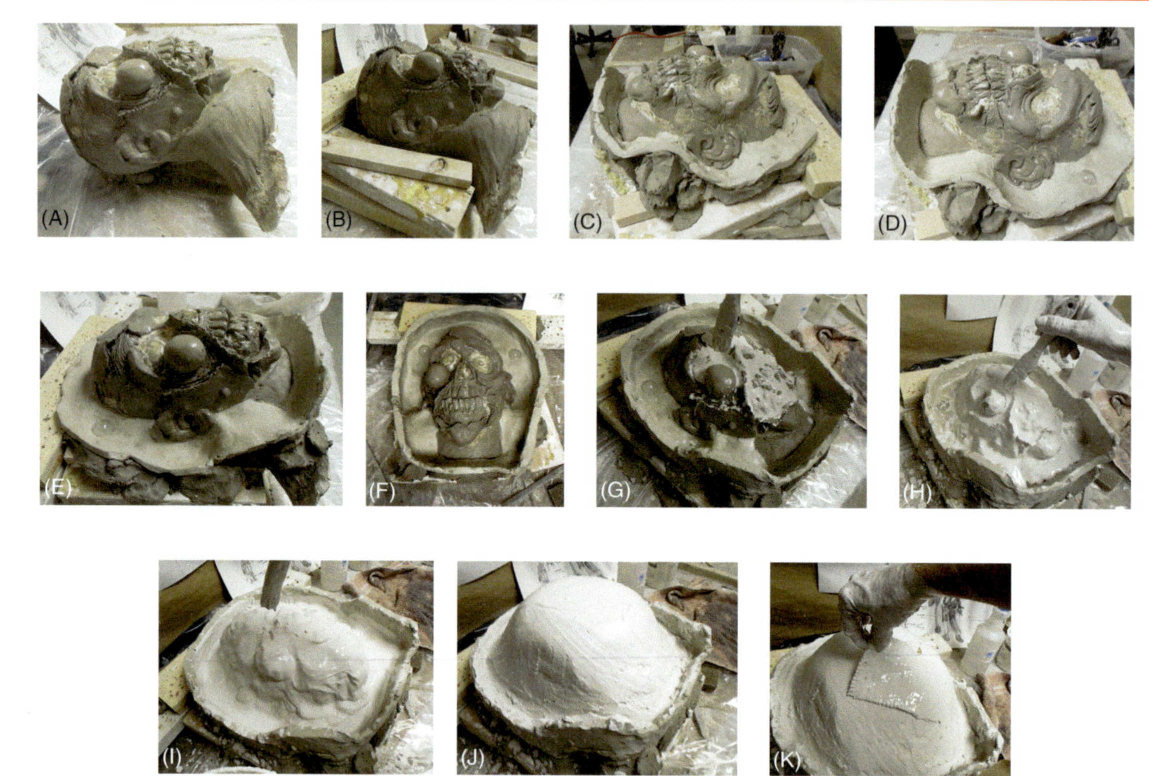

FIGURE 14-76 *A–K) Casting the front half of the sculpt. The first layer is the "splash coat." The second layer can include burlap squares or lose hemp fibers. the third layer is to smooth and shape the mold*

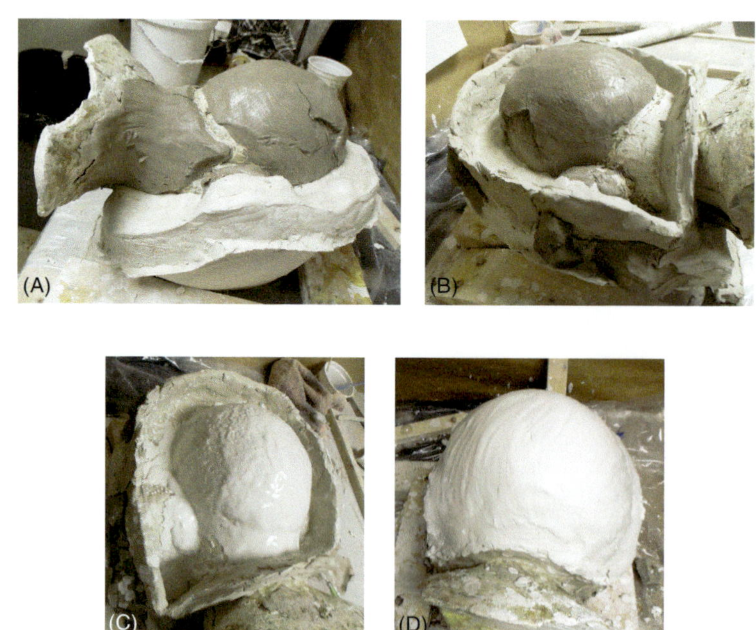

FIGURE 14-77 *A–D) Casting the back half of the sculpt. repeat all previous steps. make sure to add vaseline to any exposed plaster areas or the plaster with fuse*

9. Strap or clamp the mold together. If there is a fear of leaking, clay or hot glue may be used along the seams.
10. Place the closed and sealed mold on a stable surface such as a bucket, then fill the mold with liquid latex. As it fills, gently shake and tilt the mold to release any air bubbles.
11. Let the latex sit for approximately 45 minutes to an hour. The thickness of the latex skin can be assessed my checking the neck area.
12. When a thickness over 3/32 inches has been reached, pour the remaining latex back into the original container. Turn the mold upside down and let the excess latex drain in a bucket, a plastic lid or onto paper. Propping the mold up on scrap wooden blocks is also helpful. Let the mold stand overnight or until latex in the mold is not gooey to the touch.
13. Powder the inside of the latex mask with corn starch or baby powder. Use a chip brush or a powder puff to distribute powder.
14. Remove the clamps and strapping. If hot glue was used, it should be pulled off the seams, but if it is not coming away, add a bit of 99% alcohol to flash-freeze it, and the glue (which is plastic) will pull away. Pop open the mold halves, powder the inside, and carefully work the latex mask out of the mold. Use a blunt tool such as a popsicle stick to help wiggle out any stubborn areas.
15. When removed, powder the outside and stuff the mask with polybatting or place it on a small head form.
16. Using small scissors and a Dremel tool, trim seams, eye and ear holes, excess neck material, and any vent areas as needed (Figure 14-78).
17. Call actor in for a preliminary fitting. Trim and pad inside as needed.

TIP BOX

Patching Seams

a. Fill with cotton and latex (you can also use Pro's-Aide and cotton) and press gently in place with a metal tool.
b. Precast latex skin grafts in the plaster mold, powder, and peel off. Apply a thin layer of Pro's-Aide adhesive and carefully lay patch over the flawed area.
c. Make a putty with cabosil and Pro's-Aide. Fill and smooth on the area with a metal tool. Clean tools often with water or 99% alcohol.

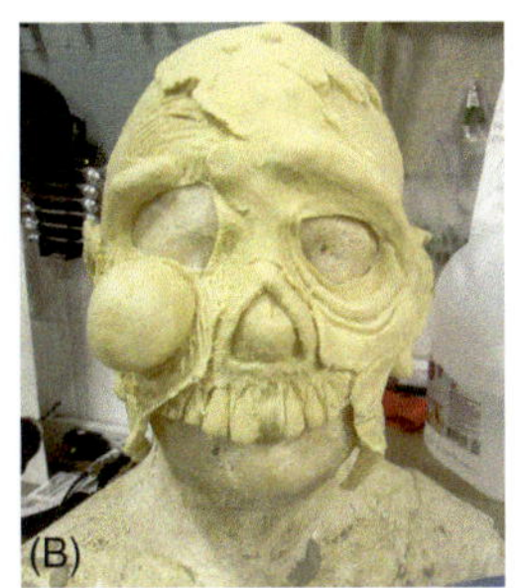

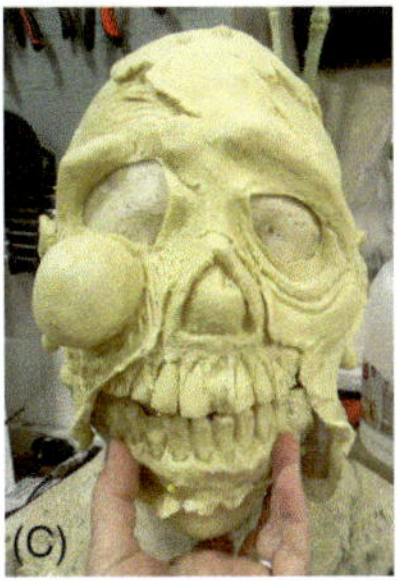

FIGURE 14-78 *A) The lower jaw cut away and pinned back in place for the fitting; B) front view without the lower jaw. eye sockets and any excess flashing are trimmed and cleaned up; C) lower jaw held in place*

18. Add any textural details as needed with cotton or fabric and latex.
19. Add vision port material in the form of black netting or screen (Figure 14-79).
20. **Painting:** The mask is painted with *lacryl* (see Chapter 10 and Figure 14-80). Adding glitter also helps make the green skin look slimy. It was important to paint the mask with severe contrast and color as it was for a big theater venue. The pupil is covered with large sequins to catch the light.
21. Add the head cloth (Figure 14-81).
22. Figure 14-82 shows the final mask and character in performance.

FIGURE 14-79 *Black stretch netting is used to mask the missing eye*

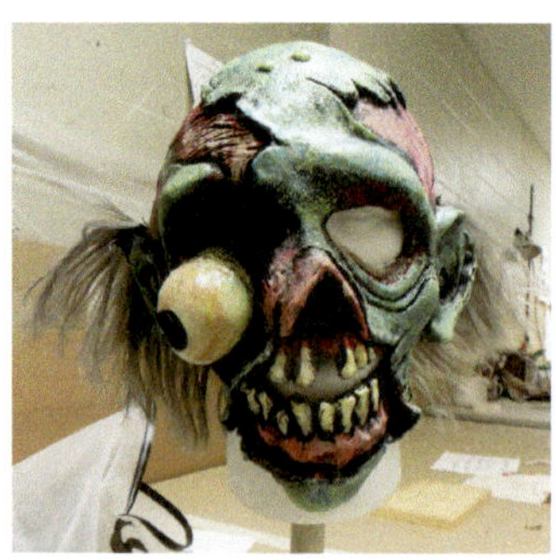

FIGURE 14-80 *Painted mask with high value color and contrast with hair attached*

FIGURE 14-82 *Character in performance*

FIGURE 14-81 *Head cloth attached*

MASK PROJECT 6: NEOPRENE COMEDIA-STYLE HALF MASK

Neoprene

Though Commedia-style masks are based on a standard group of characters, there are still many variations that can be achieved within the descriptive framework. This design is based on *Pantalone*, which is traditionally an older character with a large nose (Figure 14-83).

1. Just as with a latex mask, construction of a neoprene mask needs to start with a foundation sculpt.
2. The design was sculpted in water-based clay, but any clay could have been used (Figure 14-84).
3. When the sculpt is complete, coat it with Gloss Crystal Clear Glaze.

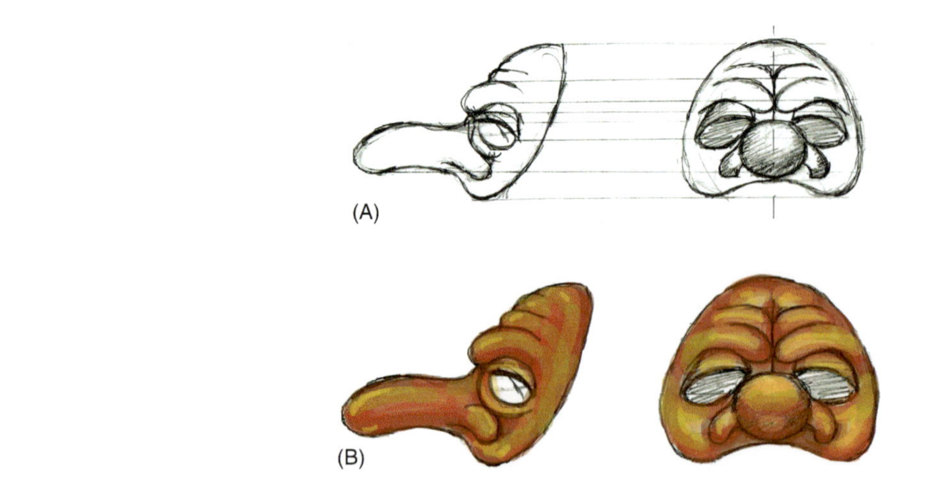

FIGURE 14-83 *A) Sketch; and B) final design*

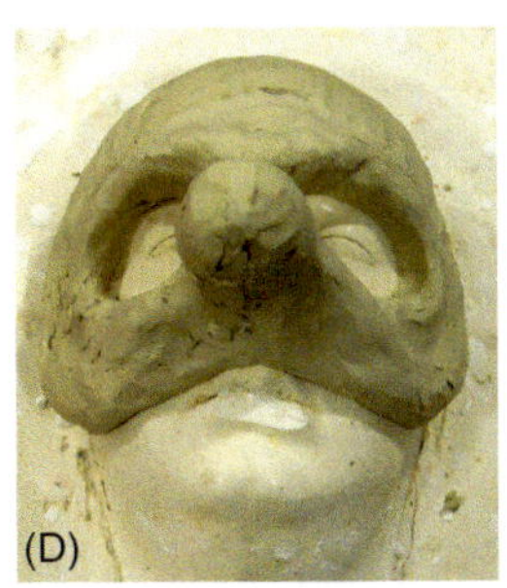
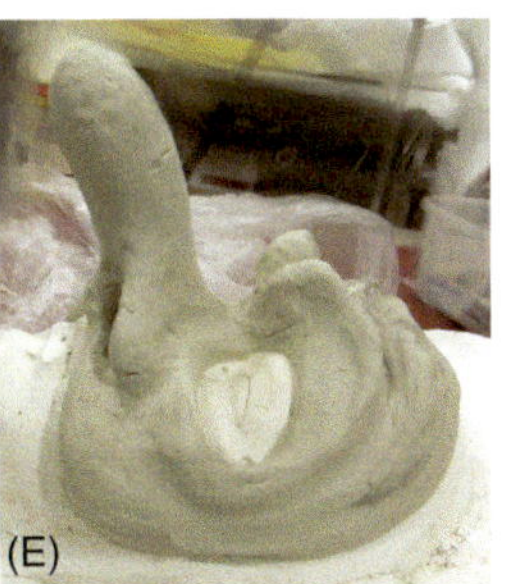

FIGURE 14-84 *A) Plaster positive of human face; B) framing the sculpt; C) filling in with clay; D) shape roughed in; E) final shape waiting for finishing*

4. This is a one-part hydrocal plaster mold. If there are especially extreme undercuts, then a two-part mold would be the better choice. Just as with latex, plaster is the desired material because the process involves "slip-casting," that is, filling the mold and leaving it so that a skin forms as the moisture absorbs into the plaster.
5. Build the clay mold walls. Using a rolling board with three-quarter-inch-thick precut sides is very helpful and will speed up the process (Figure 14-85).
6. Coat any exposed plaster with Vaseline (Figure 14-86). Drape plastic around the outside too.

FIGURE 14-85 *A rolling board, helpful for making neat molds with even thickness*

7. Just as with the latex mask, this is a "controlled pour." Add layer one: the "splash coat." Next prepare burlap squares and mix a second batch of plaster, then add this to the cast. Add the third and final layer of plaster (Figure 14-87).
8. Lift the clay off the mold and clean out the clay (Figure 14-88). Surform the mold edges, then put the mold in the sink to wash out excess clay. After the mold is dry, brush on a couple layers of 99% alcohol and wipe clean, then let it dry in front of a heater or a fan, in the sun, or if the mold is small enough, in a low-temperature oven.
9. Make a cardboard plug or build up a wall of plaster for the lower part of the mold. Hot glue the cardboard in place (Figure 14-89).
10. Place the mold on a stable surface such as a bucket, then fill the mold with neoprene. As it fills, gently shake the mold to release any air bubbles. Fill the mold to the top edge (Figure 14-90).
11. Let the latex sit for approximately 1 hour. This process may need to be repeated and the time increased, depending on the material and how damp the mold is. The thickness of the neoprene skin can be assessed by checking the top edge.

FIGURE 14-86 *A) Vaseline any exposed plaster; B) beginning of the mold wall; C) plastic surrounds the area to keep the surfaces neat*

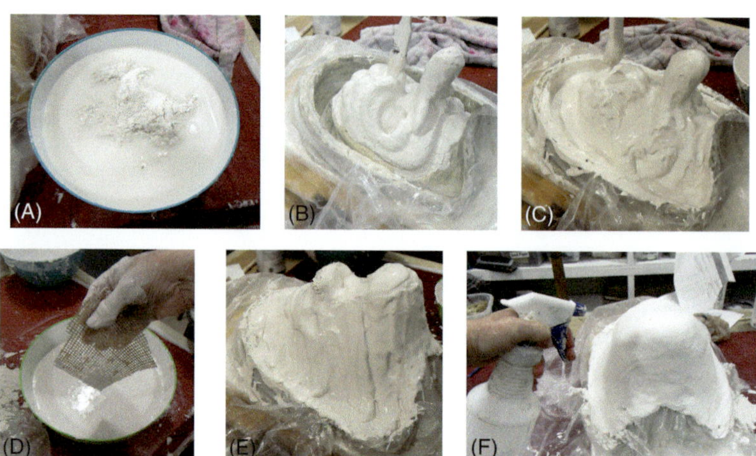

FIGURE 14-87 *A) The illusive "dry creek bed" look of plaster ready to mix; B) lightly dabbing plaster "splash coat" with a chip brush; C) "splash coat" thickening up; D) burlap layer for a second batch; E) finishing the burlap layer; F) final finishing layer smoothed with a spritz of water*

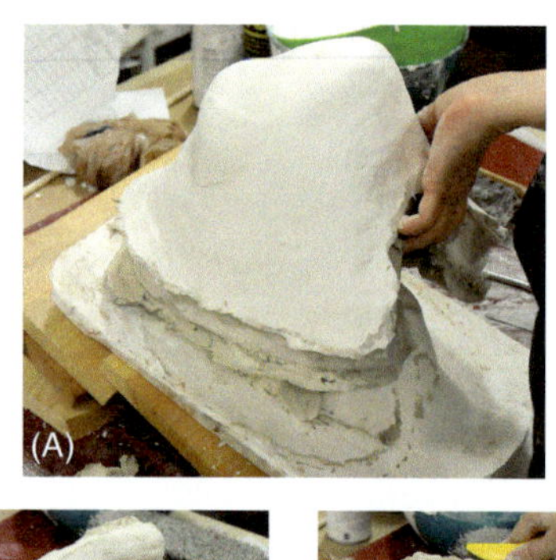

FIGURE 14-88 *A) Clay has been pulled off and the mold is pried upward; B) pulling clay out of the negative; C) using a surform tool to smooth sharp edges of the mold*

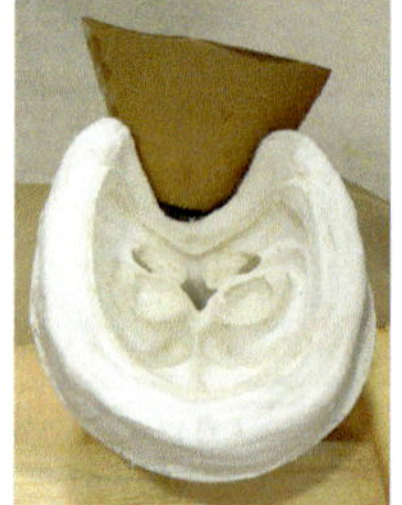

FIGURE 14-89 *Cardboard plug (or clay) may be hot glued into a void to create a bowl shape to hold neoprene*

FIGURE 14-90 *Neoprene poured into the bowl-shaped negative. Top off as it absorbs into the plaster and sinks downward*

12. When a thickness of just over 1/16 inch (but not over 1/8th inch) has been reached, pour the remaining neoprene back into the original container. Turn the mold upside down and let the excess drain out. This could be in a bucket or a plastic lid or onto paper. Propping the mold up on scrap wooden blocks covered with plastic is also helpful. Let the mold stand overnight or until the neoprene in the mold is not gooey to the touch.
13. Unlike latex, neoprene will become stiffer as it cures, so be sure to remove it from the mold no later than a day after pouring, or it may break the mold when it is removed. Powder the inside of the neoprene mask with corn starch or baby powder. *Use a chip brush or a powder puff to distribute powder.*
14. Carefully work the neoprene mask out of the mold. Use a blunt tool such as a popsicle stick or a butter knife to help wiggle out any stubborn areas. It is possible to squeeze and pull on the material to get it out of the mold if needed. Then reform with your fingers and stuff with a firmly packed material or use sand to reform.

15. Figure 14-91 shows the newly released neoprene mask. **Note:** To prevent warping, put it on the face cast as it continues to cure.

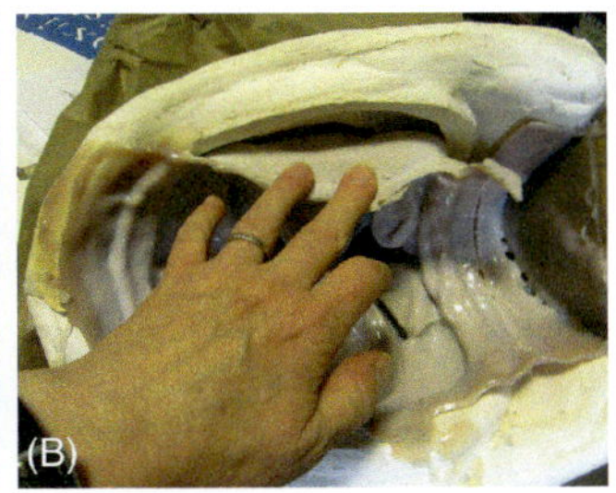

FIGURE 14-91 *A) Neoprene ready to be pulled out of a mold. Powder first to prevent it from sticking to itself; B) the mask is still curing but flexible enough to pull away from undercuts*

16. Before it cures and hardens completely, small scissors, an X-Acto, or a razor blade may be used to trim any irregularities, eyes, nostril holes, and excess material (flashing) at the edges (Figure 14-92).

17. Patch any flaws with epoxy putty or Bondo, then when cured, sand the surface lightly with fine sandpaper.

18. **Painting:** As with latex, it is possible to mix a small amount of neoprene, distilled water, and the foundation color to create paint that will adhere to itself. This formula bridges the gap between materials. Take painted finish past the edges and just inside the mask. Apply foundation layer of color (Figure 14-93). Then proceed with acrylic paint for dry brush, wet-on-wet or airbrush techniques as desired. Finish with fine brush or airbrush details.

19. After the paint has dried, seal with at least three layers of spray varnish.

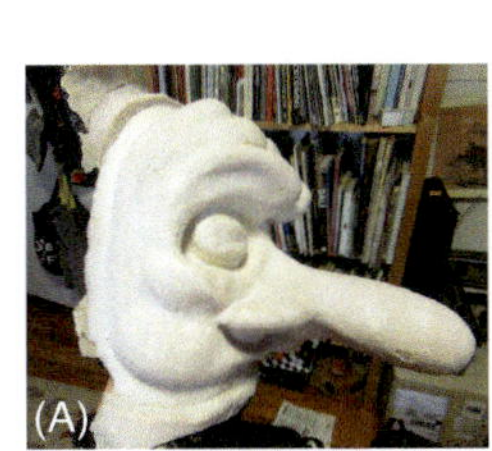

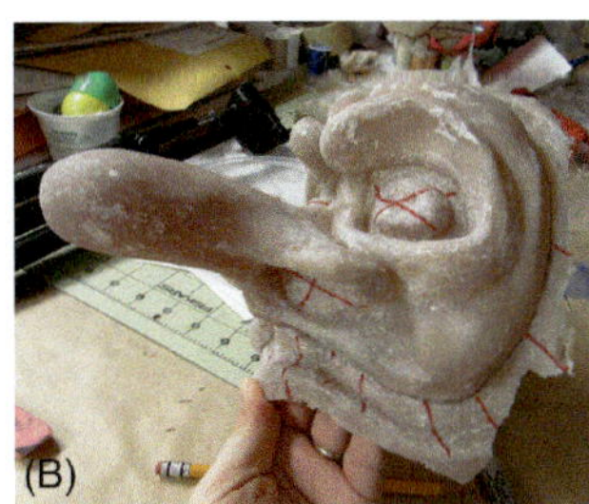

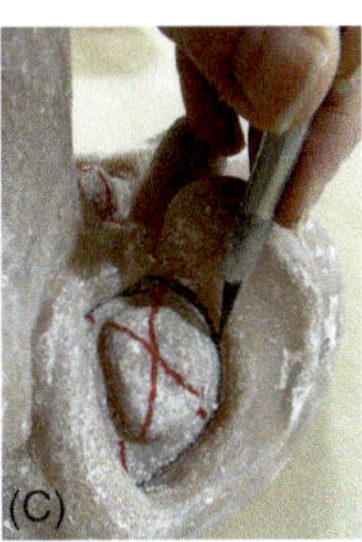

FIGURE 14-92 *A) Fresh mask newly pulled from the mold; B) a Nearly cured mask that is therefore hardened. The x's indicate areas to trim; C) cutting with an x-acto knife*

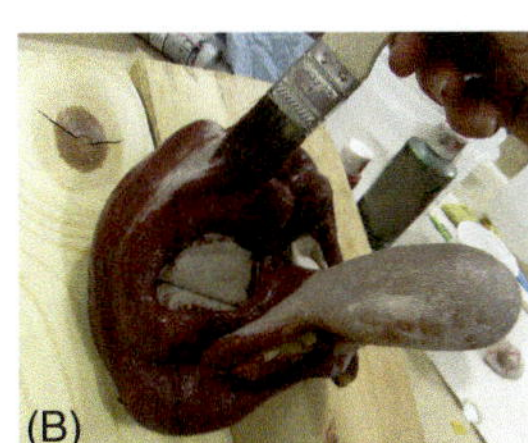

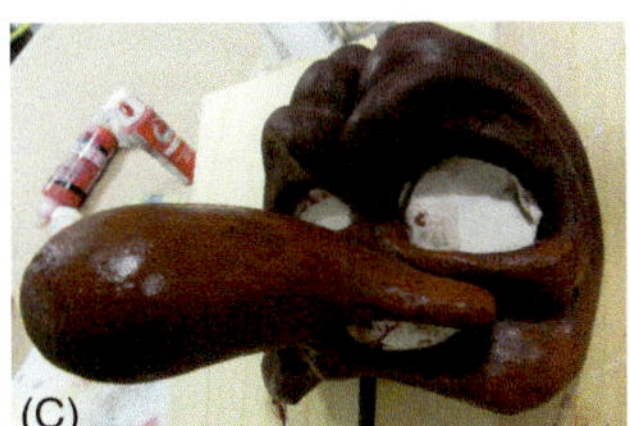

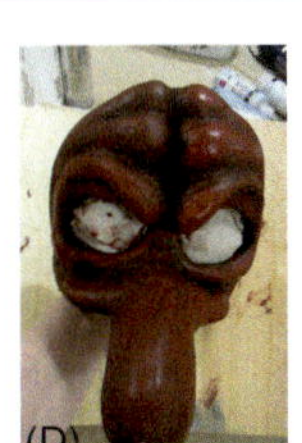

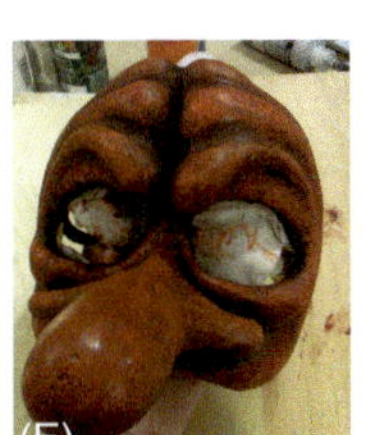

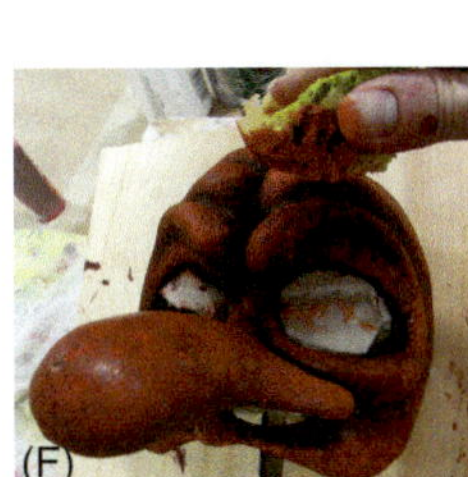

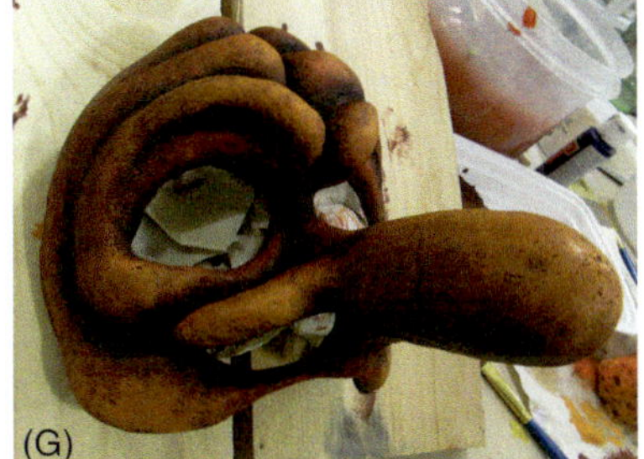

FIGURE 14-93 *A) Sanding with fine sandpaper; B) base painting with acrylic paint mixed with 10% neoprene; use only distilled water to dilute; C) adding more red; D) low lights blended in the folds; e) blending in orange highlights; F) using a sponge to hit the high points; G) painting complete; seal with a clear coat*

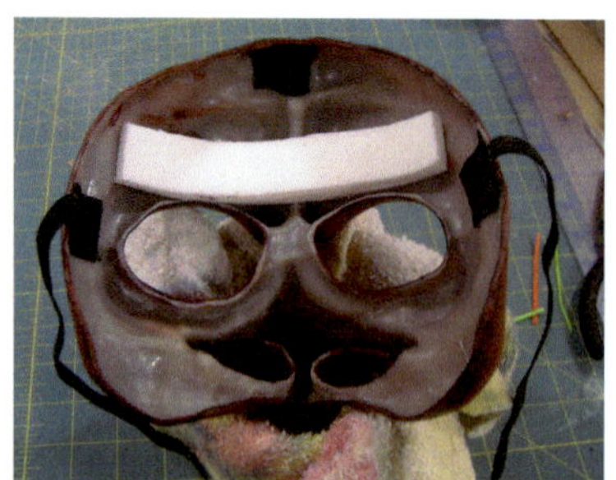

FIGURE 14-94 *Adding padding*

20. **Padding the inside:** Before starting this process, make sure to place the newly painted surface into a padded bowl or box to protect the decorative side.
21. Add padding to the forehead, cheeks, and around the eyeholes as needed. Use EVA or polyether foam and adhere with contact cement (Figure 14-94).
22. Attach elastic tight enough to stay firmly on the head, but not leave marks on the skin (Figure 14-95). A center strap over the head might also be needed for stability. Punch or drill two or three holes into the mask on the sides and stitch the elastic in place. Gluing with contact cement and then stitching through the holes helps to reinforce the strap attachment. Double the thread when sewing.
23. After the padding is complete, line with chamois for soft finish (Figure 14-95).
24. Figure 14-96 shows the finished mask, which looks like leather.

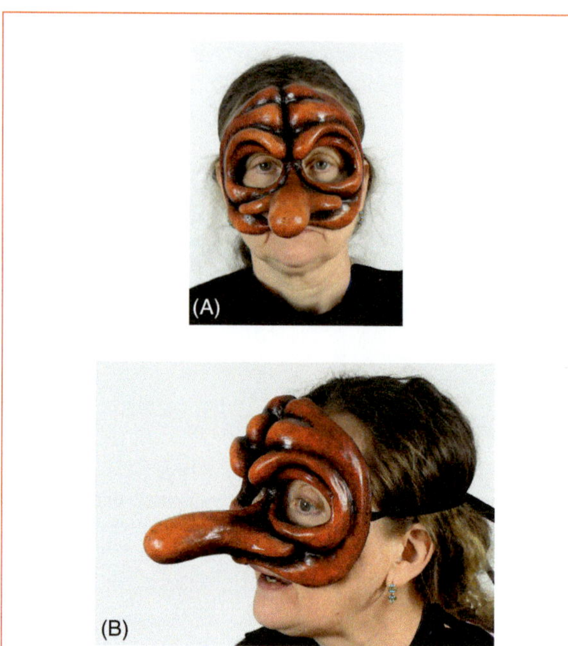

FIGURE 14-96 *The finished mask*

MASK PROJECT 7: NEOPRENE LION MASK

This is a larger style neoprene mask. The design is reminiscent of iconic medieval motifs and concrete sculptures (Figure 14-97).

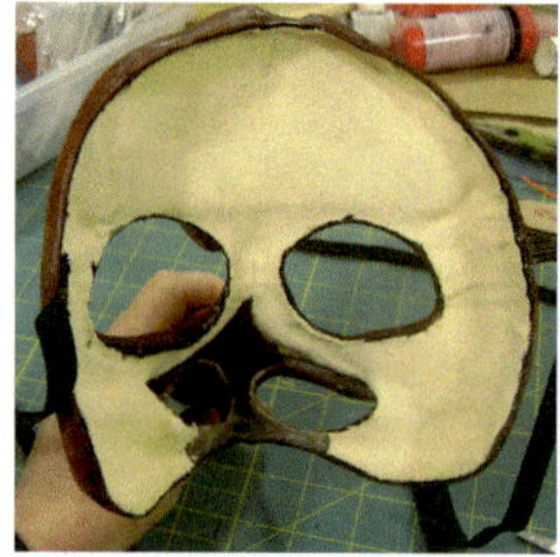

FIGURE 14-95 *Chamois is a soft sheep skin that is comfortable against the face*

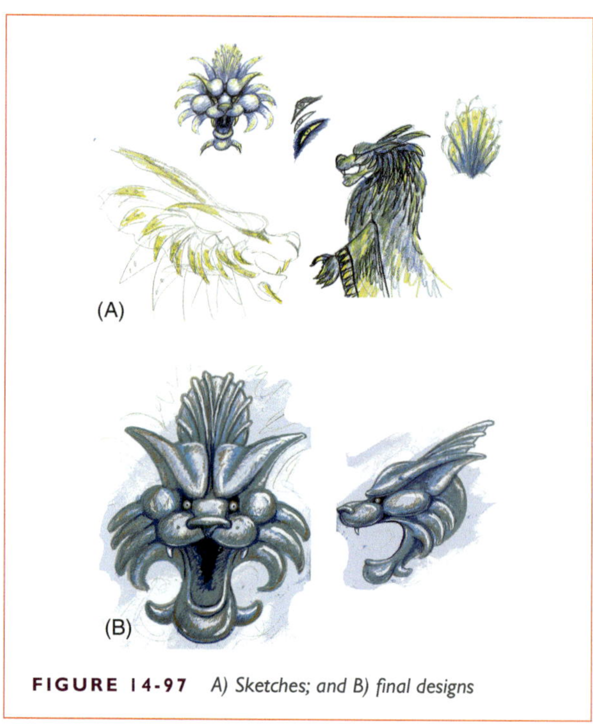

FIGURE 14-97 *A) Sketches; and B) final designs*

This project uses the same process as the Commedia mask, but many of the pieces are cast and attached separately (Figure 14-98).

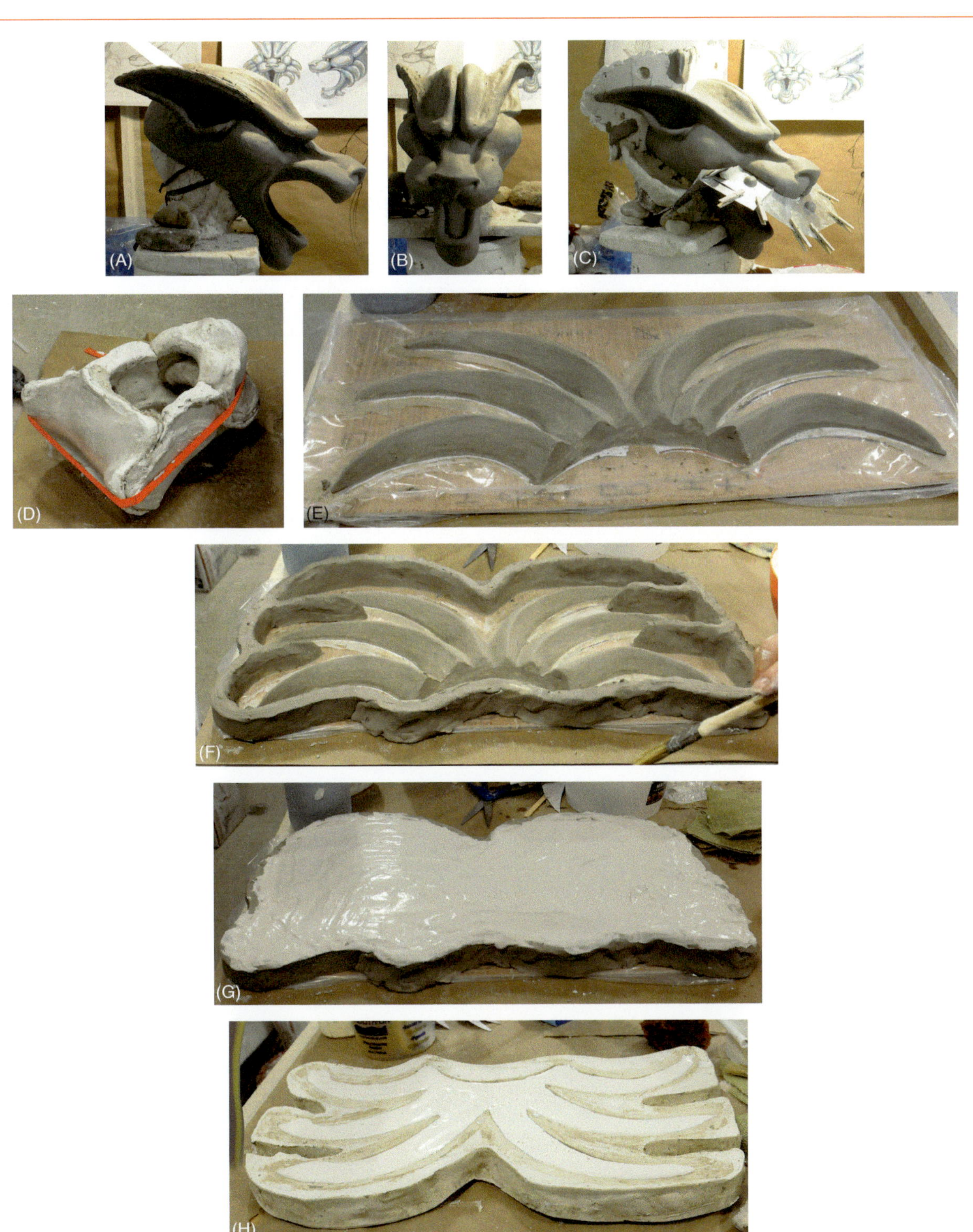

FIGURE 14-98 *A) Side view of the water-based clay sculpt; B) front; C) back side of the head is cast and the front is being divided with metal shims for additional mold sections; this is to prevent severe undercuts; D) mold is complete and ready to receive neoprene; E) separate details were sculpted and cast to attach to the mask; F) mold for the sculpt; G) cast with plaster (hydrocal) in three stages with burlap to make a strong mold; H) finished mold with neoprene; I) cast piece has been pulled from the mold. It can retain any shape that it is draped over when in this uncured state; J) cured piece; K) lion mask in process with pieces being attached; L) mask is primed with spray paint; M) mask has been spray painted with several colors; N) acrylic paint accents added; O) plain resin cabochon versus a Mylar and wooden ball eye; P) the final mask (Continued)*

FIGURE 14-98 *(Continued)*

MASK PROJECT 8: INSECT

Fiberglass

With this design, I wanted something translucent and mysterious. The mask covers both eyes (with slits for vision disguised in the wing folds) and mouth. Flying insects are sometimes hairy, slick, powdery, and jointed with a long proboscis and antenna. This version possessed an armor-like quality (Figure 14-99).

1. First decide how the mask should be approached, whether in sections or in one piece. The Insect was a big, delicate shape, so the sculpt needed to be three parts: two wings and the foundation mask.
2. The foundation mask is sculpted in water-based clay (Figure 14-100).
3. When finished, a cardboard pattern helps to capture the shape of the proboscis and how the wings fit into the socket (Figure 14-101).
4. Prepping the clay sculpts for casting in silicone. The silicone mold is called a glove mold
5. Though it could have been left on, the proboscis was cut off to be cast separately.

FIGURE 14-99 *Rough color sketch*

FIGURE 14-100 *The foundation mask*

FIGURE 14-101 *Scrap mat boards used to take a pattern of the sockets to help sculpt the wings*

6. Casting the mother mold with plaster and burlap. If a light-weight mother mold is desired, use fiber glass or silicone and Epoximite (Figure 14-102).
7. Add two to three layers of fiberglass cloth (see Figure 14-103). Let each layer become slightly rigid before adding the next layer. If this mold was being used for injection casting, an opening would need to be made at the end.
8. **Wings:** To provide a sculpting guide, draw the wing shapes before sculpting (Figure 14-104).
9. To accelerate the process of making the wings dimensional, sculpt a base out of foam.
10. Sculpt the wings in clay. Plasticene was used because the sculpting process took a bit longer. Water-based clay might have dried out.
11. Set up to cast the glove mold of the wings in silicone.
12. Cast the mother mold in plaster. If a lighter mother mold material is desired, use fiberglass, Epoximite, or opaque epoxy; one form is called Artcast.
13. **Note:** Add mold wax to any exposed areas that are not silicone, or the resin will stick permanently.
14. Cast the wings with clear epoxy and fabric netting. Keep in mind that the colored resin can overlap and either look fabulous or terrible (Figure 14-105). A blue and yellow tinted layer might turn an undesired green. Note: If a lighter-weight material is desired, use clear Worbla.
15. Pop out and trim wings with Dremel tool. Cut slots into the wings for vision ports.
16. Attach the proboscis, then trim, patch and sand the foundation mask (Figure 14-106).
17. Paint the proboscis with flat black spray paint.
18. Add padding to the interior using EVA and chamois or soft black suede or leather. Black felt can be abrasive to skin.

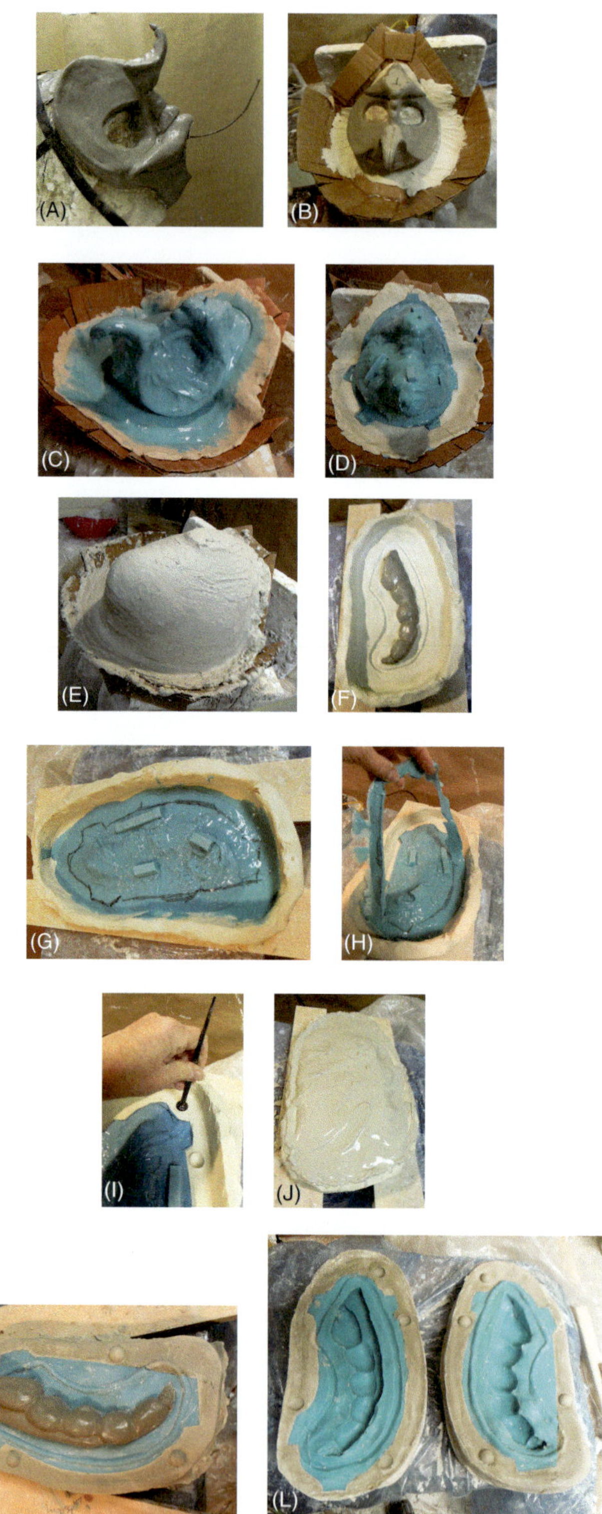

FIGURE 14-102 *A) Proboscis removed; B) clay mold floor built on a quick cardboard foundation; C) casting the mask foundation with silicone; D) silicone mold keys were added to help the blanket mold line up; E) hydrocal mother or blanket mold over silicone; F) half of proboscis being cast with a trough-like mold key surrounding it; G) silicone glove mold with keys added; lines a drawn with a sharpie to indicate where to trim off excess; H) mold trimmed with an x-acto knife, then pulled away for casting with hydrocal; I) additional keys added to help the mold line up; J) one layer of hydrocal for this small blanket mold; K) mold opened and ready to cast side two; L) mold completed and ready for fiberglass*

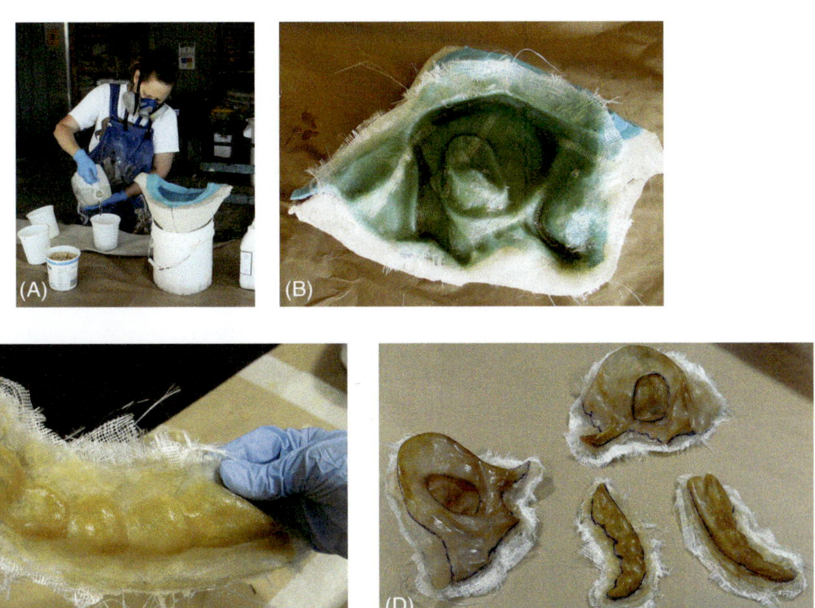

FIGURE 14-103 *A) Wear a respirator, gloves, an apron, and old clothes when working with fiberglass. Mix small amounts, as it can set up quickly in warm weather; B) add a painted layer of resin, then press or massage precut fiber squares into the mold with a resin covered brush. Two or three layers may be needed depending on the object; C) the proboscis cured and taken from the silicone mold; D) all pieces outlined and ready for trimming. wear gloves, an apron, old clothes, goggles, and a respirator when trimming. use a dremel tool*

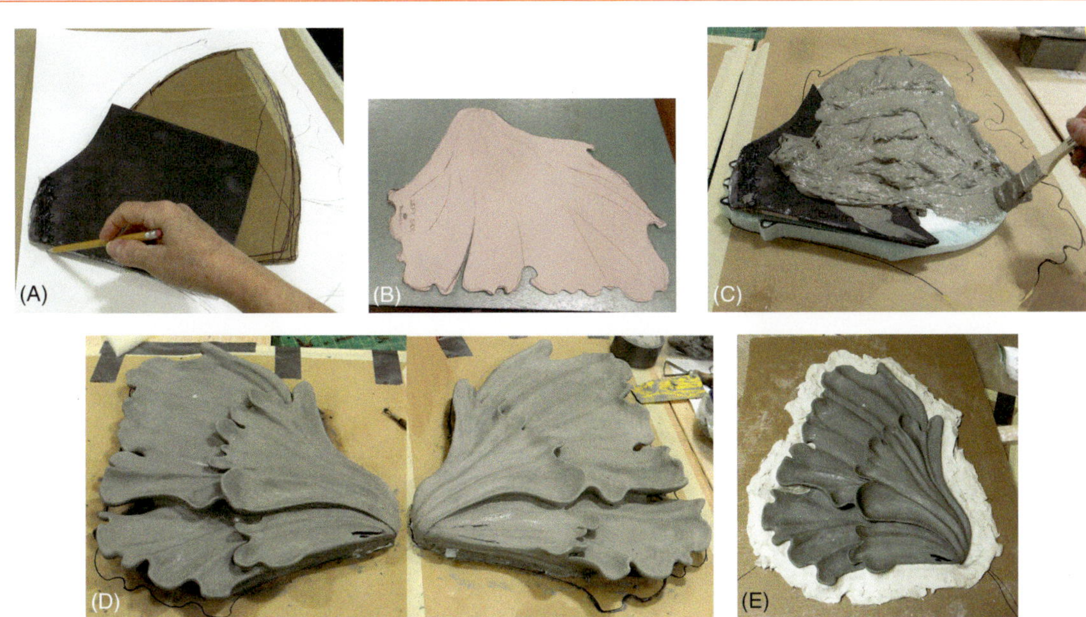

FIGURE 14-104 *A) Using the paper pattern to create a second detailed sculpting pattern; B) finished. Wing pattern. Use this pattern to cut a foundation out of foam; C) using a foam foundation to achieve the desired depth and covering with molten plasticine; D) finished set of wings; E) laying down the foundation of a water-based clay for mold; F) completed mold; G) three thin layers of silicone added, a quarter to a half-inch thick when completed; H) silicone keys premade in small plastic domes; I) trimmed silicone glove mold ready for a blanket mold; J) burlap Added to Reinforce the Mold; K) finished hydrocal mold; L) finished one-part matrix mold; M) both molds complete (Continued)*

FIGURE 14-104 *(Continued)*

19. Attach strapping (Figure 14-107).
20. Glue the wings to the mask (Figure 14-108).
21. Paint with metallic accents on the black foundation mask and on the wings, then seal with clear coat.
22. Figure 14-109 shows the finished mask with the wings attached.

MASK PROJECT 9: DODO BIRD

Mouth mover

It is an unusual experience to walk by someone while wearing a strange mask and then have its mouth move as it squawks. These masks are pretty wonderful, but they would need a wireless microphone to be heard on stage.

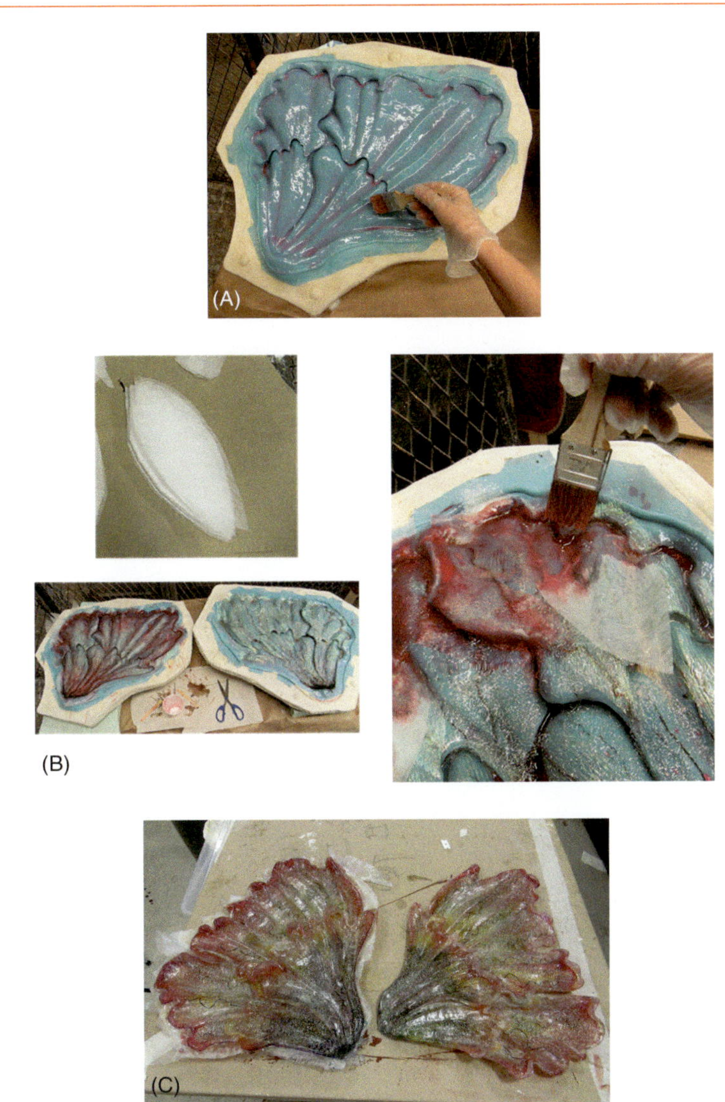

FIGURE 14-105 *(A) Laying on the first gel coat of tinted resin; B) adding layers sheer of cloth, decorative fabrics, and tinted resin. let each layer nearly cure before adding the next; C) final wings. The right wing has been trimmed*

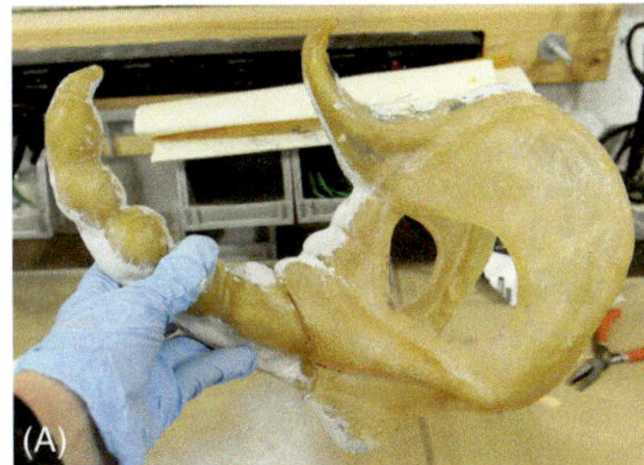

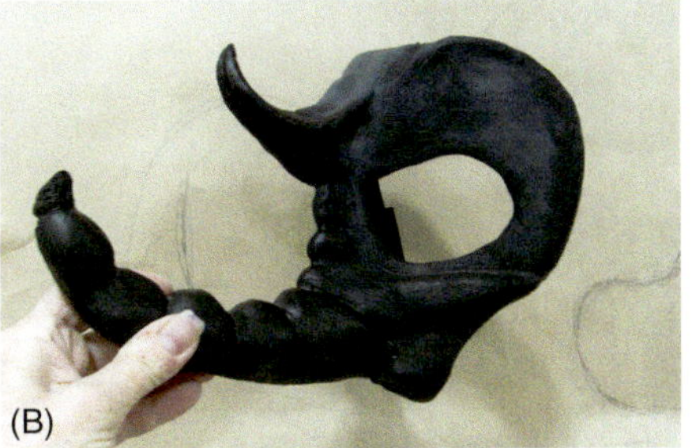

FIGURE 14-106 *(A) Trim and glue the mask together with small plastic tabs on the inside, then apply epoxy putty to patch seams; B) paint the proboscis black with spray paint. This mask is incredibly lightweight and tough*

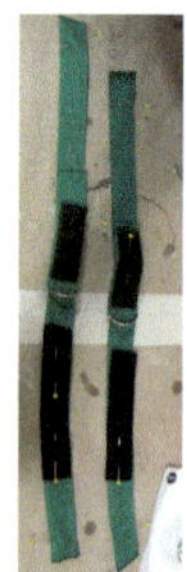

FIGURE 14-107 *Strapping with d-rings and velcro*

FIGURE 14-108 *Gluing wings to foundation mask using epoxy and additional fiber glass on the back*

FIGURE 14-109 *The finished mask*

FIGURE 14-110 *Final design*

Also, because we talk mostly with our lips and not our jaws, the movement is very subtle. Needless to say, the dodo is an extinct bird, and this project's design harkens more to a fantasy interpretation than reality (Figure 14-110).

1. First decide how the mask should be approached: in sections or in one piece. The focus of the construction at this point is the beak and forehead, so the whole shape will be cast with a two-part mold. This mask has vision ports for the wearer nestled between the wide set eyes.
2. The foundation mask is sculpted in water-based clay (Figure 14-111).
3. Prep the clay sculpt for casting in silicone. The sculpt is flipped on its back so as to get the full beak and head in the mold (Figure 14-112).
4. As each side with silicone is cured, cut off the outer flange edges in readiness for the plaster mother mold (Figure 14-113).
5. Cast the mother mold with plaster and burlap (Figure 14-114). If a lightweight mother mold is desired, use fiberglass, opaque epoxy resin, or Epoximite.
6. Repeat the casting process for the second side of the sculpt. Make sure to apply a release agent on the silicone and plaster so the fresh silicone and plaster won't stick to themselves.
7. Remove the sculpt from the silicone and plaster matrix mold (Figure 14-115).
8. This mold could be used for multiple materials: rigid or flexible polyfoam (if a hollow shape is desired, it would need a core mold, and an additional footing for back pressure), fiberglass, liquid plastic (epoxy), papier mâché, thermoplastics, and latex (with patience!). It can be used in halves or closed with bolts and wing nuts or mold straps.

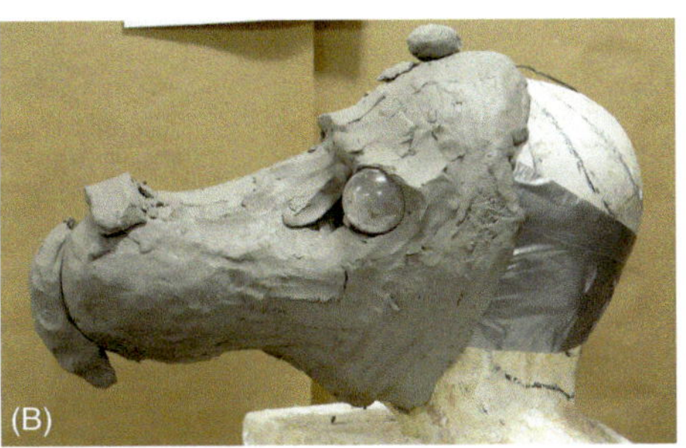

FIGURE 14-111 *A) Mapping out the basic shape; B) adding plastic domes to indicate the eyes; C) Finished sculpt with texture*

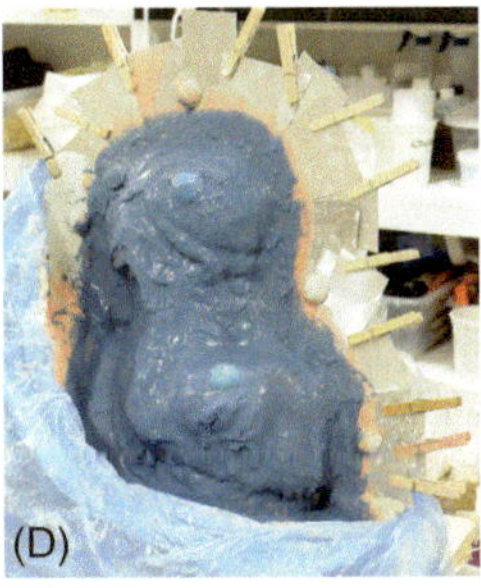

FIGURE 14-112 *A) Lay the sculpt on its back to cast; B) use a Shim metal cut into keystone shapes to divide the sculpt. add clay to bridge the gaps; C) close pins are used to keep the shim from separating; D) silicone glove mold with keys*

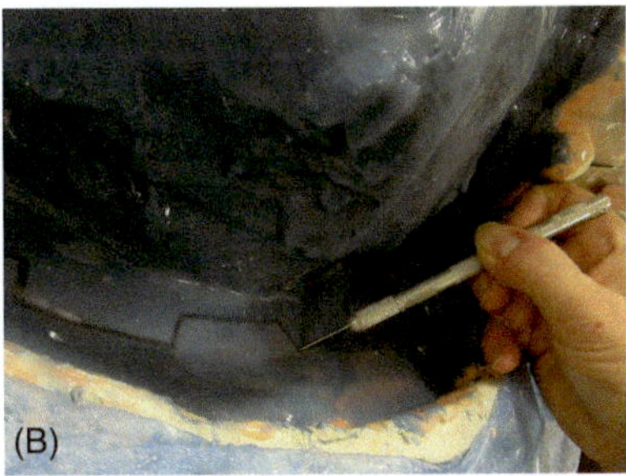

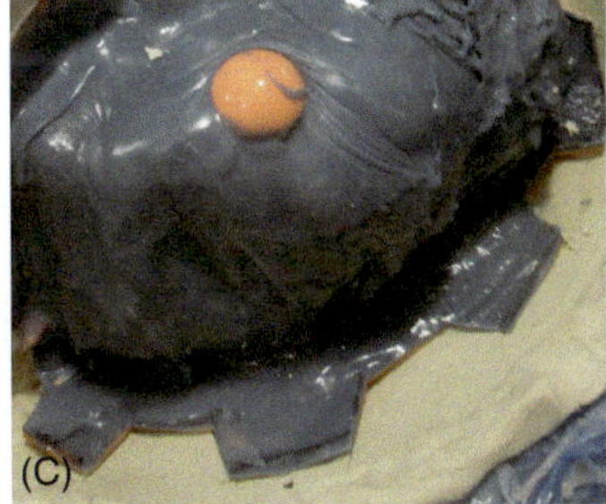

FIGURE 14-113 *A) Sketching the trim lines on the glove mold; B) cutting the excess; C) silicone trimmed and ready for the blanket mold*

FIGURE 14-114 *A) Hydrocal layer with burlap; B) as the layer begins to cure, more can be swiftly added; C) final layer smoothed with a spritz of water; D) the first half of the mold is complete, and the metal shims are removed. Repeat the steps for the second half. Vaseline any exposed plaster; E) second half complete; F) the mold pried apart*

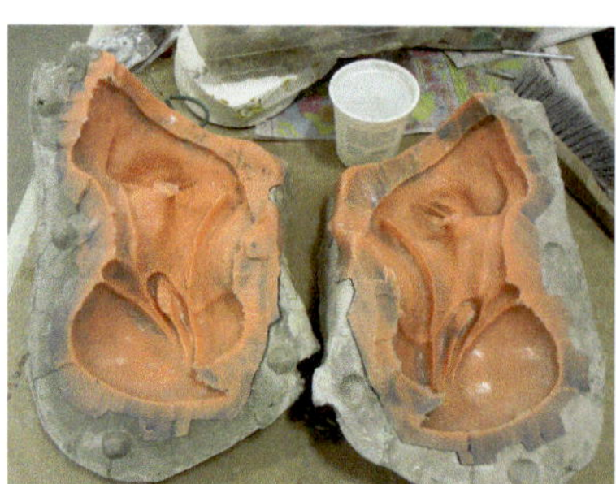

FIGURE 14-115 *Removing the sculpt from the silicone and plaster matrix mold*

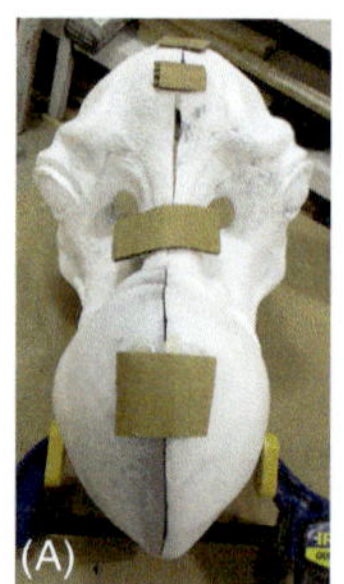

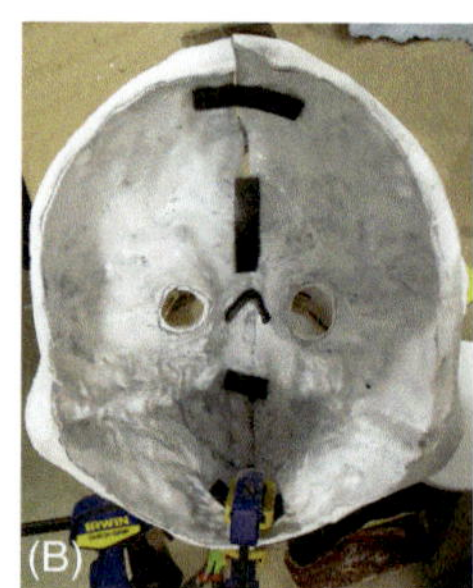

FIGURE 14-117 *A) Any materials may be used for temporarily holding the halves together. To remove hot glue, flash freeze it with 99% alcohol; B) sintra tabs epoxied across the joint*

9. For this mask, I used a two-part liquid plastic (epoxy). It was rotocast and brushed into the mold halves until it cured. Tint each layer of liquid plastic with compatible pigment, so you can tell if each new layer has complete coverage. To make this same mask lighter, use fiberglass, thermoplastic, or papier mâché.

   Note: Work in a ventilated area. Wear a respirator, apron, goggles, gloves, and sleeves when working with epoxy resins.
10. The material is ready to lift out of the mold when it has cooled (Figure 14-116).
11. Trim the flashing from the halves and sand any flaws (Figure 14-117). Cut out the vision ports and nostrils.
12. Tape or hot glue cardboard tabs to hold the halves together then adhere them on the inside with epoxy and plastic tabs. The tabs were heat bent to better fit the convex joint.
13. Patch the seam with epoxy putty. Working fast, details may be sculpted into the surface to match the sculpted texture (Figure 14-118). Sand as needed.

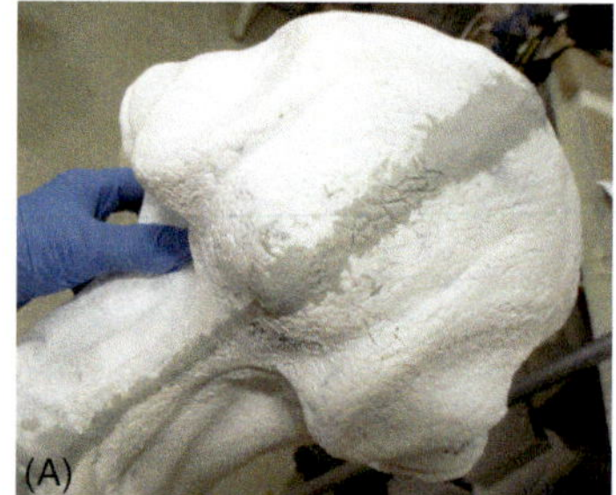

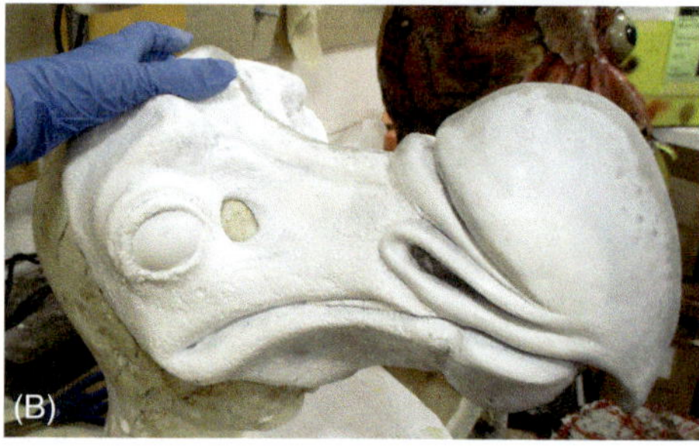

FIGURE 14-118 *A) Use a dental tool or a fine sculpting tool to add fine details; B) mask glued together, patched, and sanded*

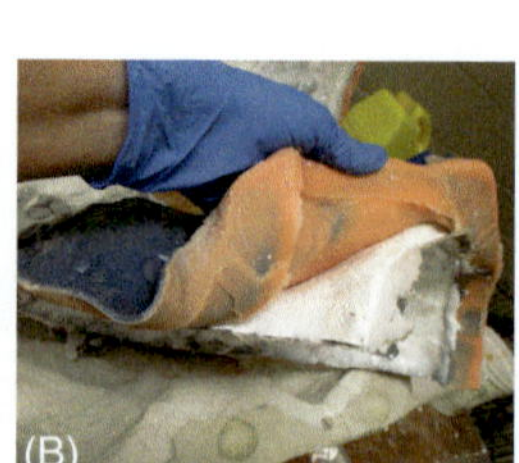

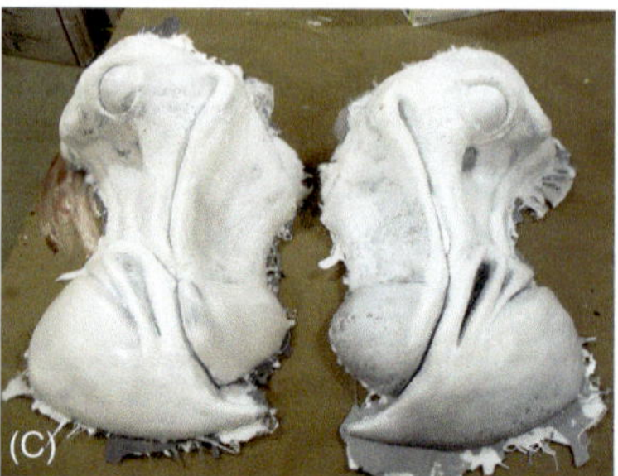

FIGURE 14-116 *A) Rotocasting and brushing on the epoxy resin, two layers; B) peeling back the silicone to reveal the positive; C) both sides pulled out of the silicone mold*

FIGURE 14-119 *Use a Dremel tool to help cut the beak apart*

14. Separate the beak with a dremel (Figure 14-119). Use the aluminum oxide cutting disk and the small carving bit to finesses delicate areas.
15. Patch and sand the beak edges. Add more epoxy putty to round out the edges of the beak as needed.
16. Tape the beak closed to gauge any trimming that might be needed at the joint of the beak (Figure 14-120).
17. Create the aluminum hinge.
18. Attach the hinge. Use lock nuts and washers to secure the rotating hinge joint.
19. Add the springs on either side about 1–2 inches in front of the jointed jaw.
20. Add padding to the interior. Pad the chin area with thin EVA foam for more support and cover with chamois.
21. **Optional:** Create a coif out of EVA foam (Figure 14-121). Add straps with Velcro closure and D-rings at the back under the cranium and over the head. To attach them, hand stitch or use zip ties. If the mask is lightweight, then not much foam is needed for padding.
22. Insert black mesh to mask the vision ports. Adhere the mesh with contact cement inside the mask. This may be done before the padding/coif is inserted or after, depending on the mask.
23. Mask the spring with spandex and line the mouth (Figure 14-122). The mouth lining is optional because the mouth doesn't open enough to see the inside.

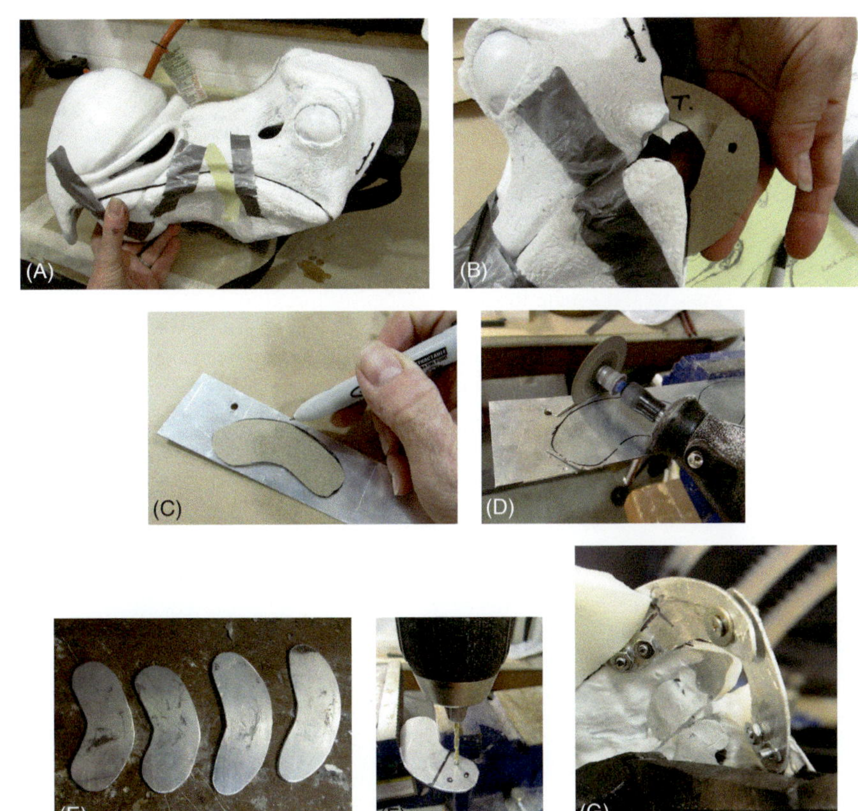

FIGURE 14-120 *A) Mask taped together for mapping out how to trim joint edges; B) mockup patterns for joints; C) transferring to aluminum; D) cutting half of the hinge; E) all hinge parts cut and filed; F) holes predrilled for attachment; G) attached with lock nuts, washers, and small screws*

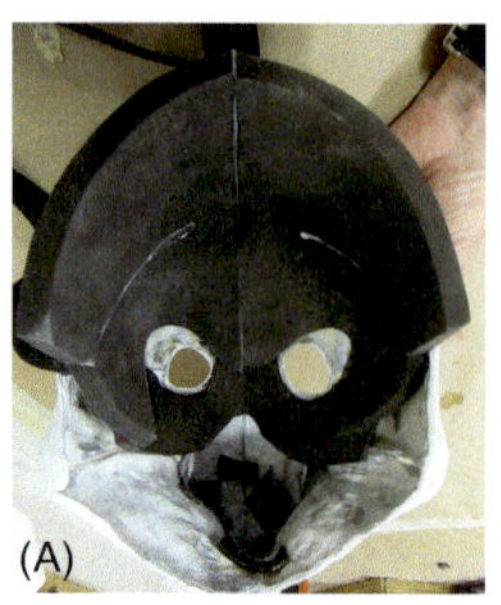
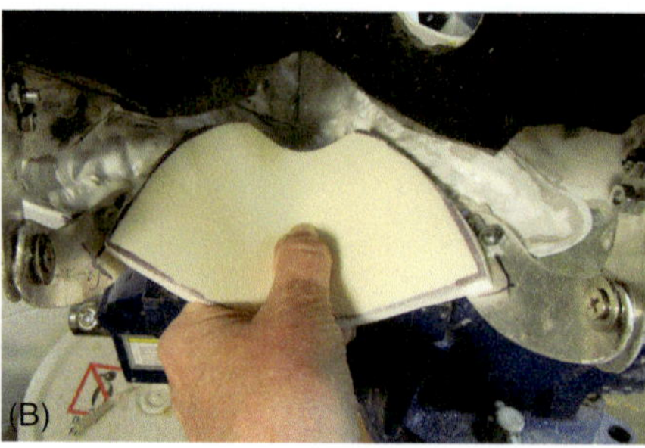

FIGURE 14-121 *A) image of an eva foam partial coif to pad the mask against the face and on top of the head; B) adding thin eva to the chin; C) zip-tying nylon compression strapping to the side of the mask*

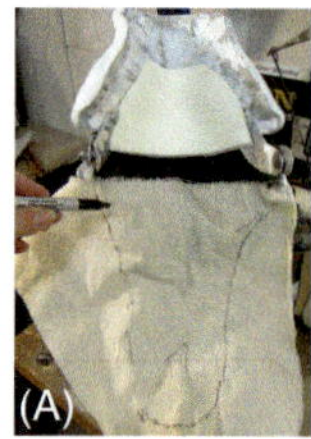

FIGURE 14-122 *A) Making a pattern of the upper interior of the mouth; B) a second pattern was made of the lower interior, then both were connected; C) dyed piece of spandex with contact cement around the edges waiting to be glued inside the mouth*

However, I lined it just in case. Adhere the lining with contact cement.

24. **Painting:** Foundation paint the beak and head (Figure 14-123). Then dry brush and stipple highlights and add fine details.
25. **Eyes:** Paint layers of color, using fine brushes for veins and small glints. Mix two-part epoxy to add a shine to the eyes or spritz with clear gloss varnish.
26. **Fur:** Pattern and sew a mockup of the faux fur coif (Figure 14-124). To get two tones, draw a line on the mockup pattern indicating where the fur colors divide, then separate the pattern for each color. Keep in mind the direction of the fur. To add additional fullness, the fur could be cut upside down/backward against the nap. After sewing together the color breaks, sew darts. **Note:** To avoid raw fur edges, add a spandex lining or a bias fabric edge.
27. If the mask is unbalanced and tends to be heavy in the front or back, stitch in a counterweight using small sandbags, metal washers, or lead fishing weights. It is miraculous how this can help!

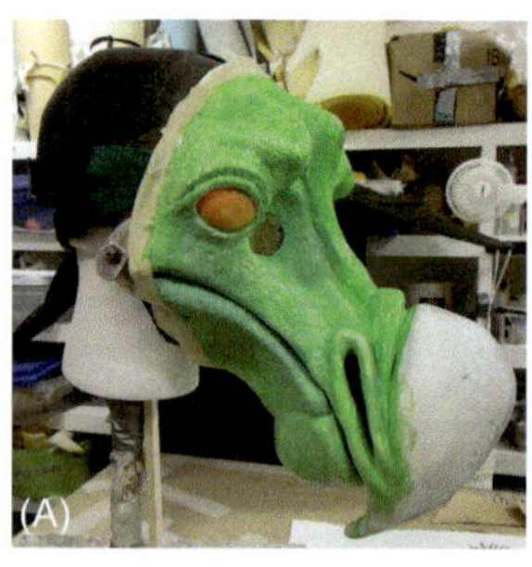

FIGURE 14-123 *A) Foundation layer of paint. note the edge is masked with tape to allow for gluing later; b) continuing to add more details; C) suggestion of eye painting; D) eye painting completed. Eye, a layer of epoxy resin was added to add a shiny finish*

FIGURE 14-124 *A) Half of the fur coif cut out of the yellow and white ombre fur. Note the darts and the notches that indicate where it connects to the green fur; B) fur pieces sewn together and glued to an unpainted edge with contact cement*

FIGURE 14-125 *Small paper sample of how to merge the edge of the fur with paint treatment*

28. Add individual pieces of fur to the transition area between fur and dodo skin to create an organic fur/hair/feather line (Figure 14-125). Then paint small dots to suggest pin feathers or pores under the surface.
29. The fur alone wasn't working for me, so I added pellon (nonfusible, fabric interfacing) cut into the shape of feathers. This was pretinted with a dust coat of spray paint – yellow and pale greens – to help meld the feathers visually with the fur (Figure 14-126). Hot glue or stitch the faux feathers into the fur.
30. *Optional:* To add sympathetic movement, use individually plucked barbules from an ostrich plume and hot glue them into the fur (see the top of the dodo's head).
31. Figure 14-127 shows the finished mask.

MASK PROJECT 10: THE ELEMENTALS

Thermoplastic: Varaform

The Elementals were created for a dance piece involving big masks and costumes along with shadow puppetry. The inspiration was connectivity of nature, Earth, fire, wind, and water (Figure 14-128). The Moon was also introduced to demonstrate yet another force: gravity. The choice of material was made because varaform is porous, allowing air to pass through so dancers would stay cool. It also allowed for very clear sightlines.

1. First decide how the mask should be approached: in sections or in one piece.
2. Though sculpted bead foam and/or clay is often used, to avoid excess mess, build the positive sculpts with coiled and compressed newspaper, then hold them together with masking tape (the dragon has a cardboard tube as

FIGURE 14-126 *A) Pellon spray-painted with yellows and greens, then cut to simulate a stylized feather. These are then inserted and glued into fur with hot glue; B) pellon feathers added and the edge of the fur painted and melded visually with hand-glued pieces of fur and feathers; C) side view; D) close-up of inserted feather pieces*

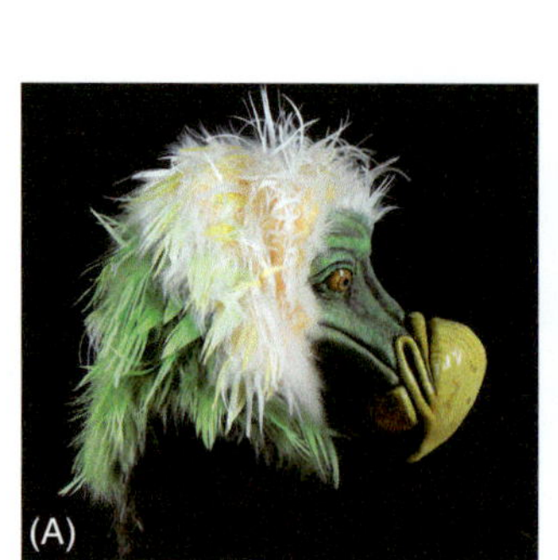

FIGURE 14-127 *The finished mask*

FIGURE 14-128 *Designs for* The Elementals *masks: A) Moon; B) Wind; C) Earth; D) Fire; E) Water*

part of the construction). Then cover the paper shapes with dry cleaner and grocery bags and hold them on with T-pins (Figure 14-129).

3. Start a small piece of varaform that is big enough to wrap around the shape and connected to itself. This is the anchor point for all the other pieces. Then large squares of varaform may be cut with tin snips and dunked in pots of hot water and/or steamed together. **Note:** A clothing steamer is a huge help!
4. After completely covering the paper mold, cut it open down the back of the shape so that the varaform can be pulled away from the plastic. Additional incisions might need to be made to help release the mask from the sculpt.
5. After the paper sculpt has been removed, use small pieces of varaform to patch the incision. Use either hot water or steam. Keep a spray bottle and a bowl of cool water handy to keep your hands from being burned. Take the time to fold back and roll any rough edges, especially in the neck opening, as this area might scratch the wearer's face when taking the mask on and off (Figure 14-130).
6. After patching the mask, begin construction on the interior helmet, also made with varaform and supported inside with three or four doubled varaform struts (Figure 14-131).
7. The interior helmet may be shaped on a padded foam head, a padded human head form, or plaster bust. It

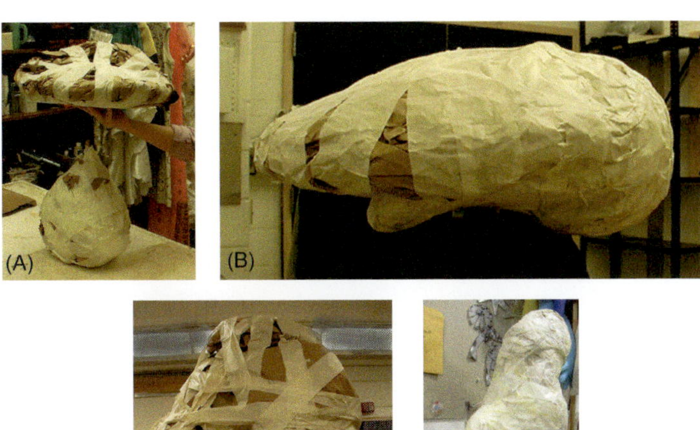

FIGURE 14-129 *A) Beginning of the paper and tape sculpt of earth. the body and head will be created separately, then connected with a small PVC tube covered with varaform; B) earth's head in the final stage. It will be covered with plastic and t- pinned, then covered with varaform; C) the rough beginning of water; D) the paper sculpt of moon*

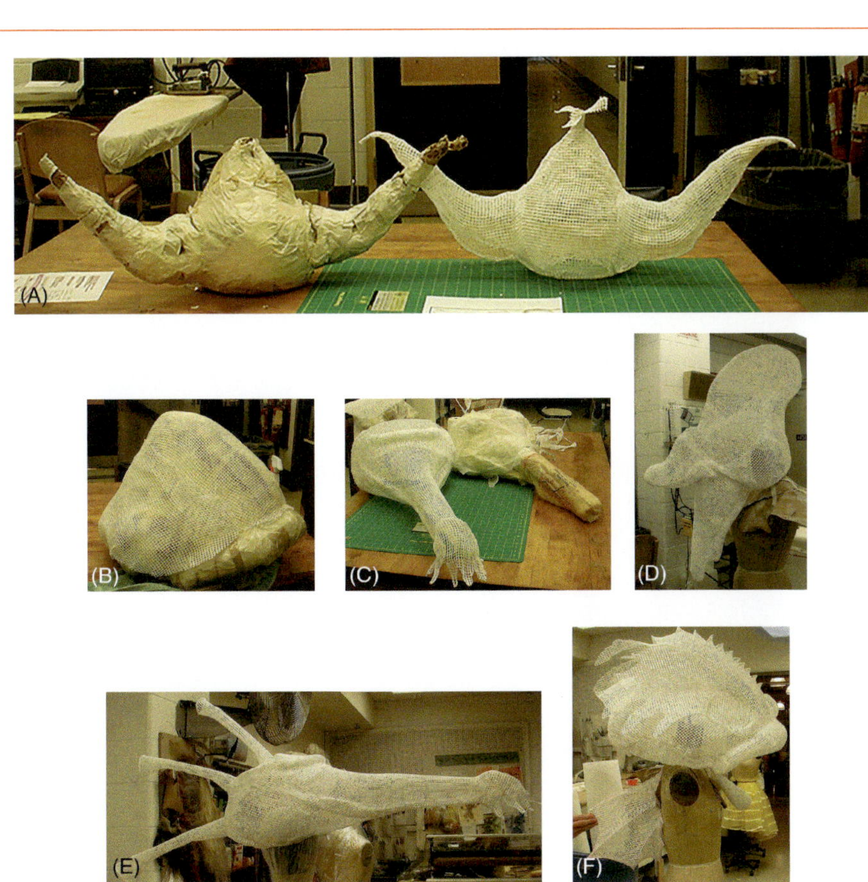

FIGURE 14-130 *A) The paper sculpt of earth's body and the varaform copy made from it; B) the beginning of water's head; C) the dragon fire. Varaform shape with the paper sculpt; D) the moon's finished varaform head; E) the dragon's final crest pieces, which will be filled with decorations; F) water's final head in varaform with a completed fin that is later sewn to a matching vest*

FIGURE 14-131 *The helmet inside water's mask (see Chapters 4 and 5)*

can also be a full helmet or just a headband with two crossed bands over the top (see Chapter 5, Figure 5-1).

8. After constructing the shape, fit it on a human head. Padding may be added using EVA foam adhered with contact cement after it is inserted. A removable spandex or terry cloth liner might also be added for cleaning purposes.
9. Attach a chin strap to the varaform helmet. Stitch a strip of 1-inch rough and soft Velcro onto one side of this strap, then machine stitch a loop (running through the side of the helmet). Machine stitch a D-ring to the other strap, and then repeat stitching to the other side of the helmet. As the strap runs through the D-ring, the Velcro strap folds back on itself and catches the Velcro (See Chapter 5, Figure 5-2).
10. A floating padded piece may also be added to the chin strap for comfort.
11. To position the helmet inside the mask takes patience and requires measuring, fitting, and eyeballing. Using a steamer, preattach doubled struts made from varaform and attach them to the helmet. If you get one in place inside the mask, then the rest will follow. It is often helpful to make cardboard and tape "mockup struts" to get an idea of how long the final supports might need to be. **Note:** Consider the focus of the character when inserting the helmet.

TIP BOX

Make A Custom Foam Helmet Liner

Make a foam helmet liner for a specific person by creating a custom pattern, cover the foam shape with plastic, then with the foam cap on the person, form it on their head. The foam will act as insulation.

12. At this point, paint the inside front of the mask with flat black spray paint. Seeing through a black vision port makes it easier for human eyes to focus on the outside. Then base coat the whole mask (the remaining inside and outside) with the spray paint of choice. Use spray paint specifically for plastic and it will bond very well. Then add hand-painted or spray-painted accents to shade and highlight eye sockets, facial contours, ears, etc.
13. Additional details such as translucent fabrics, clear dyed Worbla, hair, feathers, poly horsehair tubing, sequins, ribbons, etc., may be glued or stitched to finish the masks.
14. Figure 14-132 shows eyes made of layered fabrics and sequins.
15. Make antennas with a heat-bent nylon rod and attached with varaform strips *before painting*.
16. Figure 14-133 shows Jointed tail made with individual varaform shapes with a core of rope.
17. Figure 14-134 shows the finished masks with costumes made from recycled wedding dresses.

FIGURE 14-132 *Close-up of earth's antennae and eyes*

(A) (B)

FIGURE 14-133 *A) Side view of earth's segmented tail; B) back view. This moved really well*

FIGURE 14-134 *A) wind; B) fire; C) earth; D) water; E) moon*

MASK PROJECT 11: THE WITCH

Thermoplastic: Worbla

I have mulled over many iterations of this character all my life – they say we create what we see, so perhaps she favors me. This iteration is just larger than life-size. She seems like she is devoted to her craft, is a carnivore, and probably has foresight. I wanted her to seem pungent and in-your-face. I always think of my character designs as having some sort of sound – she would be heavy metal with moments flatulence; some windy, some cracking (Figure 14-135).

1. First decide how the mask should be approached: in sections or in one piece.
2. This positive sculpt was built in stages with water-based clay (Figure 14-136). The nose and other features were added as the sculpt progressed. **Note:** To help remove the mask from the clay sculpt, cover it with aluminum foil.
3. While constantly wetting your fingers, lay pieces of molten Worbla over the clay shapes and work slowly into the nooks and crannies. A wet popsicle stick is very helpful (Figure 14-137).
4. After the head is completely covered, go back with a heat gun or a steamer to smooth down the edges (Figure 14-138).
5. To remove the mask from the clay and foam form, make three big incisions on the back of the head and work the piece off carefully. **Note:** be patient!

FIGURE 14-135 *Final design*

TIP BOX

Working with Thermoplastics Safely

When working with thermoplastics and a heat gun, make certain to do so in a ventilated area. If the process involves softening in hot water or steaming, it does not burn the plastic and therefore there are no fumes. When using a heat gun that is literally melting plastics toward burning, toxic fumes will be produced. Use a heat gun in an area with fans and a ventilation hood or outside. Burned plastic fumes are dangerous.

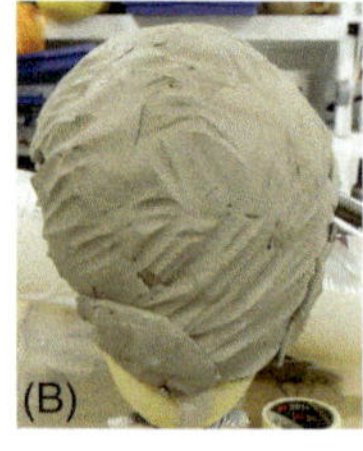

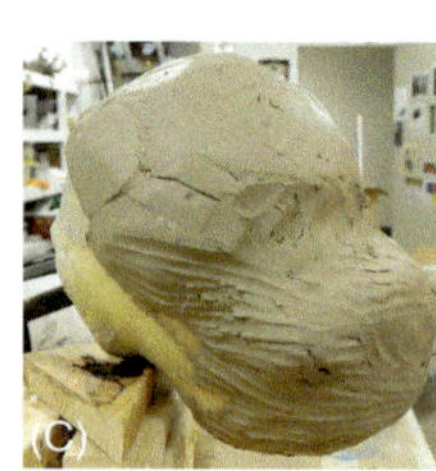

FIGURE 14-136 *A) Rigid foam head form to build up the sculpt; B) building up the general shape; C) adding bigger shapes as needed; D) adding clear eye domes and getting more specific with all areas*

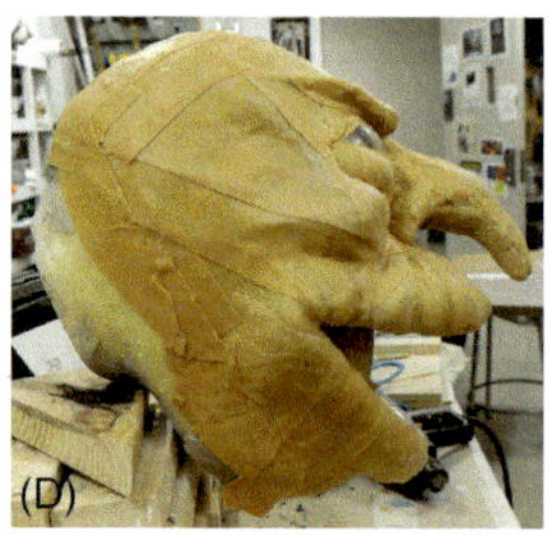

FIGURE 14-137 *A) Laying on pie-wedge sections of worbla; B) after the lips and jaw are covered, then add the sculpted nose; C) the nose and side of the head being covered. I like to start from the bottom and underneath objects, then end by finishing the top; D) the head is completely covered*

FIGURE 14-138 *Next spend time smoothing overlapping seams. It's good craftsmanship and it will make the plastic shape stronger*

FIGURE 14-139 *Cutting the worbla skin off of the clay sculpt*

6. After the Worbla is removed from the sculpt, wash out the excess clay and let the sculpt dry. Then patch the incisions and reinforce the rest of the cranium with additional pieces of Worbla (Figure 14-139).
7. Helmet placement inside the mask may be determined by starting with the front of the helmet. Measure down from the front edge to the level of the eyes. Use that measurement to help gauge how the helmet should line up with the vision port(s). This might take some time putting on the head and taking it off to determine the correct angle. Cardboard struts might also be used to help gauge the position. Tape to the top of the helmet and into the top of the mask. Add faux struts to the sides as well. When the length is determined, use heat-bent polyethylene or aluminum straps to support the helmet. Attach with bolts, lock washers, and nuts (Figure 14-140).
8. To help with trimming the excess material, always give yourself a drawn guideline before cutting. Trim the edges inside the mouth, around the back of the head, and at the eyelids.
9. It is helpful to add the net vision port in the mouth at this point; however, it may be added later in the process. Adhere the port material with contact cement.

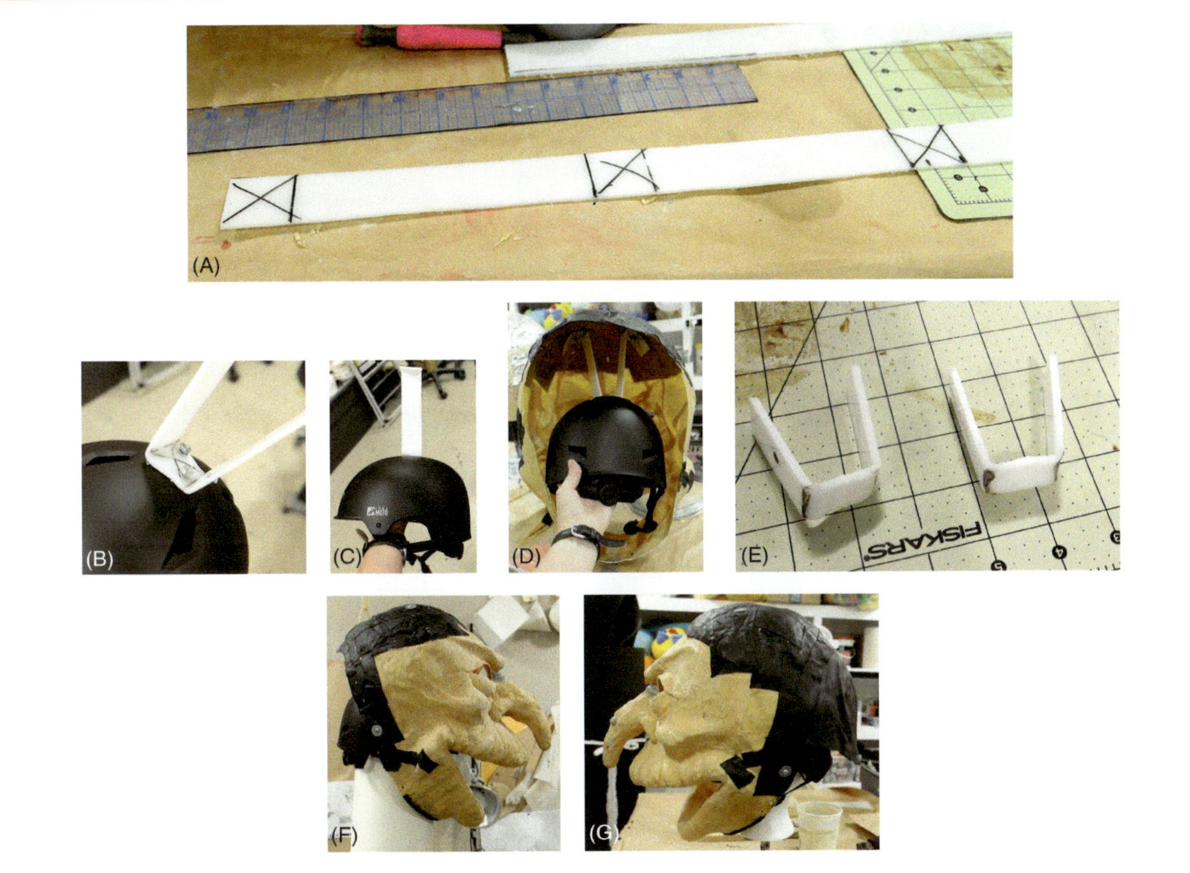

FIGURE 14-140 *A) Image of a polyethylene strut; B) the strut heat bent and bolted to the helmet top; C) what the helmet looks like before attaching to the mask; D) bolted inside the mask; E) small struts for the sides of the helmet; F) the helmet attached; G) building out the rest of the skull*

10. Spray the inside of the mask with flat black spray paint, especially the front. The inside of the mouth might also be sprayed with black paint. It all depends on the finished look. This mask has a constant grinning leer, and the inside of the mouth needs to be black to make the teeth visually stand out.

11. **Ears:** Hand-form clear Worbla with heat. Implant wire into the top of the ears, then cover them with opaque Worbla. Also add wire for interior veins. Insert bolts and wrap them with Worbla so that these might be firmly anchored to the head. Attach with washers and nuts. A coating of Worbla may also be added to cover the joint (Figure 14-141).

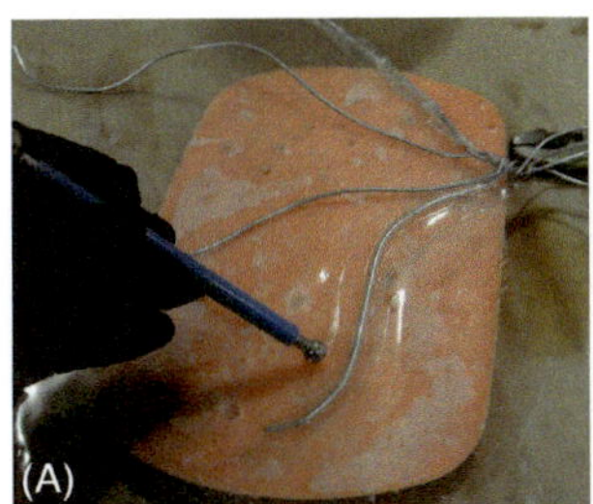

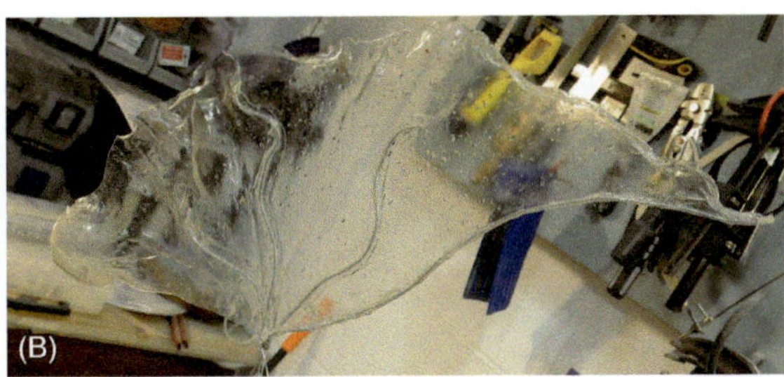

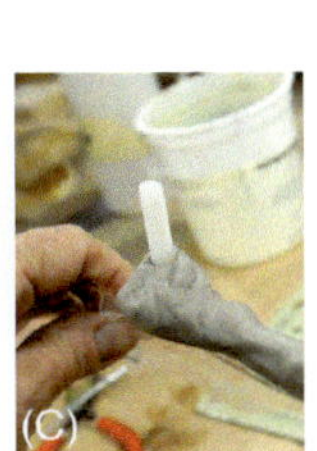

FIGURE 14-141 *A) First make a paper pattern to decide the scale of the ears, then cut the shape out of clear worbla. Pictured here a metal tool melding wires into the ears. These wires serve a structure and as veins; B) ears have been sculpted. Wires are twisted and will help with the structure when they are attached to the head; C) nylon bolts encased in soft worbla along with the twisted wire ends. The bolts will help to attach the ears to the mask; D) a finished but unpainted ear*

FIGURE 14-142 *A) Dyed pieces of clear worbla, shaped with heat gun; B) pieces being attached to the head of the mask; C) after clear pieces were adhered to the outer crest/crown with heat; D) I decided to tweak some of the flames. Hanging the mask upside down helped. The flames tended to flop over until each cooled, but this did the trick*

12. **The flaming head piece:** Dye clear pieces of Worbla with Rit poly dye in yellow, orange, and red. Then trim these pieces into the shape of flames and attach them to the top of the mask (Figure 14-142).

13. **Eyes:** Use premade oval hemispheres filled with layers of clear resin (Figure 14-143).

    To add depth, use individual layers of painted resin (see Chapter 12).

    Teeth: The teeth needed to have some translucence and stability, and resin was the best choice to get the desired look (Figure 14-144). Sculpt with plasticine and cast in a two-part matrix mold. Remove clay and fill the mold with tinted resin.

14. **Painting:** Add a foundation color, then depending on the facial area specify the paint colors. Add areas of gold and greens for an organic patina (Figure 14-145).

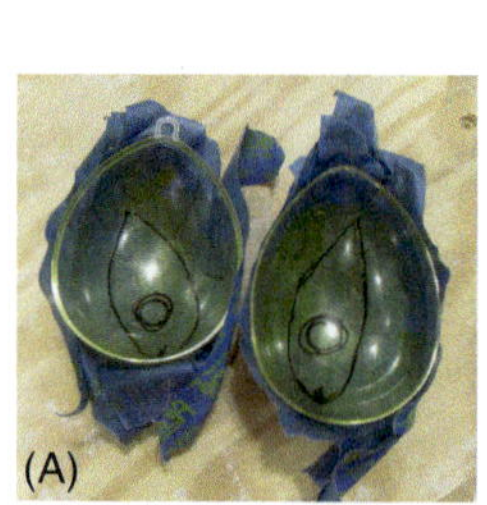

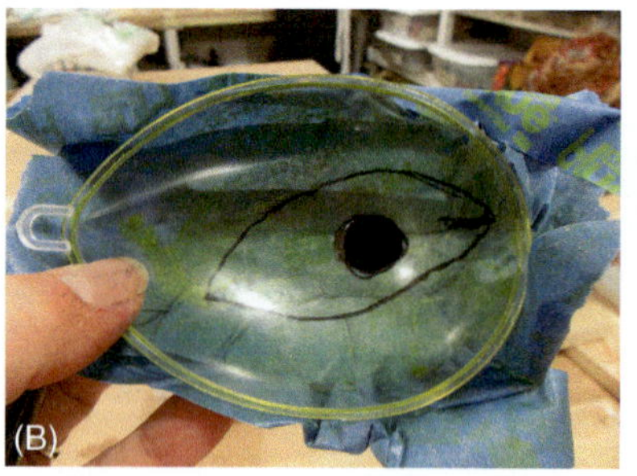

FIGURE 14-143 *A) Trace the outline of eyelids on oval domes and cover the front with tape. Add a translucent wash of sharpie ink to the inside of the dome diluted with 99% alcohol; B) glue in black plastic disks harvested from googly eyes; C) paint layers backward visually. Take a pin and scratch off some of the paint, then add an undercoat to show through. After all the layers are added, adhere gold Mylar to the back of the eye*

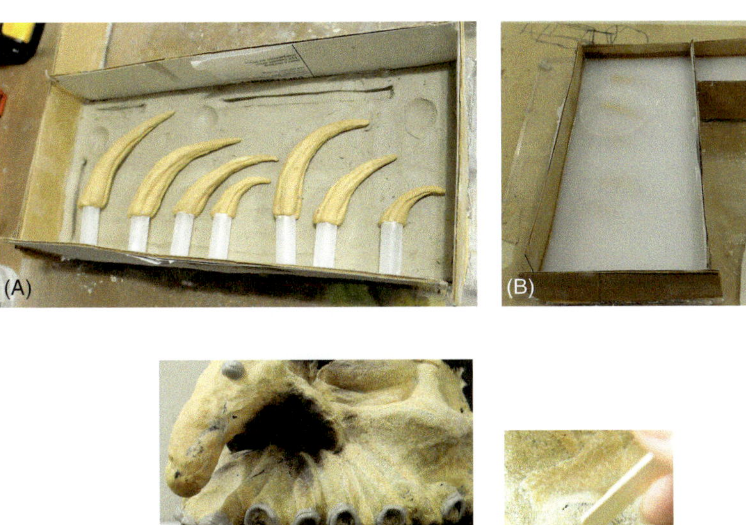

FIGURE 14-144 *A) Large sculpted plasticine teeth with tubing cut for pouring resin, set up in a water-based clay foundation with cardboard sides. This was sealed with two layers of crystal clear; B) silicone was used for the glove mold and hydrocal for the blanket mold for each side; C) sockets for teeth; D) close-up of sculpting. use a heat gun to soften the worbla foundation, which then melds with the pieces to be added. A damp popsicle stick helped to sculpt*

FIGURE 14-145 *A) Foundation layer covering the whole mask; B) low lights and highlights added to enhance the wrinkles and shapes; C) stippling complementary dots of orange and pink. metallic paints also help bring out the luminescent quality of the mask. The ears are dry brushed; D) Mylar was added to top of head at the base of the flames to add reflective depth; E) close-up of the skin*

FIGURE 14-146 *The witch's hair*

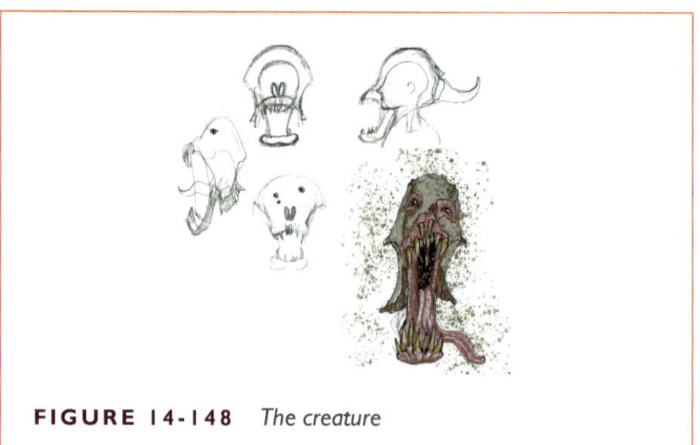

FIGURE 14-148 *The creature*

Hair: Four wigs (black and brown) were used to complete the hair. These were cut apart and attached to the mask's back and sides. Stuffed black tubes of fabric were covered with hair wefts to create the look of long, thick, weedy braids. Then gold ornaments and netting were added for finished details (Figure 14-146).

15. Figure 14-147 shows the finished Mask.

MASK PROJECT 12: CREATURE

Polyfoam with latex skin

This creature seems to be a tortured soul. Perhaps it is the result of a DNA experiment. It is not happy – perhaps it's in horrible pain. It seemed to me to be screaming or howling in agony or great hunger. Originally it was designed wearing a skin coif, but as it developed, the coif was cut from the finished mask. I wanted to be able to see the whole thing in the round.

The polyfoam mask has two great characteristics: 1) it can be custom made to fit a specific actor, and 2) polyfoam (a urethane foam) is flexible. As a result, these masks can move depending on the engineering of the sculpt. For example, the mask can lay against the actor's face for subtle movements, or if a larger mask is desired an armature shell may be built/cast out of fiberglass, thermoplastic, or fabric mâché and be hinged at the jaw.

Note: The mask in the construction example does not have a moving jaw but is posed in a specific gesture (Figure 14-148).

1. Construction of a polyfoam mask needs to start with a foundation sculpt over a plaster bust.
2. The design was sculpted in water-based clay, but any clay may be used (Figure 14-149).
3. To provide a protective skin, when the sculpt is finished, coat it with Crystal Clear Glaze.
4. Cast the clay sculpt front with plaster (Figure 14-150).
5. Open the mold and clean out the clay.
6. Sand down any sharp edges with a surform tool.

(A)

(B)

(C)

FIGURE 14-147 *The finished mask*

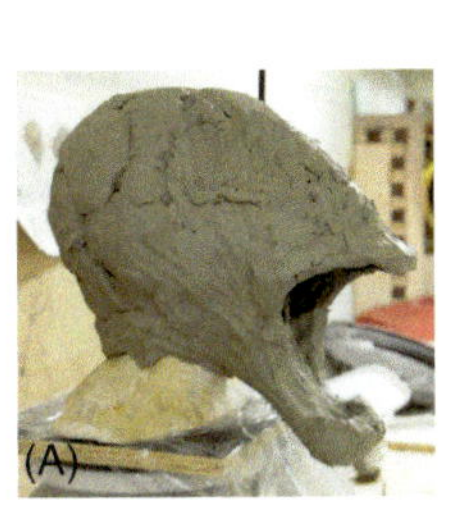

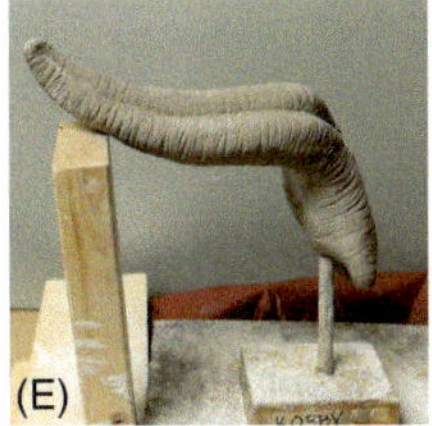

FIGURE 14-149 *A) Beginning sculpt in water-based clay. A crude armature was constructed under this clay later to help support the shapes; B) refining the sculpt; C) side view. The mask is asymmetrical; D) mask with tongue. The tongue was loosely attached inside the mouth to get the shape, then finished outside the mouth; E) tongue sculpted on a stand*

7. Wash out mold halves with dish soap and water. Using a toothbrush and a one-inch chip brush may help to remove clay from small nooks and crannies. Let mold halves dry in front of a heater or a fan, in the sun, or if mold is small enough, in a low-temperature oven.
8. **Note:** After cleaning the mold haves, plan how the mold will be positioned when expanding. Vent holes need to be drilled at this point to allow for trapped air to escape. If the air remains trapped, then the foam will not expand into those areas. The holes should be drilled at the peaks or highest points of the mold.
9. Before running foam, a release agent must be used on the inside of the mold parts *and on plaster core or positive mold*. The vent holes should also have release agent applied. Tint slightly with diluted Murphy's Oil Soap (or any mold soap) using a few drops of food coloring and dab into the mold halves with a chip brush

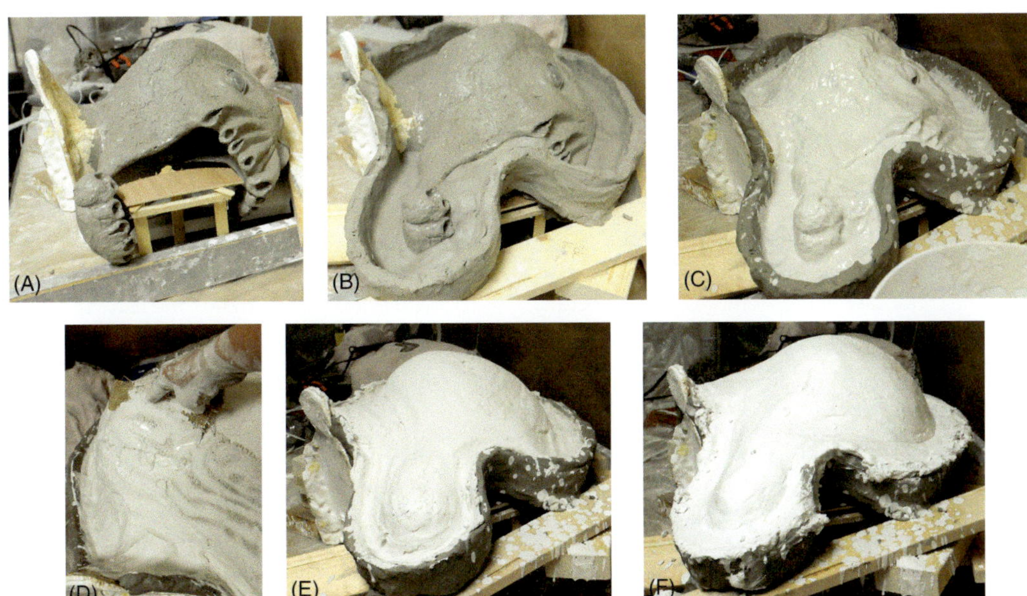

FIGURE 14-150 *A) Laying the head on its side to begin casting. Temporary scaffold built to support the clay foundation; B) clay foundation and the low wall in process; C) first layer of plaster (the splash coat) done with hydrocal; D) second layer of plaster, done with burlap embedded in hydrocal; E) burlap layer complete with a mixed batch of plaster in place; f) final layer to support and add a smooth finish to the mold; G) after plaster goes through exothermic reaction, then remove all the clay, flip the head, and repeat the casting steps for the other side; H) the last part of the mold is the inside of the mouth. careful planning should go into the mold parts as there might be undercuts and the pieces could get locked permanently if the artist is not careful; I) the completed mold in three parts; J) half of the finished mold, clean and dry; K) the completed two-part tongue mold; L) Opening the mold (Continued)*

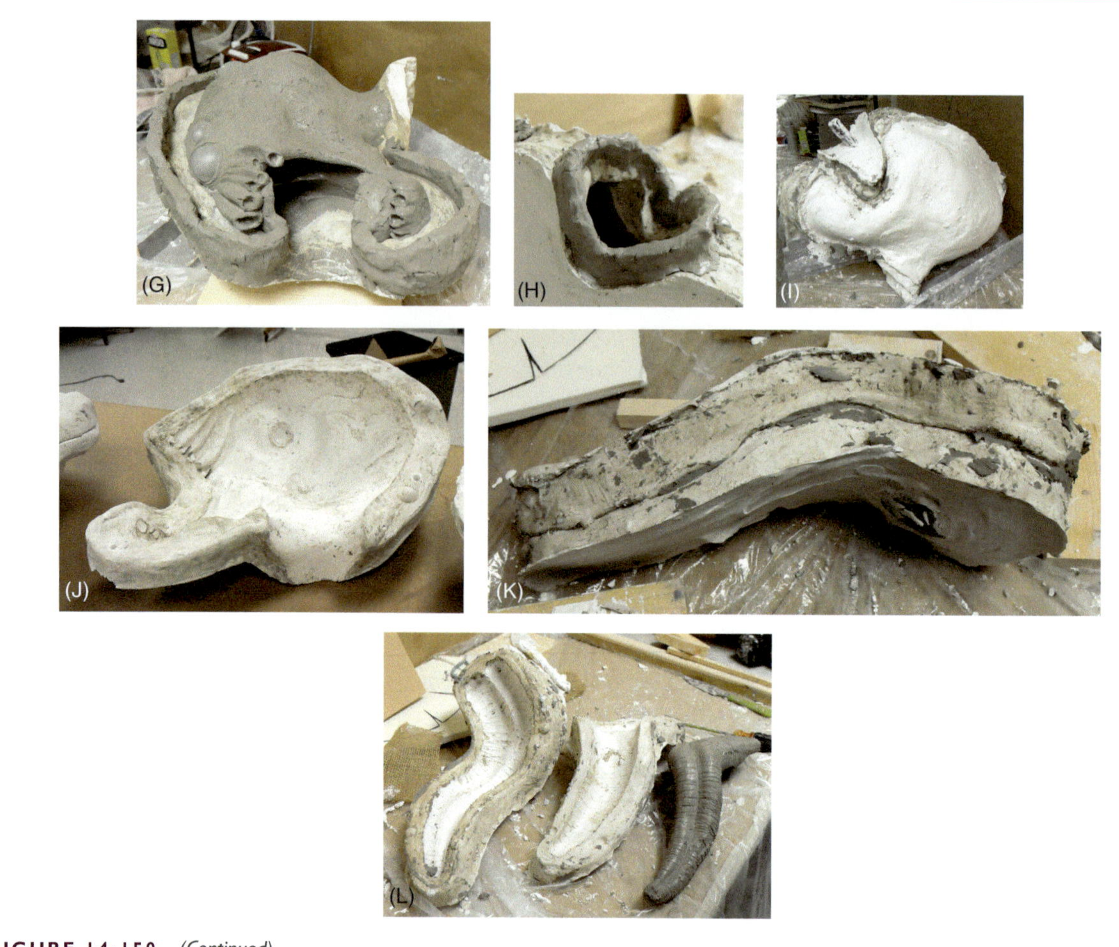

FIGURE 14-150 *(Continued)*

so you can see where the mix has been applied. Do so carefully to avoid creating bubbles (Figure 14-151). **Note:** Though I habitually use a spray release agent for silicone, if it is used as a glove mold, then no release agent is necessary for casting polyfoam. Nothing sticks to silicone except silicone. The plaster or fiberglass mother mold definitely will need a release agent.

10. After the release agent is dried, dab on a thin layer of latex to create a skin on the mold halves *and the positive mold*. This is an optional step, as the foam will expand and push against the mold; however, there are often air bubbles that can form that the latex skin might hide.
11. Running polyfoam is tricky because the working time is 30 seconds from mix to pour.

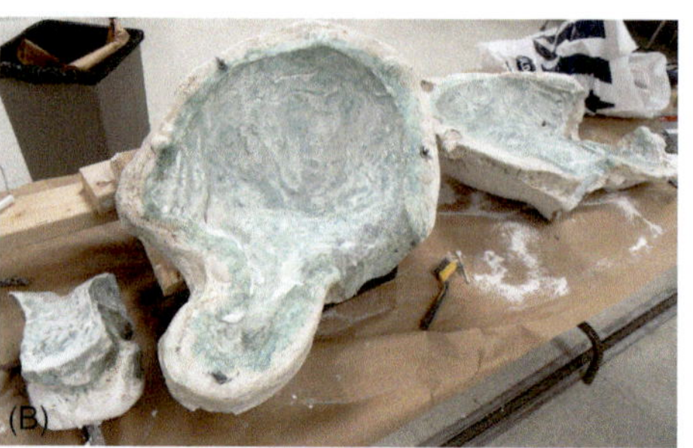

FIGURE 14-151 *A) Mold with tinted mold soap added; B) latex stippled into the mold. A latex skin is optional*

For this mask, the process was choreographed so that the foam could be rapidly poured, the core mold inserted, the remaining foam poured over the core, then the mold closed and clamped with *quick clamps*, all in just under 30 seconds (Figure 14-152). The best method is to inject the liquid foam swiftly into a closed mold.

Note: Ideally, run foam outside at or above 60° and wear a respirator, gloves, arm sleeves, an apron (or old clothing), and goggles when working with polyfoam.

12. Let the latex skin and foam cure overnight in the mold. Without the latex skin, the mold may be opened after about an hour or when the foam has cured and lost its sticky texture.
13. Remove the clamps. Slowly pry open the mold halves with a big flathead screwdriver or a metal superbar. Use a blunt tool such as a popsicle stick to help wiggle the foam out of any stubborn areas.

    Note: The positive head will stay inside until it is cut out.
14. Remove and then powder the outside latex skin. If there are tears, save all the pieces; these can be reattached later when patching and seaming occurs.
15. Using a cosmetic eyebrow or grease pencil, sketch the line where the cut will be made to release the interior core. Using small scissors or a razor blade, cut along the drawn line and work the interior core out of the mask. Then powder the inside of the mask.

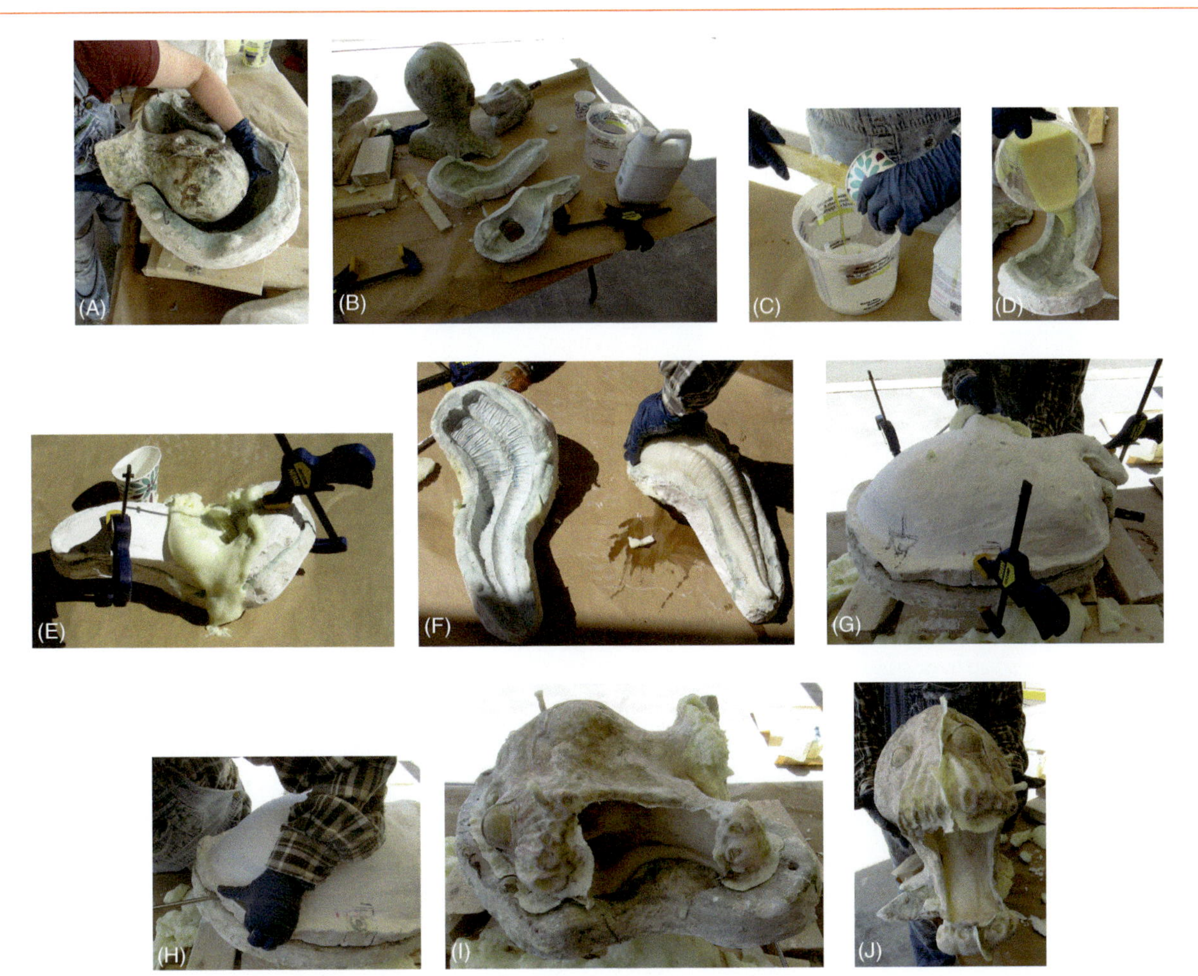

FIGURE 14-152 *A) Rehearsing the choreography for a fast layering of mold parts; B) all the mold parts are ready to be assembled; C) mixing two-part polyfoam; D) pouring the mixture into half of the tongue mold; E) the tongue mold clamped and the foam expanded and cured; F) removing the foam tongue from the mold; G) the mask ready to be removed from the mold; H) prying open the mold; I) half of the foam mask exposed with the positive head still inside it; J) the foam head removed*

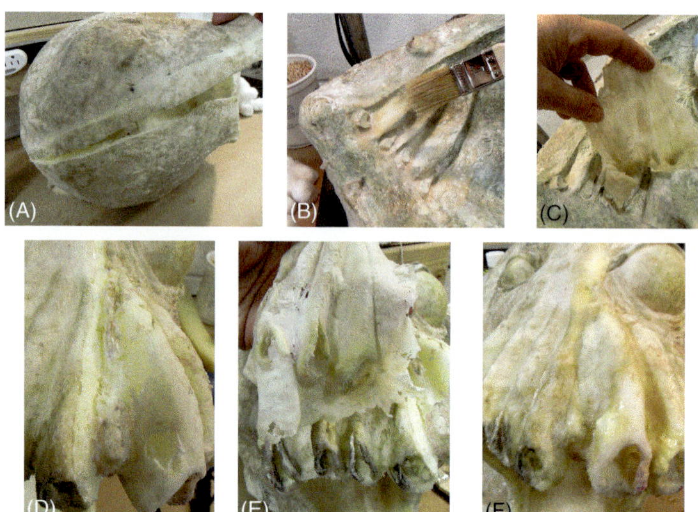

FIGURE 14-153 *A) Slicing open the back of the mask to remove the positive plaster head; B) one way to patch flaws is to create a latex skin from the mold, creating a graft that can then be glued in place with pro's-aide adhesive; C) pulling off the latex graft; D) flawed area to be covered; E) graft is powdered and ready to attach; F) finished area – smooth as a baby's bottom*

16. Trim seams, ear holes, excess neck material, and any vent areas as needed (Figure 14-153). If there are tears or seams with flashing, contoured grafts can be made and taken from the molds. Adhere grafts with stippled on and dried Pro's-Aide adhesive. This is especially helpful if the mask surface is highly textured.
17. The polyfoam eyes may be painted and used as is, or they may be cut out and replaced with resin or hand-painted domes, then glued in with epoxy or contact cement and fabric patches (Figure 14-154).
18. Call the actor in for a preliminary fitting. Trim and pad inside as needed.
19. To close the CB seam, add Velcro tabs sewn to the spandex. These should be adhered with contact cement and stitched to ensure stability (Figure 14-155). Create a latex and fabric flap to disguise the CB opening. Use the negative mold to create a custom cast shape for the placket. Stitch and glue with Pro's-Aide adhesive any additional Velcro closures needed to secure the flap.
20. Add the vision port material in the form of black netting or screen (Figure 14-156). The netting may be treated with flexible acrylic gel or latex and then painted to match the outside color.
21. **Eyes:** This mask has several sizes of eyes. The interior eye shape was painted on a plastic hemisphere (half) with pupil and veining, then nestled into another slightly larger hemisphere (half) filled with resin (Figure 14-157).
22. Attach the eyes on the inside with contact cement and a fabric backing.
23. Add any textural details such as veins or bumps with cotton or fabric and latex.

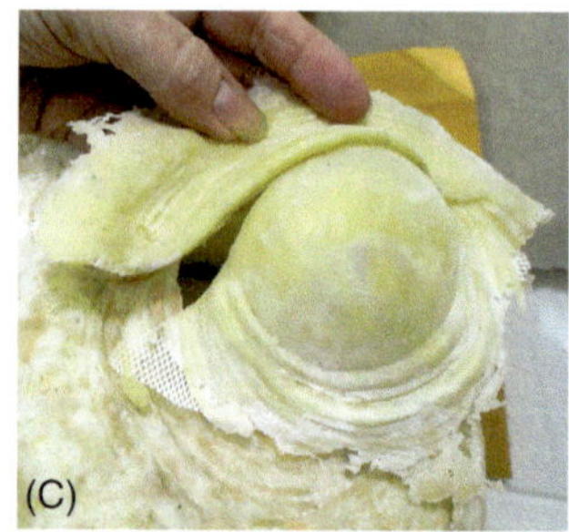

FIGURE 14-154 *A) Eye socket crudely cut out with a small tear in the upper lid; B) making an eye graft with stretch netting intrinsically added to latex layers; C) cutting away the eye from the lids, then attaching the grafts with Pro's-Aide*

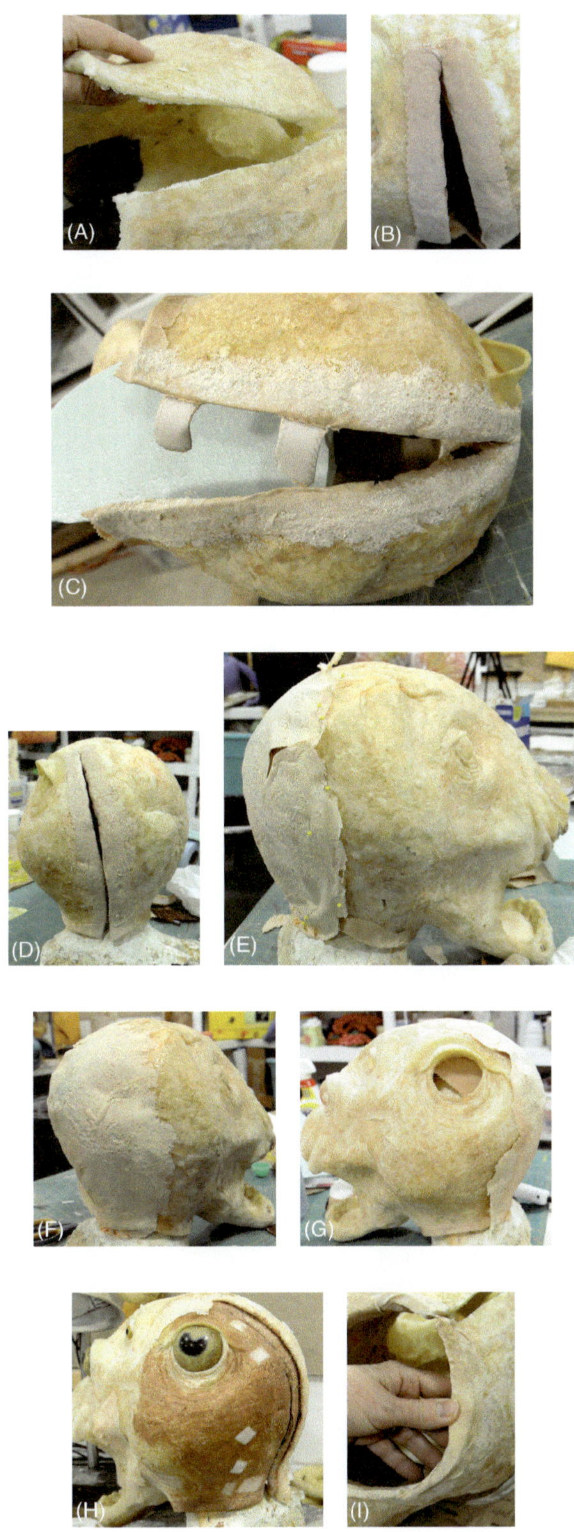

FIGURE 14-155 *A) Image of a raw CB seam; B) spandex strips wrapped and glued around the raw edge; C) Latex stippled over the edges of the spandex strips. the velcro tabs are machine stitched first to spandex strips, then hand stitched to the mask; D) the mask closed in the CB with velcro; E) a large CB graft taken from the mold is joined to one side and left open on the other to disguise the straight CB opening; F) a piece glued to the back of the head; G) the open side has small pieces of velcro tacked (where possible) and glued; H) image of velcro placement; I) raw edge of the neck wrapped with spandex*

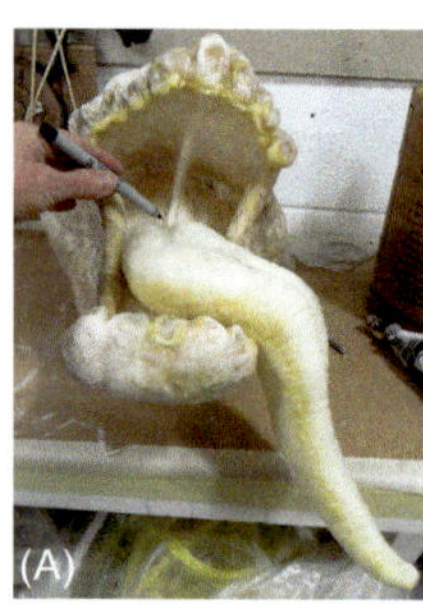

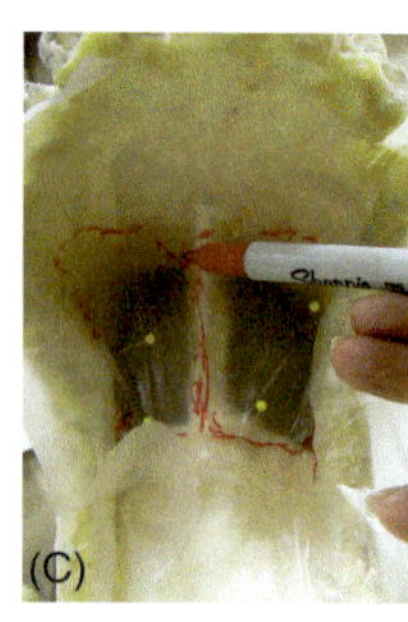
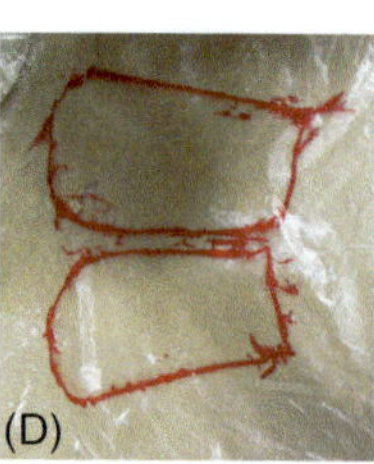
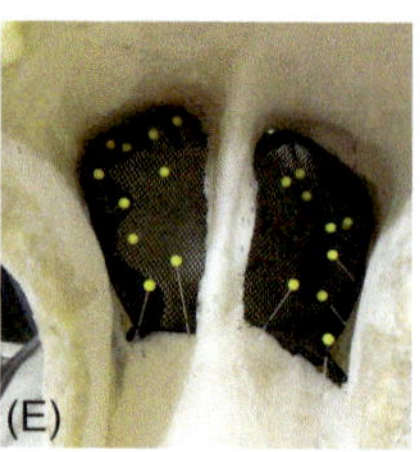

FIGURE 14-156 *A) Sketching out the vision port with still-to-be-attached tongue in place for a marker; B) the traced rea is cut out with an x-acto knife; C) sheer plastic dry cleaner bag used for making a pattern; D) pattern cleaned up and ready to transfer to the net; E) stretch net panels pinned in place, to be glued on the inside*

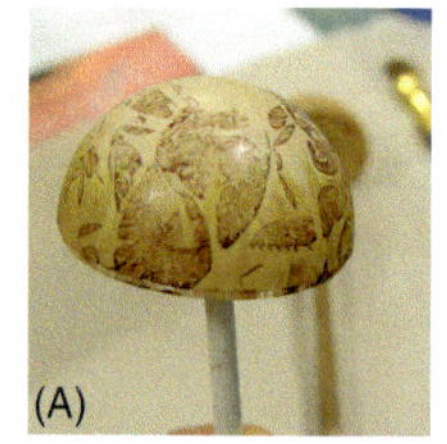
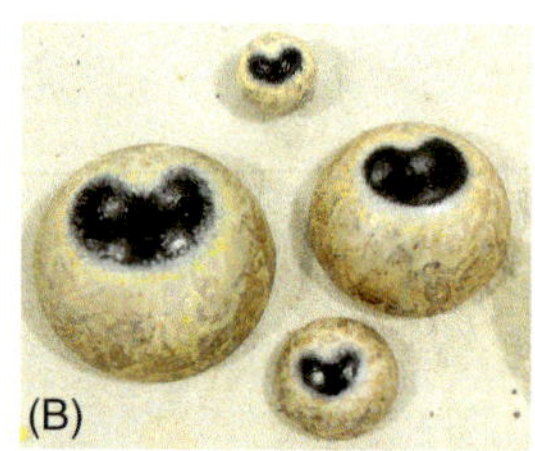
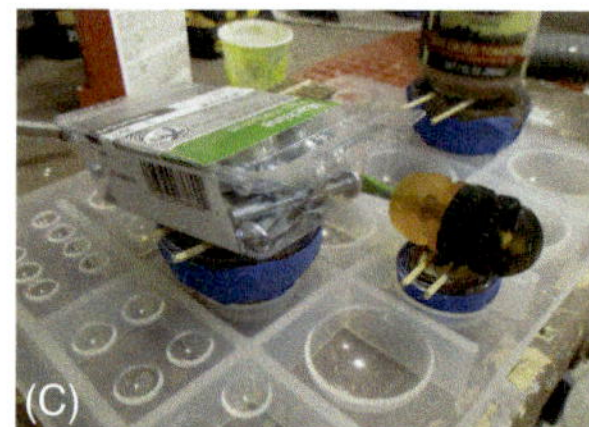

FIGURE 14-157 *A) Eye domes sanded and base painted with beige spray paint, then painted with a glaze and wrapped with crushed plastic wrap until dry; B) all the sizes of eyes that will be used. each is painted with acrylic paint. glitter paint has also been stippled on; C) using silicone mold tray as a stand for the eyes as they cure. The blue covered dome is used as a clear surface layer with the resin trapped between the two layers. this adds depth to eyes. The objects on top are being used as weight. otherwise, the interior domes would float and bob out; D) finished eyes; E) eyes inserted into the mask.*

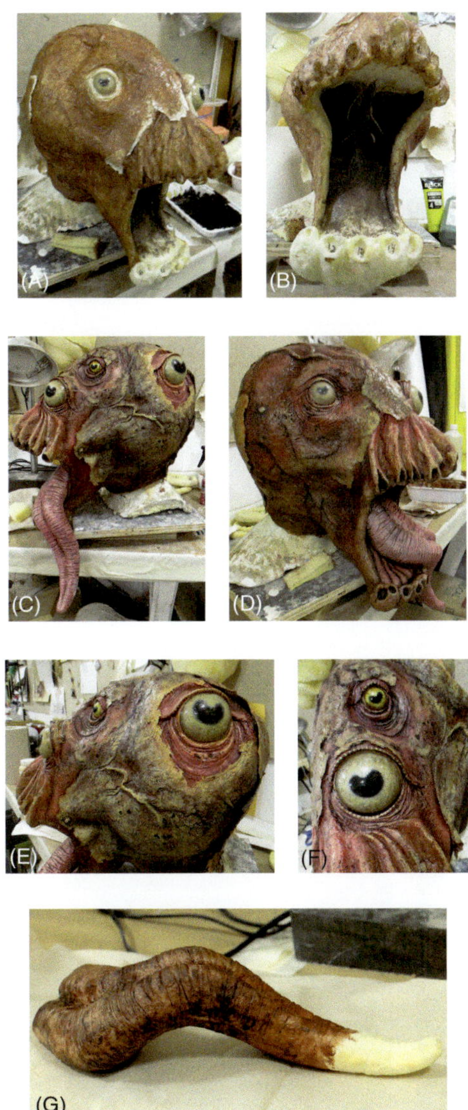

FIGURE 14-158 *A) Base painting the head with lacryl; B) painting inside mouth – melding the black vision port with the shadows of the mouth; C) building up layers of the color and then dry brushing to catch the peaks of the details; D) opposite side with one cloudy eye. veins and cracks may also be painted with dark lowlights; E) close-up of side back of a large eye and some details. the flap covering the back closure simulates flaky skin; F) close-up of eyes and detail painting; G) underpainting foam tongue*

24. Base paint the tongue first, then attach it with contact cement.
25. **Painting:** Apply a foundation layer of color (Figure 14-158). For this, Lacryl was used. Then proceed with dry brush, wet-on-wet, or airbrush techniques as desired. There are at least three techniques for painting latex that include solvents, acrylic, or latex additives (see Chapter 10).
26. A nice slimy look may be achieved with thin layers of acrylic gel coat. Glitter-infused paints were also added to heighten the light-catching reflectivity of slime.
27. **Teeth:** Each tooth/fang was sculpted with plasticine and was matched to a gum socket (Figure 14-159). A silicone mold was made for casting with tinted resin. To get the dual-color merge (purple and yellow), two colors of resin were poured into each fang mold at the same time until full.
28. Figure 14-160 shows the final mask.

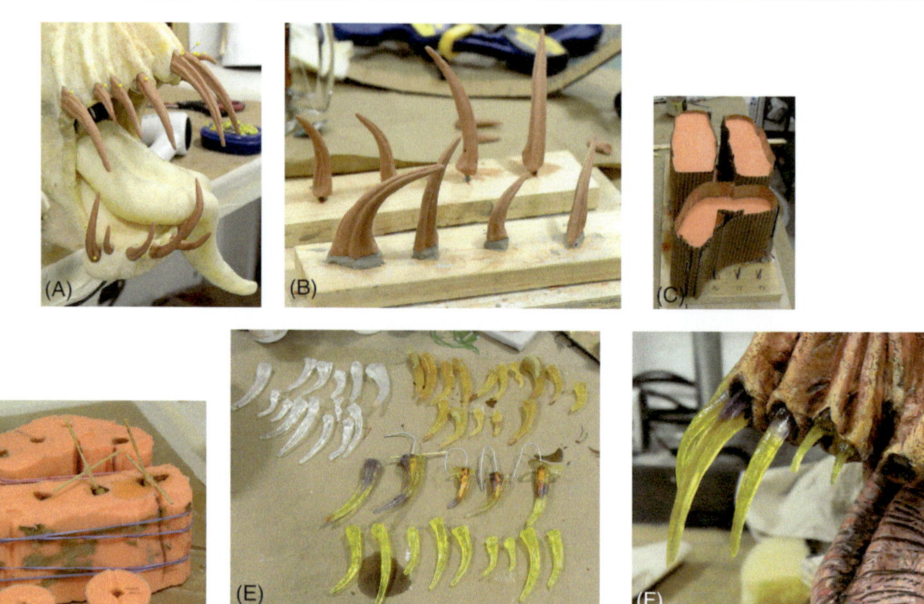

FIGURE 14-159 *A) close-up of teeth sculpted out of plasticine and pinned to a foam mask; B) teeth positioned on a mold foundation for casting with silicone; C) molds built out of flexible cardboard saved from a foam shipment; D) cut open the mold to allow for the teeth to be extracted when cured. Successive castings are done by strapping the mold together. Rubber bands work really well; E) different teeth samples cast in the molds; F) to adhere teeth, carve out a socket using an x-acto knife, then epoxy the tooth in place*

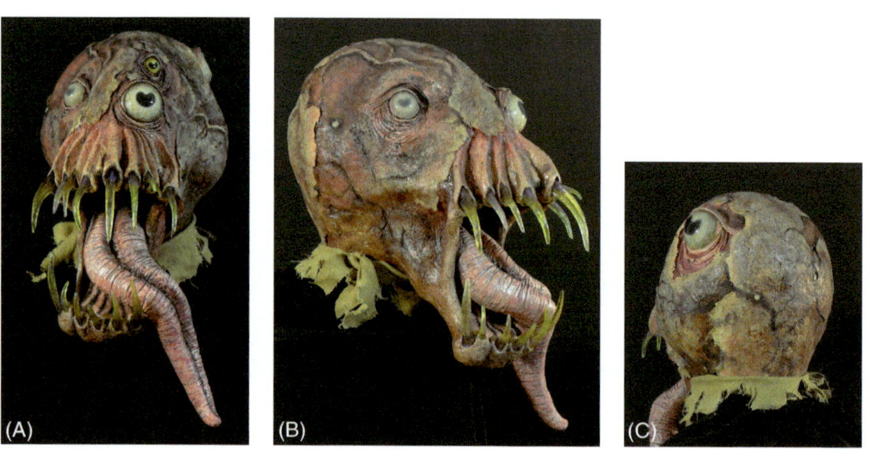

FIGURE 14-160 *A–C) The finished mask.*

SOURCES

Frog Jelly Leather
Latex Chicago latex/spartan Resources
Critical Coatings
Tap Plastics
Standard Ceramics
FXSupply
Monstermakers
Immortal Masks
Polytek
Burman Makeup Inc.
BJB Suppliers
Brick in the Yard Mold Supplies
Sy Fabrics
National Fiber Technology
Georgia Stage
Douglas and Sturgess
Spandex House
Organic Armor.com
Van Dyke's Taxidermy Supply
Manhattan Wardrobe Supply
Harbor Frieght
Reynolds Advanced Materials/Smoothon

ONLINE SCHOOLS AND TUTORIALS

Stan Winston School
Burman Inc.

BIBLIOGRAPHY

Clough, Eric C., Plaisted, Thomas A., Eckel, Zak C., Cante, Kenneth, Hundley, Jacob M., Schaedler, Tobias A. "Elastromeric Microlattice Impact Attenuators." Cell Press. URL: tascheaedler@ hrl.com. Accessed: July 23, 2019.

Definition of *Style*. *Oxford Languages English Dictionary*. URL: https://www.oed.com/ Accessed: July 19, 2022.

Definition of *Style*. Merriam Webster site. URL: https://www.merriam webster.com/?utm_source=google&utm_campaign=dictionary&utm_medium=cpc&gclid=Cj0KCQjwwfiaBhC7ARIsAGvcPe6bKmaCFx47xTpOvNakBiI12cAfFNju_mG3xaIG844R6s_aAQ53WpUaAnYVEALw_wcB. Accessed: July 19, 2022.

"Mask: Antelope (Walu)." Metropolitan Museum of Art. The Michael C. Rockefeller Wing. URL: https://www.metmuseum.org/art/collection/search/314148. Accessed: November 20, 2021.

MSDS Regulations. MSDS Requirements and Regulations site. URL: https://www.ehso.com/msds_regulations.php#:~:text=MSDSs%20must%20be%20developed%20for,chemical%20occurs%20in%20the%20product. Accessed: August 2022.

INDEX

Page numbers in *italics* indicate a figure on the corresponding page.